Functional Analysis of Information Processing

A Structured Approach for Simplifying Systems Design

Grayce M. Booth

Honeywell Information Systems
Phoenix, Arizona

A WILEY-INTERSCIENCE PUBLICATION

JOHN WILEY & SONS

New York • London • Sydney • Toronto

Library of Congress Cataloging in Publication Data

Booth, Grayce M   1931-
    Functional analysis of information processing.

    (Business data processing: a Wiley series)
    "A Wiley-Interscience publication."
    Bibliography: p.
    1. Electronic digital computers.   I. Title.
QA76.5.B62   001.6   73-12956
ISBN 0-471-08846-3

Printed in the United States of America

10 9 8 7 6 5 4 3 2 1

to Hal

Preface to the Series

Business Data Processing: A Wiley Series is intended for system analysts, programmers, and managers who desire to improve their competence in business/management applications of the computer. Treating some twenty subject areas, publications will provide a range of technical depth. The objective is to provide a series of publications that will enable readers to gain an understanding in specialized subject areas.

In the face of the growth in depth and complexity of the computer field, practitioners encounter the problems of developing and maintaining technical competence. The junior level practitioner must upgrade his competence to reach the experienced practitioner level. The experienced system analyst/designers and programmers must strive to reach senior levels. The manager must broaden his knowledge to include the new technology that is being employed by his subordinates, but at an appropriate managerial level.

The Series will draw on experienced practitioners in the subject areas to the fullest extent possible, so as to provide useful, practical information.

The Series is designed to address three major areas of interest:

System Analyst Titles. These publications are designed for the practicing system analyst/designers, who already have a knowledge of computer systems, and who desire to learn about and apply new techniques.

Programmer Titles. These publications are designed for the experienced programmers, who desire to improve their competence in program structuring, building, and testing.

Manager Titles. These publications are designed for the active data processing managers who desire to learn ways to improve the operations under their control.

To assist the authors in the preparation of their manuscripts,

Wiley has organized a small Advisory Group for providing advice and suggestions on a timely basis to the authors. Experienced system analyst/designers counsel on the System Analyst Titles, practicing programmers on the Programmer Titles, and active managers on the Manager Titles.

Within any one set of titles, say the System Analyst Titles, there will be found a rather wide range of technical content. Some publications will discuss basics, for analysts who have only recently completed their training. Other publications will address the interests of the senior analyst/designers.

Thus Business Data Processing: A Wiley Series addresses the breadth, complexity, and the dynamic characteristics of the computer field. It covers an expanding set of technical subject areas. It addresses the interests of system analyst/designers, programmers, and managers. And it provides basic as well as more advanced information.

Training, updating, and upgrading professionals in the computer field will be a continuing problem. We hope that the Series will be an effective method in helping to cope with this problem.

Richard G. Canning
J. Daniel Couger
Series Editors

Preface

This book is intended to aid the information system analyst, designer, or programmer in the analysis of complex computer systems. The seasoned professional, bearing the inevitable scars acquired while attempting to implement an unworkable design, is only too well aware that the computer users and manufacturers have much to learn. These lessons are necessary before we can analyze, design, and implement computer systems of growing complexity with any degree of confidence or guarantee of success.

In thirteen years of working with information systems, frequently with large-scale on-line configurations, I have become aware of the need for a new approach to the design problem. I was therefore very interested when Hal B. Becker described to me a technique he developed for analyzing complex network-processing systems.

Hal calls his method the Functional Approach. It is a logical, structured approach to the definition of complex information networks. The functional approach is the result of Hal's many years in the data communications environment, and it is described in the companion volume *Functional Analysis of Information Networks*, also published by John Wiley and Sons.

It was Hal's suggestion that I apply the approach to the information-processing functions. He had identified their location in his tree structure, and convinced me of the need for a companion volume.

The resulting book amplifies Hal's separation of function philosophy and represents a structured approach to the manipulation of information once it arrives in an information processor. Hal's book, a structured approach to the communications environment surrounding computer systems, treats the problem of moving the information from the source(s) in the network into the information processor and moving the results back out to the appropriate destination(s).

These two volumes can be of significant help to the designer of free-standing information systems, communications systems, and/or true information networks combining both. The structured approach is presented as a first step toward formalizing the analysis and design process. Further work in both fields is necessary to identify the various simulators, design methods, models, and analysis tools required to solve the problem now that it has, for the first time we believe, been adequately defined.

Since it is impossible to individually acknowledge all of the people whose ideas I have utilized, I would like to collectively cite my colleagues in the WEYCOS project at Weyerhaeuser. It was there that I gained much of my large-scale systems experience, and the many people involved in the project contributed to my education and hence to this book.

I wish to especially thank Hal B. Becker for persuading me to write this book and for providing continued encouragement and support when my spirits flagged during the writing process.

Phoenix, Arizona   *Grayce M. Booth*

Contents

Section IV
SOFTWARE FUNCTIONS

Section V
SUMMARY

APPENDIX

A.   Information Network Tree Structure

Functional Analysis
of Information Processing

SECTION **I**

Introduction

CHAPTER 1

Introduction
and Scope

The subject of this book is information processing, which is a subset of a larger topic, "information networking." The term information networking may be a new one to the reader. It is used here to describe the universe of what was once called data processing. The rapidly evolving use of data communications to enhance the responsiveness of computing facilities has led to the creation of geographically-distributed systems. From these the information-networking concept has evolved.

Information networking encompasses all of those functions and elements required to configure a geographically-distributed information-processing facility. Information networks range from the small and simple to the very large and complex. An example of the former is a small-scale general-purpose computer (information processor) with its associated terminals and the lines connecting the terminals and the computer. A very large network might span one or more countries, include several different information processors, hundreds or thousands of terminals of various types, and many different kinds of communication lines. The concepts used in information networking can easily be subsetted to cover systems which require only information processing (no remote communication) or only network processing (no information processing).

Information networks have already been created and are operating today. However, to date each such network has been approached as a unique problem. Even computer vendors who have installed multiple information networks for their customers have pursued this application-specific approach, which has made each such installation significantly different from all others. Compatibility between network elements (such as information processors, concentrators, terminals, etc.), even within a single network, has been less than optimum. Often the owner of such an installation finds any change difficult because of the lack of flexibility in basic design.

Treating each problem as unique significantly increases the system designer's tasks because of the complexities involved in designing information networks. The lack of a well-defined approach to network and information-processing-systems design is being felt today, as complex and/or remotely oriented systems become more prevalent.

To reduce these complexities, this book proposes a new approach to be taken in defining and implementing information networks. This approach is a functional one; it analyzes the network from the "top down" as a series of functional levels. The functional definitions used become progressively more detailed at each level, until the lowest and most detailed level defines the individual items needed in each specific network. By defining a complete set of functions, and then by using these definitions to analyze, design, and implement each new information network, we need no longer treat each system as a special case. Each will, instead, represent a subset of information networking. A subset may well be unique, but it can use common functions and techniques from other networks.

Information networking is separated into two major categories of processing: network processing and information processing. The separation of function between these two categories is an important one. Too often present day designs fail to recognize this distinction, and therefore they often provide less than optimum performance.

As an example, some general-purpose information processors handle data communications interfaces directly, rather than via a network processor. This generally detracts from the processor's main function—information processing—and often warps the software design so that successful handling of the remote interface causes its other functions to suffer. A clear distinction between the functions which are part of network processing, and those which are part of information processing, is one of the goals of the functional approach.

Although it is possible to produce a comprehensive functional definition of information networking as a whole, this book concentrates on information processing. The functional definitions used in network processing are not included in this volume.[1]

This book first describes the functional approach and the hierarchy of functional definitions which are used in this approach. It then describes in detail that subset of the total set of definitions which deals with information processing.

These detailed descriptions cover the total set of functions, hardware and software, which exist in information-processing systems. Although the external world of network processing is not described, the interfaces and relationships between network processing and information processing are identified and explained.

These are the functions from which the analyst or designer must choose whenever he works with a new system. Which functions he chooses, how he arranges them, and their specific implementations will characterize the new system and differentiate it from other information-processing systems.

It is assumed that the reader has some background in information processing and is familiar with the terminology in general use within the industry. Within that context, a broad range of readers will find the information presented here useful.

For the experienced system designer, this book will provide an insight into the functional approach, which is really a method of logically structuring the system analysis and design process. It will also furnish him with the complete set of hardware and software functions which he can evaluate when designing an information-processing system.

For the less experienced designer or programmer, the detailed functional descriptions will also provide a comprehensive, generalized explanation of information-processing systems. Each of the hardware and software functions is described in terms of its basic purpose. Examples are given, where appropriate, of the use of these functions in specific implementations. These functional descriptions can therefore be read as a survey of current information-processing techniques, as well as in the context of the functional approach.

Preceding further definition of the functional approach and specific functions, Chapter 2 presents a brief description of the evolution of information-processing systems. This will give the reader a perspective as to where information-processing systems are today and how they arrived at this point.

[1] See *Functional Analysis of Information Networks* by H. B. Becker, John Wiley and Sons, New York, 1973 for a description of network processing.

Evolution of Information- Processing Systems

Information-processing systems have a relatively short history. The first commercially used computer was the Census Bureau's Univac I, which was installed in 1951. However, these systems have evolved rapidly through a variety of forms. Their history is interesting, both intrinsically and because few of the important developments have completely disappeared.

While it is common practice to speak of the reckless pace at which new designs are created and discarded in the computer industry, it is apparent on closer examination that this cliché is only partly true. The industry has certainly innovated at a great rate, but it has discarded comparatively little of the old while embracing the new.

We can illustrate this using examples from computer hardware technology. Integrated circuits have not completely replaced transistors; semiconductor memories are unlikely to completely eliminate core; core has not eliminated drum memories; discs have not made tape obsolete; even the original punched card is still used in substantial quantities. Generally, each new development or technology becomes prominent and pushes aside the older ones to some degree (often changing their use), but few significant technologies disappear entirely.

Information-processing systems in general, and operating-systems software in particular, have followed this same pattern. Although more and more complex system techniques have been developed, older systems and methods have not been scrapped. Therefore, much of the following discussion, although historical in nature, also serves to describe systems still in existence.

Because information-processing-systems development is mirrored in the evolution of operating-system software, operating-system evolution is also discussed. Early information processors did not use operating systems because there was no apparent need to do so. Computer hardware was originally of limited capability, with no ability to multiprogram or multiprocess, even if software had existed to support those features.

More important, early computers were not usually operated in what would today be considered a production environment. Often the programs run were one-time jobs, created to solve a specific, nonrecurring problem. One person (often an engineer, mathematician, or scientist) had a problem which required solution, wrote a program to solve it, and ran the program and data through the computer to obtain the solution. This mode of operation was at first satisfactory because computers had adequate capability to run their limited workloads, even when they were not operated efficiently.

As time passed, however, the inefficiency of programmers as computer operators became more noticeable. Efficiency also became more important because the workload continued to grow, and it could no longer be accommodated on systems operated in this way. The closed-shop computer room was one attempt to solve this problem. In a closed shop, specially trained operators run the computer equipment. If programmers and/or users are admitted to the computer room, which they often are not, they are only allowed to watch the operators. The development of the closed shop made computer operation take on more of a production aura, and the urge to operate efficiently increased as time passed.

One of the next steps in improved information-processing efficiency was the creation of between-job monitors, one of the earliest forms of operating system. A between-job monitor allows the computer operator to stack the available jobs in the correct sequence for execution and input them as a group to the computer. The monitor initiates each job, regains control at job termination, initiates the next job, etc. as long as there is work to do. The monitor requires that some of its code remain in memory permanently, to gain control whenever necessary. However, each user program effectively controls the entire computer system while in execution. In any case, it was not safe with the early monitors for more than one job to be concurrently resident, because the hardware provided no way to protect such jobs from each other. In fact, the resident-monitor coding was sometimes destroyed by a malfunctioning user job, causing the entire system to fail.

Another early operating-system development was "spooling." This was one of the earliest forms of multiprogramming, that is, the sharing of hardware use between multiple (usually two) programs executing concurrently. This mode of operation allowed better use of computer resources than was previously possible. The principle of spooling is that the subsidiary program needs little processor time, while the main program is selected for heavy processor use, with little need for I/O (Input/output) time.

Even the simple form of multiprogramming used in spooling requires two hardware features not previously implemented in most computers. First, the computer must be able to execute instructions and I/O processes simultaneously. As long as hardware performed these functions sequentially, multiprogramming techniques were of no use, since the main feature of multiprogramming is to overlap I/O for one program with processing for the same or another program.

Another hardware ability needed for multiprogramming is a signal to indicate that an event, generally an I/O operation, is complete. This type of signal is called an interrupt. Early computers, which had no I/O overlap, did not need interrupt capabilities. Even with I/O overlap, uniprogramming systems could issue I/O, then go into a timed program loop and wait for the I/O to complete. Since only one program was executing, this worked well. However, the use of I/O overlap to provide multiprogramming made apparent the need for an interrupt capability. With the interrupt, I/O can be started, then other processing can continue until an interrupt signals that the I/O is complete.

Additional information-processing-system developments pointed out the need for an overlay capability. This was recognized in application-program development, when programs too large to fit into main memory were needed to solve complex problems. It was also noted in operating-systems development. Only in very simple operating systems, such as between-job monitors, can the entire operating-system code remain resident in main memory. The ability to overlay a block of code in memory with another set of code was a considerable breakthrough, although it remained relatively useless as long as the only available overlay media were cards and magnetic tape. The advent of mass-storage devices made overlays feasible and proved to be a basic tool necessary in development of the extremely complex information-processing systems of today.

Another important programming development which occurred during the early days of commercial computer use was the creation of standard I/O routines, which could be inserted into any program and used via standard linkages from the user's coding. Typical of these I/O routines was IOCS (Input/Output Control System), used on a wide range of IBM equipment, including the 700, 7000, and 1400 series.

Packages such as IOCS were needed for two reasons: to eliminate the requirement for each programmer to write his own I/O routines and to standardize operator actions during program execution (tape mounting, error correction procedures, etc.). In early versions IOCS was loaded with each user's program and executed as a part of that program, but routines similar to these soon became part of the evolving operating systems. A single set of I/O routines was made available to be shared by all user programs, including those executing concurrently in multiprogramming mode. Considerable savings of main-memory space were achieved by this technique.

In the late 1950s and early 1960s, experiments with interactive systems began. Interactive systems are those which provide direct contact between the computer and an individual operating a terminal such as a teletypewriter. Interactive systems require much more rapid response than noninteractive (batch) systems, simply because the user is waiting at the terminal for each answer from the computer and will tolerate only a reasonable delay (a few seconds, generally). A notable early time-sharing system was created by Dartmouth College using the GE-225 and DATANET-30 computers.

Interactive systems, which were initially used for computational time sharing, presented the first need for true multiprogramming. Even the capability of a small or slow computer would obviously be wasted if one person sat at a keyboard and fed commands to the system at less than typewriter speed. The need to share one computer's power among many users led to operating systems with both multiprogramming and swapping capabilities.

In some cases multiprogramming is accomplished serially; i.e., one program occupies memory for some period of time, then is swapped out and another is swapped in and allowed to execute, and so on. In other cases, multiple-user programs are allowed to reside in memory concurrently, with multiprogramming achieved by allowing each to use the processor part of the time. The term "time slicing" was coined to describe this form of processor sharing. The more complex interactive systems use both concurrently resident multiprogramming and swapping, substantially increasing the number of users that can be handled concurrently on a single system.

Interactive time-sharing systems began the evolution toward remotely oriented or geographically-distributed systems. Remote job entry, consisting of batch job input from a terminal (usually a small computer) rather than the card reader soon came into use. Early transaction-processing systems also developed at roughly the same time. One of these early transaction-processing systems was a management information system developed by the Weyerhaeuser Company using General Electric computer equipment.

The need to use data communications to expand information processing capabilities was generally recognized, but two different approaches were taken in merging communications and information processing. One approach was to attach the communication lines directly to the information processor; the attachment generally consisted of a multiline controller, so this will be referred to as the multiline-controller approach. The other approach was to attach the communication lines to a separate computer, specially structured for data communication functions, and then interface that computer with the information processor. The data communications computer was called a front-end or network processor, so this will be called the network processor approach.

Both the multiline-controller and network-processor approaches have survived until today. Each has a place in the full spectrum of information networking. The multiline controller is suited to applications in which a very small number of lines are required; the cost of a network processor cannot be justified in such cases. The network processor is suited to all large or heavily loaded applications and those in which a wide variety of communication techniques are used; the multiline controller places too great a burden on the information processor in these cases.

Another development was the evolution of multicomputer information-processing systems. The term "multicomputer system" is used in at least two ways. Originally, it was used to refer to two separate computer systems, usually of different types, connected via hardware link. The software systems of the two computers cooperate to achieve common goals. There is usually specialization of function; i.e., one computer processes I/O while the other computes. There is also generally a master/slave relationship; one system controls (indirectly) what the other does. The software used in the two computers is sometimes referred to as a distributed operating system.

This type of multicomputer configuration as a rule consists of a small computer, used for media conversion (reading job input, printing job output, etc.) and sometimes for controlling all I/O devices (tapes, discs, etc.), and a large computer used for rapid, high volume computation. A typical multicomputer system using second generation equipment was the IBM ASP (Associated Support Processor) configuration, using a 1401 or 1410 I/O Computer and a 7090/94 or 7040/44 processing computer. Contrary to expectations, the smaller computer was the master while the larger processor was the slave; control over job input inevitably led to master status being given to the I/O-system computer.

The second type of multicomputer is of much later development. It consists of two or more computers, generally but not necessarily of the same type, linked via some type of hardware interface. Each runs under its own operating system, which may or may not be identical with the operating system(s) of the other computer(s). There is little or no specialization of function and no master/slave relationship. The computers operate independently, but they cooperate to do whatever processing is required. Very few examples of this type of system exist, at least partly because of the complexity of the software required.

Another considerable increase in system complexity occurred with the advent of multiprocessor hardware, in which two or more processors share access to the same memory. Multiprocessor operating systems are not simply a logical extension of multiprogramming systems; in practice they present a whole new set of problems. These difficulties revolve around how to use multiple processors effectively without generating unacceptable interference between them, and how to prevent the processors from destroying each other's work. These problems, although complex, have been effectively solved in some current systems. Particularly notable in this respect is the GCOS operating system used on Honeywell Series 6000 computers. Multiprocessor configurations provide considerably more computing power than do monoprocessor systems at less than the added cost of another complete computer.

To close this history, we should mention one of the most complex of relatively recent information-processing-system developments, the virtual machine. A virtual-machine system is a ruse by which users and/or operating systems are made to execute as though they are on different hardware than that equipment physically present.

Probably the outstanding example of such a system is the CMS (Cambridge Monitor System) which runs on the IBM 360/67. The CMS is a super operating system within which other operating systems, OS/360 for example, can execute. Given sufficient hardware, multiple operating system of the same or different types can operate concurrently under virtual-machine monitor control.

Such systems are useful principally for testing and experimental purposes and in cases where the facilities of two or more different operating systems are needed by users at a single installation.

SUMMARY

Although information-processing systems have evolved within the last 20 years, a significant variety of software and hardware technologies has been developed. This has led to great diversity in current systems.

The foregoing history is not by any means complete, but it includes major milestones of the development of information-processing systems from the 1950s until 1972. Many of the system types described still exist in some form. All, without exception, were formed from some subset of the functions which are described in the following chapters.

Functional Approach and Level Definition

CHAPTER 3

Definition of
the Functional
Approach

The design of information networks, and of information processing-systems, is an extremely complex process. It involves defining the results expected from the system and the data and procedures needed to provide those results. Central to this process is the choice of hardware and software which will receive information, process it, and output the desired results.

As hardware and software become increasingly complex, and an ever wider selection is available from which to choose, the designer's task becomes forbiddingly difficult. This often results in choices being made for a variety of illogical reasons since the application of logic seems impossible.

The functional approach is presented as a step toward simplifying the design process itself, as well as simplifying the subsequent choice of obtaining or creating hardware and software elements.

The functional approach to information processing requires, first, that all possible functions be defined. It is obvious that this cannot be done at an extremely detailed level since the list would be literally endless. However, defini-

17

tion in extreme detail is unnecessary; what is required is definition at a level of sufficient generality to be universally applicable. Functions, in this context, may be performed by either hardware or software, so both types must be defined. The body of this book consists of such a list of functions.

With the aid of this complete list of functions, the designer can define the subset needed for his system. It is possible to form an endless number of subsets from this same list of functions. For example, a user wishing to implement an on-line order entry application system will need a particular subset of the total list of functions. He will select hardware to perform some of these functions. Since he will probably use an operating system, he can determine which of the remaining functions will be provided by the operating system. Those which are not provided must be included in the application programs he writes or in software which he acquires in some other way.

In exactly the same way, the designer of an operating system can choose functions from the same complete list. His problem is slightly different; he must decide which subset is appropriate for the stated aims of his software system. An operating system intended to support only batch processing, for example, will require a different set of functions than will one which supports computational time sharing.

When the operating-system designer has selected the appropriate set of functions that his software will provide, he has also defined the set within which the users of his system must work. As a very simple example, media conversion is one of the functions used in information-processing systems. If the operating-system designer includes it in his chosen set of functions, users need not provide it. If he does not, then any users of his system must provide their own media-conversion software if they require that function.

The functional approach does not, of course, solve all of the designer's problems. It does not deal with the quantitative or performance factor which is necessary to completion of design. That is, the elements chosen to perform the needed functions must do so at acceptable levels of throughput. However, performance data is only important after the required functions have been defined. It may then be the deciding factor in choosing between two otherwise equivalent implementations of the same function.

The definition of functions is only one of the steps needed in a methodical approach to the design of information-processing systems. The next step is the development of tools and techniques which the designer can use to apply the functional approach to his specific problem. These tools and techniques will include information-gathering methods, models, simulations, etc. These tools have not yet been defined or developed, but they are clearly needed to ease the designer's task.

One of the important features of the functional approach is that it removes the distinctions among types of software during the system-analysis phase. Software is generally divided into the classifications of operating system, other vendor-supplied software, and user-created software. These distinctions are unimportant when the total set of functions needed is being defined.

The total set, defined in this volume, includes all software functions. In a few information-processing systems, all of the required functions will be provided by specifically written user (problem program) software. More generally, some of the functions will be part of the computer's operating system and some of them will be installation-written routines, while the remainder will be part of the standardized software furnished by the computer manufacturer or by another software vendor(s).

In considering the distinctions generally made between operating-system functions and user-program functions, we see that they are often arbitrary. Some vendors, for example, consider a compiler to be an integral part of the operating system. Other vendors provide one or more compilers, but they consider these a different class of software than the operating system. Other vendors do not provide any compilers, and when one is used it is the same as a problem program while executing, receiving no special treatment from the operating system.

Since these different definitions of operating-system versus non-operating-system software are arbitrary, they are treated as unnecessary in the functional view. In the analysis of an information-processing system, we can define certain functions as necessary. Those functions found to be missing when the definition is used to match against an already existing operating system and perhaps against other vendor-supplied software, will be provided as user (or other vendor) software. When the definition is used to create an entirely new information-processing system, including an operating system as well as other software, then a logical separation can be made on the basis of the particular system's characteristics. Generally, functions basic to the hardware interfaces will be part of the operating system, while functions unique to applications will be user software.

The fundamental premise of this approach is that certain definable functions are necessary in all information processing. In spite of the enormous apparent diversity of existing systems, all will be found to have basic similarities if superfluous external detail is stripped away.

It is difficult to eliminate this complexity, but it is a rewarding task if clarity results.

It seems reasonable to assume that future information-processing systems can be made less complex if the system organization is as simple as possible. This can only be achieved when there are explicit definitions of the functions required. This is particularly important in the design of operating systems and large, complex application systems.

The question of simple system organization is not an academic one. Present day operating systems are, almost without exception, so complex that any change is a major undertaking. Significant change, such as adding interactive capabilities to an operating system designed for batch processing, is almost always impossible. The current state of the art in operating-system design requires that all major uses of a system be visualized before the system structure is defined. Major application systems suffer from the same problem, generally to a lesser, but still significant, degree.

Since it is generally impossible, in practice, to foresee all of the uses to which a large information-processing system will be put, it is necessary instead to make it sufficiently flexible to change as required. This is very difficult to do, but the functional approach will assist in achieving this goal.

The functional approach leads naturally to the use of very formalized design principles, since the functional definitions are themselves formalized. The design method required consists of defining system functions at a very generic level, and implementing those functions so that they can be used in a great variety of ways, only some of which are originally known. In this sense, one can think of an information-processing system as consisting of a series of interfaces between various logical levels of functions, as shown in Figure 3-1.

USER INTERFACES

↓

APPLICATION SPECIFIC FUNCTIONS

↓

GENERAL OPERATING SYSTEM FUNCTIONS

↓

BASIC MACHINE DEPENDENT FUNCTIONS

Figure 3-1   Concept of functional levels.

A system may actually have many more logical levels than shown in the example; this is simply a presentation of the idea of progressing from symbolic functions through more and more specific functions, finally arriving at the machine-level functions. If the items which belong in each level are properly defined, and if explicit, formal interfaces are maintaincd between them, a given system should be able to support an almost infinite variety of functions at the most symbolic (user interface) level.

Some attempts at formal, hierarchical structures for operating systems, have been made. So far these experiments have been more noted for elegance than for operating efficiency. However, at least one such system, MULTICS,[1] has demonstrated that major changes can be made fairly easily within its structure. As experiments of this type continue, we can expect that flexibility and simplicity of design will be achieved without an unacceptable loss of efficiency.

In summary, the functional approach offers an orderly method for determining the functions required in any information network or in any information-processing system. This is intended to aid the designer in performing his task of system definition. In addition, it is felt that viewing a system functionally will lead toward simpler, more flexibly designed systems, which are more readily adaptable to the change which occurs continually in the normal course of events.

The remainder of this volume describes the functional levels which have been defined as part of information processing. It then describes in detail the specific hardware and software functions which form the full set required for information-processing systems.

---

[1] *MULT*iplexed *I*nformation and *C*omputing *S*ystem, jointly developed by MIT and the General Electric Cambridge Lab, for use on the Honeywell (formerly GE) 645 and 6180 computers.

CHAPTER 4

Definition of Information Network Levels

The first step in the functional approach is to define the logical levels at which functions exist. This book describes six levels which allow functions to be defined in enough detail for system design. The six levels are named:

Level I   NETWORK LEVEL
Level II PROCESSING LEVEL
Level III MACRO FUNCTIONAL LEVEL
Level IV MICRO FUNCTIONAL LEVEL
Level V   ELEMENT LEVEL
Level VI DEVICE/TECHNIQUE LEVEL

LEVEL I. NETWORK LEVEL

At this level, we determine whether or not the system is an information network, based on its characteristics. A system which has no remote-processing requirements is identified at this level as being an information-processing system. For example, a small batch computer using only local I/O does not form an information network. Its characteristics can be defined under the Level II entry Information Processing.

Systems in which both information processing and communication requirements exist are identified at this level as networks. These are then analyzed further using the lower-level entries of this structure.

LEVEL II. PROCESSING LEVEL

This level provides the initial separation of function between information processing and network processing. Systems which consist only of network processing, a message-switching system for example, can be defined by following only the network-processing side of the tree from this point. Systems which are only information processing, for example the small batch system mentioned earlier, can be defined using only the information-processing side. Systems which include both types of processing are information networks, and they must be defined using both sides of the tree structure.

As Chapter 1 stated, this volume is dedicated to describing the functional approach as it relates to the information processing side of this structure. *Functional Analysis of Information Networks* by Hal B. Becker similarly describes the use of the functional approach in network processing.

LEVEL III. MACRO FUNCTIONAL LEVEL

At this level, hardware and software functions are separated. Under Network Processing, the Level III entry Network Functions includes all hardware elements, while the Control Functions entry covers software. The Level III entries under Information Processing are titled simply Hardware Functions and Software Functions.

At this point system requirements are evaluated and separated into those best handled via hardware and those most effectively performed by software. Although preliminary decisions may be made here, these will be subject to revision as lower-level analysis continues. It is important that hardware and software functionality, although separate, be considered together as subsets of a total system.

The first three functional levels of the information networking tree structure are shown in Figure 4-1. These three levels are enough to identify any system as belonging to one of three categories:

- Information Networks
- Free-Standing Network Processing Systems
- Free-Standing Information Processing Systems

Level

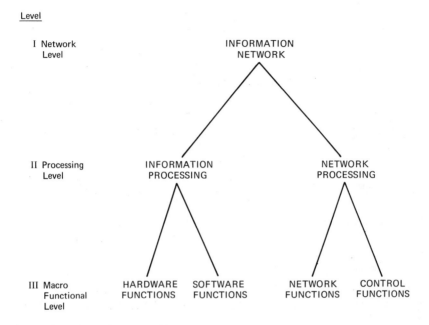

Level		
I Network Level	INFORMATION NETWORK	
II Processing Level	INFORMATION PROCESSING	NETWORK PROCESSING
III Macro Functional Level	HARDWARE FUNCTIONS SOFTWARE FUNCTIONS	NETWORK FUNCTIONS CONTROL FUNCTIONS

Figure 4-1   **Information networking.**

The network processing side of the functional definition tree is not described further in this volume. The remaining levels are described only for information processing. The complete tree structure functional diagram is given in Appendix A, and subsets are included in later chapters associated with the explanatory text.

LEVEL IV. MICRO FUNCTIONAL LEVEL

At this level, the hardware and software entries are broken into major logical functions. The entries at Level IV are still quite general, and most systems will require all of the Micro Functions defined at this level.

The Level IV items which appear under each of the Level III Macro Functions are described briefly here. More detailed descriptions form the body of this book, beginning in Chapter 5.

Level

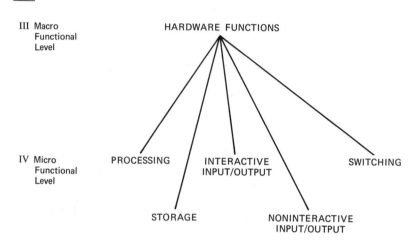

III Macro
     Functional
     Level
                              HARDWARE FUNCTIONS

IV Micro   PROCESSING   INTERACTIVE   SWITCHING
    Functional   INPUT/OUTPUT
    Level

                        STORAGE   NONINTERACTIVE
                                             INPUT/OUTPUT

Figure 4-2 Hardware functions.

Hardware Functions

The Level III entry, Hardware Functions, is separated into five Level IV functions, as shown in Figure 4-2. Each of these items is explained as follows.

Processing is the function of performing computations, addition, subtraction, logical operations, etc.

Storage provides a semipermanent method of saving information, either within the information processor or separate from it (i.e., on magnetic tapes, disc packs, or other media).

Interactive Input/Output includes devices used to provide interaction between the information processor and a person using the system. This is one of the interface points between information processing and network processing.

Noninteractive Input/Output is the function of providing transient input to the computer and removing transient output from the computer. No interaction is involved although the I/O may be remote. In the latter case this represents another interface with network processing.

Switching is the function of moving hardware components within the information-processing system, that is, reconfiguring it.

Software Functions

The Level III entry, Software Functions, is separated into nine Level IV functions, as shown in Figure 4-3 and described in the following paragraphs.

Languages are the interfaces provided between machine coding and the computer programmers. The simplest languages are assemblers; these are often very closely related to machine languages. The compilers, such as Fortran and COBOL, are much more machine independent than the assemblers. Still another level removed from the actual computer hardware are the data management languages which provide the means for data base creation, manipulation, and use.

Applications form the second software function. These group all programs (written, of course, in languages) which execute application-specific functions. A payroll program is a good example of an application. It may be a generalized one, suited to the needs of many companies, or it may have been created specifically to process a particular payroll.

Utility, as the name implies, consists of features needed to support the user and/or other system functions. Media conversion, program loaders, I/O routines for general use, and debug tools all fall into this class. This function includes items whose status is traditionally ambiguous; they may be part of the operating system, part of system software, or user supplied.

File Management is the function which handles files at the logical level. Files of many types, stored on many different types of devices, can be treated in the same manner by this function. File management does not deal with file content or structure, but only with the file as a logical entity.

Task Management is the function which exercises control over the various tasks (also called jobs or processes) executing or waiting to execute. System users and operating-system components may define and execute tasks. A user job may consist of sequential or concurrent execution of one or more programs, each of which may consist of one or more tasks. The task management function must maintain awareness of all of these relationships and manage processing accordingly.

Resource Management deals with available computer-system resources, logical and physical. Logical resources include peripherals,

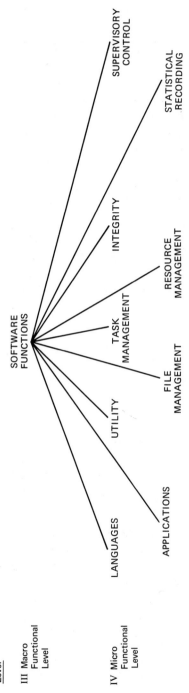

Figure 4-3 **Software functions.**

processors, etc. The hardware functions managed are I/O operations, processor interrupts and faults, etc. Resource management is always an operating-system function in large information processors, but it may be part of problem-program coding in small systems.

Integrity is the function which ensures that the level of reliability and availability required by the owner of the information-processing system is provided. This function includes error detection/correction and similar features which protect the integrity of information processed or stored by the system. It also includes features such as restart/ recovery and fail soft, by which computer failures are prevented, minimized, and/or recovered from. Finally, it includes security functions which protect data privacy, prevent unauthorized data modifications, and prevent unauthorized use of system resources.

Statistical Recording is the function of accumulating, in detail and/or in summary form, the data needed to monitor and control system operation, to bill users for resource expenditures, and to evaluate system performance. This function also includes report preparation and dynamic evaluation and feedback to alter processing based on analysis of earlier performance.

Supervisory Control, the final software function, includes all interactions between the system and those personnel who have varying degrees of control over its operation. This control requires information logging by the system and features to allow operators to inquire about system status, etc. These are functions which support the basic interaction between people and software to control the computer's operations.

LEVEL V. ELEMENT LEVEL

At this level, the micro functions of Level IV are separated into specific forms or elements. Each of the Level V elements is described briefly in the following pages. Under each element is a list of the associated Level VI devices and/or techniques. First the entries under the Level III item Hardware Functions are described, followed by the entries under Software Functions.

These are the levels at which the system is defined in detail. They are therefore extremely important. Each of the items in Levels V and VI is described in detail in Chapters 5 through 14.

Processing

Level IV

PROCESSING

Level V

PROCESSORS

Processors are the only Level V entry under Processing. These are the hardware devices which perform the processing function: that is, arithmetic, logical operations, data moves, and similar processes. The following major types have been defined:

Level VI—INTERRUPT-DRIVEN
            —SYNCHRONOUS
            —MICROCODED
            —MULTIPROCESSORS

Storage

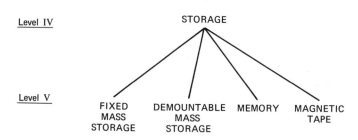

Fixed Mass Storage includes those devices in which randomly-addressable storage media are connected directly to the information processor and are never disconnected. The devices which fall into this category include:

Level VI—DISC
            —DRUM
            —BULK STORE
            —TAPE STRIPS, ETC.

Demountable Mass-Storage devices are identical to the preceding group, with the added ability to be selectively connected to or disconnected from the information processor. Data stored on these devices remain unchanged while the device is demounted. Demountable mass-storage devices include:

Level VI—DISC PACKS
          —TAPE STRIPS, ETC.

Memory devices provide relatively temporary information storage. Their significant characteristic is the information processor's ability to execute instructions stored in these devices. They include the following major types:

Level VI—BASIC MEMORY
          —EXTENDED MEMORY

Magnetic Tape is the final Level V entry under Storage. It is the most significant storage device for sequential access. It has the same characteristics as the demountable mass-storage devices except for the lack of random accessibility. There are no Level VI entries under this item.

Interactive Input/Output

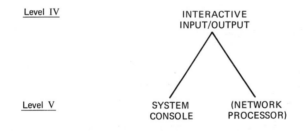

System Console is the interactive interface between the software and the personnel controlling the system. Many types of devices may be used to perform this function: for example, typewriters, CRT's (Cathode Ray Tubes), teletypewriters, etc. There are no Level VI entries.

Network Processor is the interface between the information processor and remote interactive terminal devices. It appears in parentheses because it may or may not be present, depending on the architecture of a particular information processor. If it is not, the remote devices are handled directly by the information processor. Teletypewriters are typical of the remote interactive devices. There is one device entry under this:

Level VI—INTERACTIVE REMOTE TERMINALS

Noninteractive Input/Output

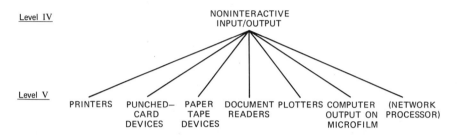

Printers include devices which produce printed copy output. These devices may operate on-line (directly connected to the computer) or off-line (not connected, but printing from tape or other storage media). There are no Level VI entries under this item.

Punched-Card Devices process that old standby, the punched card. Several types of cards are in general use; the most common is the 80 column Hollerith format. Two classes of punched-card devices are included:

> Level VI—CARD READER
> ————— —CARD PUNCH

Paper Tape Devices use punched paper tape as I/O. Several paper tape formats are used: 5 level, 6 level, 8 level, and others. These two device types are included:

> Level VI—PAPER TAPE READER
> ————— —PAPER TAPE PUNCH

Document Readers obtain computer input data directly from printed documents without any intervening data preparation step. Two basic techniques for reading are used:

> Level VI—MICR (Magnetic Ink Character Recognition) READERS
> ————— —OCR (Optical Character Recognition) READERS

Plotters include devices which produce graphs and similar charts from digital input. These devices operate on-line or off-line, and sometimes are used as remote noninteractive terminals. There are no Level VI entries.

Computer Output on Microfilm (COM) includes devices which produce a microfilm record from information-processor data. These devices generally operate off-line, but they may also be used on-line. There are no Level VI entries under COM.

Network Processor, the last of these Level V entries, covers the non-interactive interface with remote devices. This is another of the interface points between information processing and network processing. The device entry under this item is:

Level VI—REMOTE BATCH TERMINALS

Switching

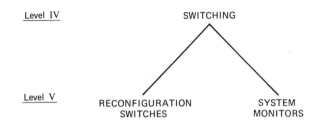

Reconfiguration Switches are devices used to charge physical connections between hardware components, causing reconfiguration. These switches may be manually and/or automatically controlled. There are no Level VI entries defined.

System Monitors include devices which maintain watch over an information processor and notice if it fails, so that recovery action of some type can be taken. There are no Level VI entries under this item.

Languages

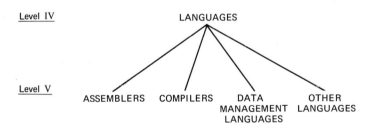

Assemblers are the lowest-level languages; they are very similar to machine coding. They provide the programmer with features such as mnemonic operation codes, symbolic addressing, and macro instructions. Assemblers can be categorized into the following types:

Level VI—BASIC
          —MICROPROGRAMMING

Compilers, often called higher-level languages, are relatively much less dependent on a particular machine's characteristics than assemblers. They are generally procedure oriented and designed for easy use, machine independence, and standardization. Fortran and COBOL are the most generally used compilers. The following types of compilers have been identified:

Level VI—BATCH
　　　　—INCREMENTAL

Data Management Languages are specifically designed to give the user a means of describing and using data structures. These languages exist both as free-standing software packages and as extensions to compiler languages. The following techniques are included:

Level VI—DATA DESCRIPTION
　　　　—DATA MANIPULATION

Other Languages include programming languages less generally used than the three categories already described. The following types of languages are included:

Level VI—GENERATORS
　　　　—SIMULATORS
　　　　—META LANGUAGES

Applications

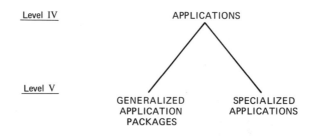

Generalized Application Packages are software systems written in a generalized manner to serve a number of users with different needs (within reasonable limits). Customization of the software for a particular installation is performed, generally using input parameters to define exact requirements. The following parameterization techniques are used:

Level VI—APPLICATION GENERATORS
　　　　—INTERPRETIVE APPLICATIONS

Specialized Applications are those software packages written specifically to accomplish a particular job. The vast bulk of existing software falls into this category since the majority of all programs are written to solve only a specific problem. No Level VI entries are needed.

Utility

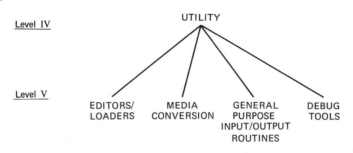

Editors/Loaders consist of all the routines required to prepare source and/or object coding for execution. Loaders may be used for problem programs, for system software, or for both. This entry includes the following techniques:

    Level VI—SOURCE EDITOR
           —OBJECT EDITOR
           —SYSTEM EDITOR
           —LINKAGE EDITOR
           —LOADERS

Media Conversion includes those routines which move data from one peripheral device to another. Examples of media conversion are card-to-tape and disc-to-printer. There are no Level VI entries defined.

General Purpose Input/Output Routines are utility packages provided to ease I/O processing by applications and other types of software. The following types of I/O routines are defined:

    Level VI—LOGICAL INPUT/OUTPUT
           —PHYSICAL INPUT/OUTPUT

Debug Tools are utility software provided to aid in the testing of other software. Debug tools may operate interactively or in batch mode, and they include the following items:

    Level VI—POST MORTEM DUMP
           —SNAPSHOT DUMP
           —EXECUTION TRACE
           —TEST GENERATOR

File Management

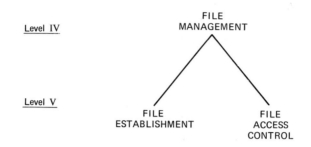

File Establishment consists of the functions required to uniquely define a file and assign it space within the available storage devices. It also includes the creation of catalog entries for the file. These entries are used to store basic data identifying the file and sometimes also to describe hierarchical relationships among otherwise separate files. File establishment includes these subsets:

    Level VI—FILE DEFINITION
              —CATALOGING

File Access Control allows a previously defined and cataloged file to be read, written, executed, or otherwise processed. File access control deals with the file as a logical entity, while data manipulation (under Languages) deals with the file content. The following items are included:

    Level VI—SECURITY CONTROL
              —CONCURRENT ACCESS CONTROL
              —FILE LOCATION

Task Management

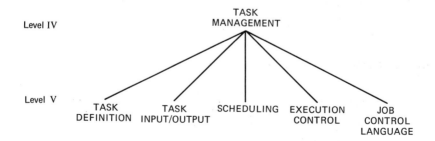

Task Definition is the process of describing a task to be executed by the information processor. Definition includes providing the code to be executed, listing resources required (memory, peripherals, etc.), and perhaps providing data to be used in execution. Definition may take place just prior to execution and be immediately followed by it, or it may be a completely separate function. Task definition requires no Level VI entries.

Task Input/Output is a specialized form of media conversion, specifically designed to read task input into the computer and to process task output directed to peripheral or remote devices. It includes the following items:

Level VI—INPUT PROCESSING
————————————OUTPUT PROCESSING

Scheduling is the function which determines how tasks will be executed. This includes examining precedences, priorities, and response requirements and deciding the sequence of execution for available tasks. When multiple information processors are available, load leveling is also part of this function. The following subsidiary items are included:

Level VI—QUEUEING
————————————LOAD LEVELING

Execution Control includes the functions which initiate task executions, control these while in process, and handle task termination. Execution control consists of the following techniques:

Level VI—INITIATION
————————————INTERTASK COMMUNICATION/
SYNCHRONIZATION
—TERMINATION

Job Control Language (JCL) is the primary external interface to task management. It provides the user with a method of defining the functions required, specifying options to be used, etc. JCL has both interactive and batch versions, although the same general functions are required in each. JCL is also associated with other software functions, but it is most closely related to task management and is therefore included here. There are no Level VI entries defined.

Resource Management

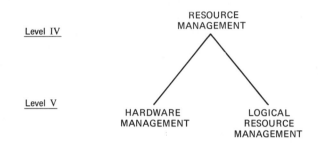

Hardware Management covers control of the computer hardware interfaces. It is the level of software directly sensitive to the physical characteristics of the information processor used. Hardware management covers the following:

> Level VI—INPUT/OUTPUT CONTROL
> —FAULT HANDLING
> —CONFIGURATION CONTROL

Logical Resource Management controls the allocation of resources to tasks. Although the resources are essentially hardware—peripherals, storage, processors, etc.—they are treated as logical rather than physical entities by this function. The following items are included:

> Level VI—MEMORY MANAGEMENT
> —PERIPHERAL ALLOCATION
> —SECONDARY STORAGE SPACE MANAGEMENT
> —PROCESSOR ALLOCATION

Integrity

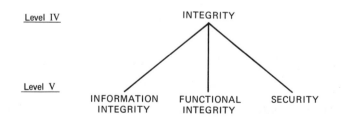

Information Integrity includes the techniques required to protect the integrity of data processed or stored by the information-processing system. The following techniques have been identified:

Level VI—ERROR DETECTION/CORRECTION
        —FILE PROTECTION/RECOVERY
        —CONTINUITY

Functional Integrity includes features used to protect the integrity of the information-processing system and of the tasks executing within it. This is closely connected with information integrity. The following items are included:

Level VI—TEST AND DIAGNOSTICS
        —CHECKPOINT/ROLLBACK
        —RESTART/RECOVERY
        —RECONFIGURATION
        —FAIL SOFT/BACKUP

Security is provided to protect the information-processing system against unauthorized access, use, or data modification. Information-processing security is closely associated with network-processing security. The following techniques have been defined:

Level VI—USER IDENTIFICATION
        —ACCESS CONTROL

Statistical Recording

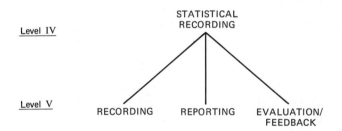

Recording is the accumulation of statistical and historical data during system operation so that system performance and loading can be reported and evaluated. There are no Level VI entries.

Reporting consists of selecting, formatting, and other manipulation of recorded data to produce the reports needed for system evaluation. The following items are identified under reporting:

Level VI—BILLING
        —PERFORMANCE DATA

Evaluation/Feedback consists of analyzing accumulated data, comparing it against norms, goals, or other measurements, and determining actual versus expected or desired performance. When significant deviation is found, feedback may be required to attempt to adjust system performance. Evaluation and/or feedback may be performed manually rather than automatically via software. There are no Level VI entries defined.

Supervisory Control

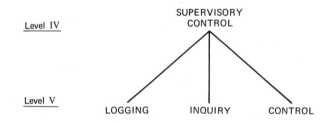

Logging is the software function of displaying data which may be of interest to personnel responsible for controlling the information-processing system. Items logged may be for information only, such as notice of successful job completion, or they may require action, such as notice of unrecoverable I/O error. The following subsidiary functions are included:

Level VI—HISTORICAL LOGGING
        —ACTION REQUESTS

Inquiry is the means by which control personnel determine system status. Inquiry allows operators to ask a wide range of status questions which are responded to by software. There are no Level VI entries required.

Control allows supervisory personnel to modify the information processor's actions via a set of commands. Actions which can be caused include starting or terminating job executions, changing the system scheduling algorithms, changing the destination of waiting task output, and many others. No Level VI entries have been defined.

SUMMARY

This chapter has presented brief descriptions of functional Levels I through V, with lists of the Level VI items. The following chapters, which make up Sections III and IV, define in detail all of the Level IV, V, and VI functions of information processing. These lists of functions form the complete set from which subsets can be selected to form particular information-processing systems.

SECTION **III**

Hardware
Functions

CHAPTER 5

Hardware Functions

A great many hardware functions and devices are required to form an information-processing system. Often the choice of hardware is given either too much or too little weight in system development. The average computer user often has less choice of hardware than of software, because he can create at least some of the latter. He may spend a great deal of time evaluating hardware since it is somewhat easier to evaluate hardware than software. Other users confronted with the same dilemma may simply select what appears to be appropriate hardware from a major vendor and spend much more effort on software functions.

Realistically, hardware and software functions should be evaluated in equal depth. In a well-designed information-processing system, each has equal importance. The user must keep in mind how closely hardware and software are related and how each affects the other. A poor choice in either area may affect the price/performance characteristics of the entire information network.

It is undoubtedly true that the average owner of an information-processing system is constrained in his choice of hardware by the availability of software support, particularly operating-system support. It is a rare user who can afford to create from scratch the full complement of software needed. For example, a particular computer may have all of the hardware capabilities needed for interactive use. However, if the available operating system(s) for this hardware supports only batch processing, the additional capabilities of the hardware are simply unusable for the average customer.

The selection of hardware and software is therefore, in practice, an iterative process. Both hardware and software functions must be evaluated and selected, or created, with the aims of the entire system firmly in mind. As an example, an on-line system with a requirement for high availability will generally need fail-soft capability; that is, the information processor must be able to survive the loss of redundant, nonessential elements. A fail-soft multi-processor computer configuration may be chosen in such a case, so that a processor failure will not halt the entire system.

Simply selecting multiprocessor computer hardware may not, however, solve the problem. Both the hardware and software must be structured so that failure of one processor does not affect the other(s). The hardware elements, for example, must not be interdependent so that a failure of one processor makes it impossible for the other to continue. The software must similarly be structured to use multiple processors when available, but it must be able to survive loss of one without complete failure.

Throughout the evaluation and/or design of information-processing-system components, the interrelationships between hardware and software must be considered in detail. One of the aspects of this relationship is the effect of hardware architecture on software structure. (The reverse is also true, but more generally in an evolutionary sense.) For example, a computer with hardware paging and segmentation requires very sophisticated operating-system software, but it may remove some of the burden from the average application programmer. Such a hardware architecture supports certain types of software functions extremely well and other types very poorly. Deficiencies of function and/or design in either hardware or software can be compensated for to some degree by the other, but serious failings can seldom be compensated for successfully.

There are five Level IV functions under the Level III Hardware Functions entry; they are shown in Figure 5-1.

Level

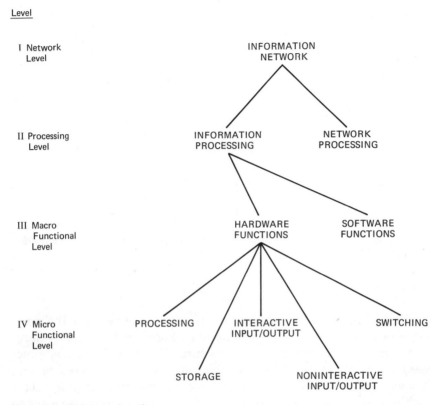

Figure 5-1 Hardware functions.

5-1 PROCESSING

Certainly one of the most basic hardware functions is Processing, which has only one Level V entry, Processors. The several significant categories of processors are listed in Level VI, as shown in Figure 5-2.

The processor is that portion of the computer which decodes and executes instructions, and performs arithmetic operations, data moves, logical operations, and other similar functions. The capabilities of processors in different computers vary widely; however, the largest, most complex processors simply perform supersets of the basic processing capabilities, and they also perform them more rapidly than smaller processors do.

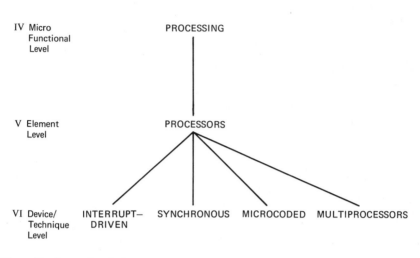

Level

IV Micro Functional Level

V Element Level

VI Device/ Technique Level

Figure 5-2   Processing devices.

Basic differences in computer architecture, which affect the processor, exist between classes of computers. Some systems, particularly small ones, are of monolithic architecture. This means that the processor is directly involved in I/O operations as well as processing, and it may also be completely integrated with the main memory. This architecture produces less expensive systems; however, it also leads to reduced flexibility and reliability. It is not possible, for example, to add a second processor to an existing configuration since the processor does not exist independently, for practical purposes. Also, a failure of any component will, as a rule, cause the entire system to fail. Although serious, these drawbacks are often accepted in return for reduced system cost.

The central system components of larger computers generally have much more modular architecture than those of small computers. The processor is a unique entity, sharing no circuitry or logic with the I/O controllers/channels, etc., and each of these devices is functionally independent of main memory. This type of architecture, by its modularity, provides much greater flexibility than monolithic architecture. Configuration changes (permanent or temporary) can easily be made. Failure of a nonessential component does not cause failure of any other component(s), provided of course that the software also supports this capability. Increased cost is incurred, so only large-scale computers are generally designed in this manner.

Several different forms of computer architecture are discussed in *Computer Architecture* by Caxton C. Foster.[1]

When considering processing, the most important point is to determine, in detail, which capabilities are most needed. Individual processors can then be evaluated on their ability to perform the most important functions efficiently, of course within the framework of the entire information processor.

In spite of much advertising and propaganda to the contrary, computers today are still oriented toward either business data processing or scientific processing. The cost of building a system equally able, as is Illiac IV,[2] to perform 64 simultaneous arithmetic functions, and, as is the Honeywell 6080,[3] to perform a COBOL MOVE command with format conversion in a single instruction, would be prohibitive. Realistically, each computer must be aimed at some type of processing and made most efficient for that mode. It may perform a wide range of other functions, but it is not optimized for these.

It is important, therefore, to match a given processor's strong points against the needed range of functions. This match is less important if the information-processing system as a whole is oriented toward data manipulation and file management. Even in these cases, however, processor capabilities should not be taken for granted; they should be evaluated seriously.

The Level VI items under Processors represent specific characteristics which are important in an evaluation of processors.

Interrupt-Driven Processors

Interrupt-Driven Processors, which form the first Level VI entry, are one of the basic forms used today. These systems are organized around the theory that each significant event is accompanied by an interrupt. This causes other processing to be interrupted; the event which caused the interrupt is analyzed and necessary action is taken. This type of system operates asynchronously, and the sequence of events at any given point cannot be predicted. This contrasts strongly with the synchronous processors described next.

The IBM System/360 is one example of an interrupt-driven proc-

[1] Van Nostrand Reinhold Company, New York, 1970.
[2] Slotnick, D. L., "The Fastest Computer," *Scientific American*, Feb., 1971, pp. 76–87.
[3] *Series 6000 Summary Description*, Order No. DA48, Honeywell Information Systems, Waltham, Massachusetts.

essor. Its use of interrupts is described in *IBM System/360 System Summary*.[1]

Synchronous Processors

Synchronous Processors form the next Level VI category. Processors in this group are not basically interrupt-driven, although they may have some interrupt capability. The basic processor cycle is synchronous; that is, certain events happen in a fixed sequence and within rigid timing constraints. Few general-purpose processors today are synchronous; the majority are interrupt-driven. One of the problems associated with synchronous systems is timing difficulties. Since the main processor cycle must occur within a fixed timing increment, any violation of that increment by the software may cause a system failure. Second-generation systems were often plagued with problems of this type.

Microcoded Processors

The next Level VI entry includes Microcoded Processors, which are becoming increasingly prominent today. Microcoding allows processor functions to be defined with more range and flexibility than when using the conventional hard-wired processor techniques.

Each processor has a basic set of gates, lines, registers, etc. In hard-wired processors, a set of operations called the instruction repertoire is defined. For each instruction so defined, a set of actions involving the registers, lines, and gates is defined and wired into the processor. For example, an LDA (Load A Register) instruction involves a set of actions in the hardware, and whenever an LDA is encountered this same set of actions is triggered.

Exactly the same result can be achieved in microcoded processors, except that the hardware-level actions involving registers, lines, etc. are called micro instructions. There are no prewired sets of these instructions. Instead, each desired operation is microcoded and the microcoding is loaded into a control storage area. Until recently, the control store was a read-only device called ROS (Read Only Store) or ROM (Read Only Memory). Newer systems now have writable

---

[1] Order No. GA 22-6810, International Business Machines Corporation, White Plains, New York.

control stores so that the microprogram can be modified without manufacturing a new control store.

It is theoretically possible to create a processor in microcoding which performs exactly as though it were hard-wired. Generally, however, microprogramming is used for one of two purposes: to emulate another information processor or to provide enhanced flexibility.

The use of microcoding for emulation has proven to be a very useful tool. Creating a hard-wired processor capable of executing code for two or more different instruction repertoires would be very expensive. However, hard-wiring native mode operations and microcoding the emulation(s) greatly reduces this cost. The computer is able, either concurrently or sequentially, to behave as if it were different computers. Often the processor emulated may have characteristics which are strikingly different from the native mode processor, but microcoding can generally overcome these differences.

Increased flexibility is possible when the control store is writable. This feature makes it possible, although perhaps not reasonable, to modify a given information processor for particular operations. For example, a frequently used routine or instruction sequence can be microcoded and executed in response to a newly defined instruction. Because of the decreased number of instruction-fetch cycles, plus the often more efficient use of registers at the micro operation level, considerably improved performance may result.

The pitfall in this type of flexibility is the resulting processor uniqueness. A customer may literally have a one-of-a-kind system using this technique. This may cause incompatibilities with vendor-furnished software, and it may also cause maintenance support problems. It is only in rare cases, therefore, that this sort of microprogramming would be justified in today's state of the art.

Another type of emulation points up the flexibility of the microprogramming approach. It is possible by judiciously combining hard-wired and microcoded instructions to obtain a truly dual personality machine, equally able to execute two distinct instruction repertoires. This is an expansion of earlier systems in which a degree of duality existed: for example, the ability to do arithmetic in either binary or BCD (Binary Coded Decimal), the ability to handle character-strings in BCD or ASCII (American National Standard Code for Information Interchange), etc. The completely dual personality processor emulates neither mode; both are native to it and execute with equal performance.

The technology of microprogramming is only in its infancy, so these uses will undoubtedly be expanded significantly as time goes on.

The techniques currently used are well described in *Microprogramming: Principles and Practices* by Semir S. Huson.[1]

Multiprocessors

The final Level VI entry under Processors is Multiprocessors. These are computers in which two or more processors operate completely independently and in parallel. Theoretically a multiprocessor system with two processors should be able to do twice as much work as a uniprocessor system. In practice this is never the case because there is bound to be some interference caused by competition for memory cycles. In fact, one must have a multiple-module main memory in order to effectively use multiple processors; otherwise the memory interference completely destroys the usefulness of the additional processor(s).

Memory interference may be a significant problem if the operating system is resident in one memory module and if there is a high rate of access to that module by all processors. This can be such a severe problem that it limits the practicality of the multiprocessor approach. The simplest solution to the problem is to distribute the operating-system code across available memory, so that accesses are similarly spread and interference is minimized. Of course this is not as easy to do as it might appear, but it is feasible.

The Burroughs B4700 computer is one example of a multiprocessor system. It is described in *Borroughs B4700 System Highlights*.[2]

5-2   STORAGE

The second major hardware function is Storage, which breaks into the Level V and VI entries which are shown in Figure 5-3. This function may be considered to overlap with the Noninteractive Input/Output function described in Section 5-4. It is impossible to completely resolve the resulting ambiguity since considerable overlap exists, and has always existed, between the two functions. It is often necessary to arbitrarily define which devices belong in each function.

For example, consider a strip of paper tape or a deck of punched cards. Are these storage media, to be classed under the storage function? Or are they I/O devices and therefore classed with the I/O

---

[1] Prentice-Hall, Englewood Cliffs, New Jersey, 1970.
[2] From 1057809, Burroughs Corporation, Detroit, Michigan.

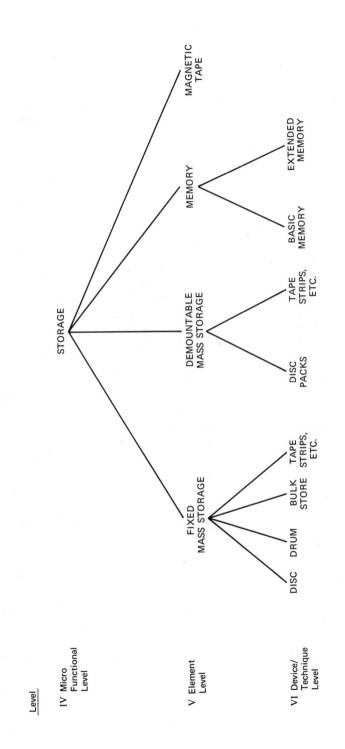

Figure 5.3 Storage devices.

function? For purposes of this volume, they are considered part of noninteractive I/O, in accordance with the following definition.

The storage function includes all types of devices which are under direct computer control and which can be used for relatively permanent storage of file data. While this is an arbitrary definition, it follows general usage quite closely. Although paper tape and punched cards can certainly be thought of as file data and can be permanently retained, they are only under computer control when actually read into the system. At all other times the files are manually controlled.

I/O media generally cannot be updated easily by the computer, nor can they be randomly accessed. These are traits which they share with magnetic tape, which is rather a special case. Tape is classed here with storage devices as its primary purpose is relatively long-term file storage. Again, the definition is arbitrary, but it follows general usage.

A fairly recent development which potentially affects all types of storage is the use of microcoded storage controllers. Generally, a storage device or set of devices interfaces with the main system through a controller. Figure 5-4 shows a typical configuration.

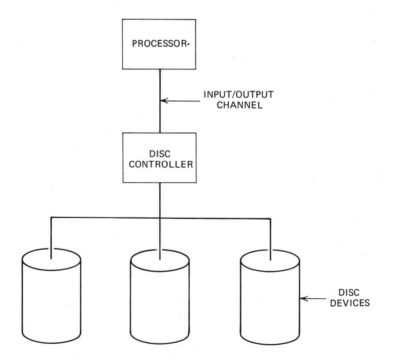

Figure 5-4   **Typical disc configuration.**

The controller's function is to act as a very special purpose processor which decodes I/O instructions directed to the attached device(s), issues commands, provides a level of data buffering, and performs other similar functions.

Until recently, each type of controller was built with hard-wired logic designed to perform its specific functions. Lately, the microcoding techniques described under Processing, in Section 5-1, have also been applied to peripheral controllers.

This approach has two advantages. A single basic controller architecture can be used for multiple purposes by providing only a different microprogram for each. Although this type of modularity can also be achieved using hard-wired logic, it is more reasonable and less expensive to achieve this with firmware. The other advantage lies in the ability to add features to the controller at much less cost than in a hard-wired implementation. For example, on-the-fly code transliteration can be performed in the controller, so that nonstandard peripheral code sets are not seen by the central system. Flexibility of this type can be extremely useful.

Another technique which applies to mass storage, and occasionally to magnetic tape, is the concept of shared access to the same device(s) by multiple processors. Figure 5-5 shows a classic application of shared access called the "delta" configuration.

The term delta comes from the three-sided, or triangular, shape conceptually formed by the two processors and the shared disc. This type of configuration allows the processors to exchange large volumes of information via the disc, rather than via direct channel interface. This smooths out the transfer load and also increases system availability by making it more feasible for one processor to continue running if the other fails.

This type of configuration is occasionally used to provide shared-file access for two information processors. However, the software problems are much more complex than in the information processor/ network processor delta, and so this type of system is rare. Section 6-3, Data Management Languages, discusses the software implications of the delta configuration.

Fixed Mass Storage

The first Level V entry under Storage is Fixed Mass Storage. This includes devices which are always directly accessible from the information processor. These devices are generally, but not always, capable of being randomly accessed.

Fixed mass storage has been available for a longer period of time

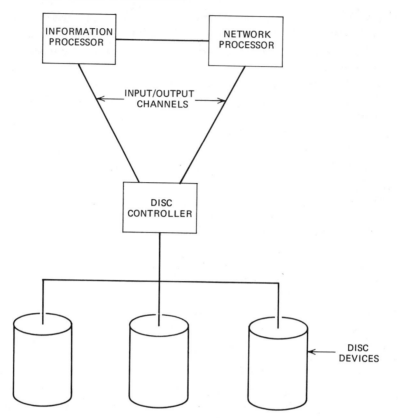

Figure 5-5 Delta configuration.

than demountable storage has. The IBM 305 RAMAC system, which used fixed disc as its only storage medium, became available in 1957. Since disc packs and other demountable mass-storage devices have been developed, larger and larger use has been made of demountable storage. Fixed storage is now most commonly found in extremely high throughput and/or fast access storage: head-per-track disc and drums, for example. The following Level VI entries fall under Fixed Mass Storage.

Disc is the first of the Level VI items. Discs can be divided into two classes, the head-per-track discs and movable-head discs. The former, although they may take the physical form of a disc, are logically equivalent to a drum. They require no seek time, except possibly a minimal head switching delay, and so average access time consists of half the rotational delay time. Devices of this type often offer extremely high performance and have correspondingly high cost.

Movable-head fixed-disc systems have much slower average access times than head-per-track disc, since the time required to move the access mechanism must be added to the rotational delay. These devices are generally correspondingly less expensive. The movable access mechanism may consist of a series of independently movable arms or of a set of arms which all move together. The latter leads to data organization in cylinders to minimize access times; the former may support much more flexible data organization.

Several different types of disc systems are described in *OS/360 Job Control Language* by Harry W. Cadow.[1]

Drum is the second Level VI entry. Drums are generally very rapid access, relatively small capacity, head-per-track devices. They are most frequently used for fast access data, such as program-swap storage or frequently used tables, subroutines, etc. Drums are among the most expensive storage devices, and so they are not normally used for large volume data.

There are exceptions to this, most notably the use of very large, relatively slow drums as the main mass-storage devices on certain Univac systems. This type of drum has moving read/write mechanisms, and therefore it is almost completely equivalent to a disc file. These Univac drums are described in *Univac Fastrand II/III Magnetic Drum Subsystems Operators Reference*.[2]

Bulk Store is the third of the Level VI entries. Until recently this class of device was referred to as bulk core, since it consisted of magnetic-core storage. Bulk-storage devices are now becoming available which are formed of integrated circuits (semiconductors) rather than magnetic core, but they are used in exactly the same way as bulk core.

Bulk store is the most rapid access of the storage devices since there are no moving parts to cause delay. Direct access can be made randomly to any location within the store. In effect, the only differences between main memory and bulk store are that the latter is slightly slower in access, and instructions cannot be executed from it by the processor.

Tape Strips and other unusual fixed mass-storage devices are grouped to form the final Level VI item. Randomly-accessible card-storage

---

[1] Prentice-Hall, Englewood Cliffs, New Jersey, 1970.
[2] Document UP-7801, Sperry-Rand Corporation, King of Prussia, Pennsylvania.

devices (punched or magnetically encoded) also fall into this category. A number of devices of this type exist, but none are widely used. Their characteristics and uses are too unusual to cover in a general discussion; it is sufficient to point out that such devices exist. They can be investigated if more common types of storage prove inadequate in a particular information system.

An example of this type of device is the data cell, which is described in *IBM 2321 Data Cell Drive*.[1]

Demountable Mass Storage

The second Level V entry under Storage consists of Demountable Mass-Storage Devices. Devices in this group have characteristics identical with those in the preceding class (fixed mass storage), and in addition they have the ability to be temporarily disconnected from the computer.

Demountable devices have several significant advantages over fixed storage; their content can be protected by removal from the computing system (preventing update and/or access); they can be used interchangeably on two or more computers or even types of computers; and more storage can be purchased at less total costs (although obviously not all can be accessible simultaneously).

Disc Packs, the first of the Level VI devices, are widely used today. In fact the general trend in mass storage seems to be toward this type of device, to the apparent exclusion of all others. The advantages listed above are significant enough to explain why this is so. A typical example of modern disk-pack systems is the IBM 3330, which is described in the *Reference Manual for IBM 3830 Storage Control and IBM 3330 Disk Storage*.[2]

The only disadvantages attached to disc packs are relatively minor. These discs do not normally achieve the extremely rapid access of head-per-track discs or drums because they use moving access mechanisms. (Usually the access mechanisms are of the type which move in tandem, leading to cylindrical data organization as explained earlier.) New hardware techniques, which speed up the access mechanism's movement and pack data more closely so that transfer rates into and out of memory are increased, are closing this gap. However,

---

[1] Form A26-5851, International Business Machines Corporation, White Plains, New York.

[2] Form No. GA 26-1592, International Business Machines Corporation, White Plains, New York.

it is probable that small, very rapid, and relatively inexpensive drums will continue to find many uses.

Another minor disadvantage is demountability itself, when viewed from the aspect of security protection. Fixed mass-storage devices which are immovably attached to the information processor cannot be physically transported away; i.e., they cannot be stolen by removal. Disc packs can (as can magnetic tapes). Physical, rather than hardware/software, security safeguards are required to circumvent this danger in cases where security is extremely important.

Tape Strips and other similar devices form the other Level VI entry. These devices are identical to those which appear under fixed mass storage, except that the storage media are demountable in the form of cassettes of other similar mechanisms.

Memory

The third Level V entry under Storage is Memory. The most common memories, at present, are formed of magnetic core, although computers (the IBM 370, in particular) are now appearing with semiconductor main memories. A few systems still exist which use drum as main memory. Regardless of type, memory of this class is directly addressable by the processor, and it is also distinguished by the ability of the processor(s) to execute instructions from this memory.

Basic Memory, the first Level VI item, covers computer main memories. One of the significant memory attributes is whether memory is packaged as a single module or as multiple modules, which means effectively how many simultaneous accesses to memory are possible.

In a single module memory, any concurrent accesses cause cycle stealing. That is, if processing and I/O are going on simultaneously, only one can actually obtain a given memory cycle. When an I/O channel obtains a memory cycle, the processor must wait until the next cycle to obtain a memory reference. Because it is, in a sense, time dependent, the I/O operation is given priority. If I/O were forced to wait for the processor, data might be lost; the processor can always wait.

In a memory with two modules, an access can be made to each module in each cycle. I/O references to one module and processor references to the other can occur simultaneously. Of course it is not always possible to arrange the software to take advantage of this capability, but even a little care can produce much improved simultaneity in a multiple module memory. This simultaneity is also important in multiprocessor configurations.

Another aspect of having two or more memory modules is that when one fails, the other will continue to operate, preventing a total system failure. Fail-soft systems generally require multiple module memories. This type of system is discussed in Chapter 12, Integrity.

Extended Memory, the other Level VI item, is a catch-all group which covers other memory techniques, generally used to improve information-processor performance.

One of the most impressive of these techniques is the cache memory. This is a two-level memory system in which a relatively large, medium speed memory and a small, very fast memory are combined. Main data storage is in the large memory, but instructions and operands are pulled from there into the cache for execution. This is essentially a paging technique which is software invisible, since it is handled entirely by the hardware.

A typical example of the cache approach is found in the IBM 360/85 computer.[1] With a 960 nanosecond (nsec) main memory and an 80 nsec cache, 95% of all operands are estimated to be found in the cache. This makes effective memory speed much closer to the speed of the cache than to the speed of main memory. A single-level memory of comparable speed would be unreasonably expensive, so the cache produces a very impressive price/performance improvement.

Another extended memory technique is virtual memory. Virtual-memory systems allow a multiple-level memory, that is, a memory consisting of multiple types of storage, to be addressed and used as though it were a single-level store of very large size. This generally requires support in both the hardware and software.

Virtual memory provides an address space which is conceptually very large (16 million pages of 1K (1,000) words each in the Honeywell 6180 system). Any use of data in virtual memory causes a mapping process into actual memory. (Again using the Honeywell 6180, actual memory size is 512K words.) Data is moved back and forth between secondary-level (and theoretically tertiary, etc.) storage and main store as needed. The cache is a simplified version of the multilevel virtual memory.

These and other extended memory techniques are being developed continually with the basic aim of improving the information proces-

[1] Lystay, J. S., "Structural aspects of the system 360, Model 85; part II—the cache," *IBM Systems Journal,* 7, 1968, pp. 15–21.

sor's price/performance characteristics. Memory, and in particular extremely high-speed memory, is very expensive. It is therefore desirable to conserve its use, while still obtaining an illusion of more and/or faster memory than is actually present. Developments such as the use of cache are very promising in reducing the cost of main memory, thus making it economically feasible to have larger memories.

Magnetic Tape

The fourth and final Level V entry under Storage is Magnetic Tape. This element, because of its unique properties and broad range of uses, deserves an independent entry. Perhaps more than any other item, it can quite well be classed either under the storage function or as an I/O device. However, general use of magnetic tape leans more strongly toward storage, and so it is included here.

Magnetic tape is still the most widely used medium for large size sequentially-processed files. Disc packs are being used increasingly for jobs which formerly required tape, but only when file size is below some reasonable limit. For larger files, tape has such great economic advantages, both in purchase price and in the cost of storage space, that it is unlikely to disappear from use.

Magnetic tape, like demountable mass storage, has some inherent advantages. Very large amounts of data on tape reels can be stored in relatively small areas. The fact that reels are inexpensive makes them the ideal medium for backup copy storage. For example, file dumps of mass-storage data bases are normally taken on magnetic tape. These tapes may then be removed to a remote site, so that they will not be lost even in a catastrophe which destroys the entire computer installation.

Tape reels are also easily transported. Compatibility between the tape handlers and recording techniques of all major computer manufacturers is becoming a reality today. A file on tape may be used at more than one site; sometimes it can even be used with different types of information processors. It is, generally, the ideal medium for data exchange between unlike systems, except where distance and speed requirements make direct data transmission necessary.

New tape techniques are continually being developed. Sixteen hundred bits per inch (bpi) tapes are common today, and 65,000 bpi systems have now been proven feasible. No doubt this medium will continue to be used where random access is not a necessity.

5-3   INTERACTIVE INPUT/OUTPUT

The next Level IV entry to be considered is Interactive Input/Output. It breaks into only a few lower-level entries, as shown in Figure 5-6.

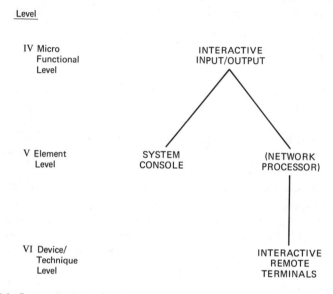

Figure 5-6   Interactive input/output devices.

The interactive I/O function includes those elements by which a person—a user at a terminal, a system operator—can appear to converse with the computer system. Perhaps the best known form of interactive operation is that used in computational time-sharing systems. Many new forms of interactive systems are now coming into use—on-line banking, point-of-sale recording, order entry, and others.

System Console

The first level V entry under Interactive Input/Output is the System Console. Although the console is not generally thought of in the same light as a terminal, it is as truly interactive. The console operators and other control personnel interact very closely with the operating system via the console.

The devices used as system consoles are quite varied. The electric typewriter is the most common, but its popularity may soon be matched or exceeded by CRT (Cathode Ray Tube) display devices.

Large-scale computers may have two or more devices grouped to form a large, complex console, sometimes referred to as the system control center. Such a center may include one or more CRT's for inquiry and display, and one or more line or incremental printers for permanent recording of status data.

Some systems do not provide a conventional console but simply use a terminal as the console. The terminal, usually a teletypewriter, may be physically close to the computer, or it may be remote from it. This approach is commonly used with low cost minicomputers, since it may be less expensive to attach a terminal than to provide a specialized console device.

Large systems often distribute the operator/system interaction to several consoles, some or all of which may take the form of terminals. It is becoming increasingly common, for example, to place a console in or near the tape reel/disc-pack library and to display peripheral requirements at that location. Another specialized console may be located near the unit record peripherals—readers, punches, printers —so that messages regarding these devices can be input and output there.

Still another specialized console may be furnished for technical staff personnel who interact with the system to monitor and control performance. The users of this type of console may be privileged to change the operating system's scheduling algorithms, to add or subtract peripherals and/or terminals as needs change, and perhaps to direct job exchange with another computer for load-leveling purposes. In cases where security is important, this type of privileged console may be in a locked area, accessible only to authorized personnel.

Network Processor

The second Level V entry is Network Processor, which is the special purpose communications processor used to interface the information processor with data communications facilities and devices. Figure 5-6 shows this entry in parentheses, since a front-end network processor may or may not be used to interface the information processor with remote terminals. If a network processor is not used, the terminals are connected directly to the information processor via single line or multiline controller(s) or other similar connection methods.

This is the point at which the separation of function between information and network processing (described in Chapter 1) occurs. This is true regardless of whether or not a network processor is used to handle the network interface. If one is not, the network-processing functions exist in the information processor, and they should be formally separated from the true information-processing functions.

There are several ways in which an information processor and network processor can be connected to each other. Probably the most common is to attach the network processor to an I/O channel of the information processor. This type of connection is shown in Figure 5-7.

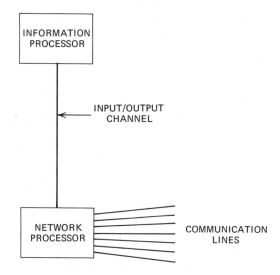

Figure 5-7   Information processor/network processor connection.

Another less common method connects the network processor directly to the main memory of the information processor. Figure 5-8 shows the layout of the Honeywell Series 6000 information processor and DATANET[1] 355 network processor which are connected in this way. This type of connection allows very high-speed transfers into and out of the information-processor memory.[2]

Finally, either of the above connection methods can be combined with the use of shared-mass storage. This is the delta configuration described earlier in Section 5-2. Although it may be possible to interface *only* via shared storage, this is seldom practical. A more direct interface is needed so that the two processors can inform each other when there is data to be picked up from shared storage and where it is located.

[1] Trademark.
[2] See the DATANET 355 Systems Manual, Order No. BS03, Honeywell Information Systems, Waltham, Massachusetts.

Interactive Remote Terminals form the only Level VI entry under Network Processor. (This effectively becomes a Level V entry if there is no network processor and terminals are directly connected to the

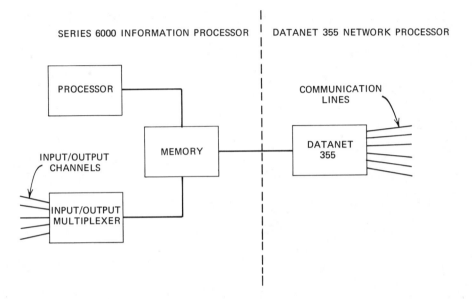

SERIES 6000 INFORMATION PROCESSOR ¦ DATANET 355 NETWORK PROCESSOR

Figure 5-8   Network processor/memory connection.

central processor.) The common characteristic of this group is the ability of the terminal user to converse, or work interactively, with the information-processing system.

The most common interactive terminal is the teletypewriter, which exists in a variety of forms. Other terminals in this class are CRT devices, which range from teletypewriter replacements through very complex graphics devices. Also included are on-line banking terminals, manufacturing recording/feedback devices, and many others. Detailed descriptions of terminal devices are part of the definition of network processing, and so they are not included here.

5-4 NONINTERACTIVE INPUT/OUTPUT

The fourth Level IV entry under Hardware Functions is Noninteractive Input/Output, which breaks into Level V and VI entries as shown in Figure 5-9. Noninteractive I/O consists of devices which provide transient input data to the processor and which receive similar

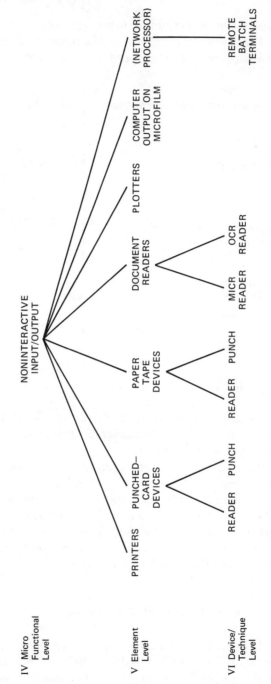

Figure 5-9 Noninteractive input/output devices.

output data from it. There is no human interaction in the process as there is with the devices described in Section 5-3. Rather, these devices can be considered to work more in a batch mode, transfering logical data increments without manual intervention (except, of course, to handle error conditions which may arise).

There are seven Level V entries, most of which share the capability of sometimes being used as on-line computer peripherals and sometimes being used as off-line devices operating as subsidiaries to computers. For example, a printer can be used as a free-standing device attached directly to a magnetic tape handler from which it receives its input. It can only print data from the tape, in this configuration; the tape must have been created on a computer at an earlier time.

Many of these devices are also used both as computer peripherals and as remote batch terminals. A plotter, for example, may be a peripheral, or it may be remotely located with data transmitted to it for output.

Printers

The first noninteractive Input/Output Level V entry is Printers. This category covers all devices which produce printed data on some type of paper form. The most common printers are the line printers used for high-speed, high-volume output.

Some incremental printers are also in use. These operate by sequentially printing characters across the platten, to produce a line. These are essentially output only typewriters, and in fact sometimes they actually consist of a typewriter mechanism. Their speed is of course slow, but their cost is considerably less than that of line printers.

New, high-speed forms of nonimpact printers which use photographic techniques to produce printed output a page at a time are being developed. While still rare and too expensive for general use, they promise very great increases in output speed.

Punched-Card Devices

The second Level V entry, Punched-Card Devices, includes mechanisms which read and/or punch cards. The cards used are most often in the 80 column Hollerith format made so popular by IBM punched-card accounting machines. They may also be in the 96 column System/3 format more recently introduced by IBM. Or they may be in the 90 column card format used in Remington Rand accounting machines. A few other nonstandard card formats exist but are not widely used.

Although the Card Reader and Card Punch are considered separate Level VI entries, they are sometimes consolidated in a single piece of hardware. The consolidation may go even farther so that the same card which is read can later be punched, presumably with the results of some calculations performed on data read from it.

These devices often include the added feature of multiple card stackers into which cards can be fed selectively. This allows either input or output to be separated into as many groups as there are stackers under control of the information-processor program. If this hardware feature is present, it may or may not be supported by the software. Multiprogramming software often makes the close timing needed for stacker selection difficult or impossible.

Paper Tape Devices

The third Level V entry includes Paper Tape Readers, punches, and devices which combine these functions. The medium used is punched paper tape, in any of a number of formats—5 level, 6 level, 7 level, and 8 level are common. The format indicates how many holes per character are punched into the tape, and this generally implies the code set used. Eight-level paper tape, for example, is usually punched in ASCII code, consisting of seven data levels plus parity.

Paper tape is not a very popular I/O medium except when it is also used as an auxiliary storage medium with remote terminals such as teletypewriters. It is most often used in applications where devices such as adding machines, cash registers, etc. are set up to produce paper tape as a byproduct of their normal operations. In these cases, computer input on paper tape can be a very inexpensive and satisfactory medium.

Document Readers

The next Level V entry consists of Document Readers. These devices read data printed on paper directly without any other input preparation. There is a Level VI entry for each of the major document reading methods, MICR (Magnetic Ink Character Recognition) and OCR (Optical Character Recognition).

Document readers may have other capabilities such as sorting. MICR check sorters are widely used in the banking industry, both as off-line devices, where they simply place documents in order, and as on-line computer input devices.

MICR Readers, the first Level VI devices, are used mainly in banking. Banks in the United States have almost universally adopted this technique for speeding check handling. Basic data is imprinted in magnetic ink characters on batches of checks when they are originally printed, and the check amount is later imprinted on each check after it is cashed and returned to a bank. Together, these two sets of data supply enough information to process the check mechanically without converting it to a punched card or other input device.

MICR readers require that printing be within very exact tolerances, so MICR is a relatively expensive printing process. When this is weighed against alternative input methods, however, the cost appears much more reasonable. Within banking, and in other businesses where a turn-around document (such as a statement) is used, MICR is very successful.

OCR Readers form the other Level VI entry. Optical character reading does not require special ink as MICR does, but it does require that recognizable printer fonts be used on the input documents. OCR is used principally where turn-around documents can be prepared by computer and later returned and used as input via OCR.

OCR is still a relatively expensive input method, except where volume makes reduced input preparation costs significant enough to pay for the readers. One of the drawbacks to date has been the limited ability of the readers to handle different fonts. However, these limitations are being removed, and as development continues the effective cost of OCR will decrease. In the long run, these devices offer one of the most promising input technologies. There are experimental OCR devices which can read hand-written documents reasonably well, and if this eventually proves feasible (particularly in reading hand-written numbers) for commercial applications, it will be an extremely useful tool. Additional information on the techniques and use of OCR can be found in *Optical Character Recognition*.[1]

Plotters

The next Level V item is Plotters. Plotters produce graphs or charts from digital input. They are sometimes used on-line, although since

---

[1] Edited by Fischer, G. L., Jr., Pollock, D. K., Kadack, B., and Stevens, M. E., Spartan Books, Washington, D. C., 1962.

they are rather slow devices they tend to waste the computer's peripheral I/O power. For this reason they are perhaps more often run off-line from magnetic tape, or as remote batch terminals via communication line.

Plotting is coming into more general use in business applications as an alternative to reports consisting of data accumulations. Even reports containing only exception data may be difficult to analyze because they consist of rows and columns of figures. The same data displayed in the form of a graph is often much easier to comprehend. This is an interesting technique, worthy of investigation in many applications.

Computer Output on Microfilm

The sixth Level V entry is COM, or Computer Output on Microfilm. COM devices are a relatively recent development, but they are already receiving considerable attention.

These devices operate to translate digital input, usually coded in records on magnetic tape, into a page image (similar to a CRT image), then photograph that image to form a microfilm picture. More advanced versions are not limited to alphanumeric images but have graphics capabilities as well. Graphs, charts, designs, etc. can be drawn and microfilmed by these devices. Like many of the other noninteractive I/O devices, COM is most often used off-line, but it can also be an on-line computer peripheral. A description of COM and its uses can be found in "Computer Output Microfilm," by Don M. Avedon.[1]

COM devices seem to have a promising future, because they are much faster output devices than line printers, and output is often an information-processor-system bottleneck. When output is historical in nature and/or will be consulted repeatedly over a period of time, direct translation to microfilm is both faster and less expensive than printed output. As the price of COM decreases, this technique may come into more widespread use.

Network Processor

The final Level V entry is Network Processor. This item is identical to the Network Processor entry under Interactive Input/Output. All of the discussion of that entry in Section 5-3 applies equally to this entry.

[1] *NMA Monograph* No. 4, 1969.

Remote Batch Terminals form the only Level VI entry. This group includes batch terminals of many types, ranging from remote card readers (unprogrammed) to general-purpose computers able to converse with another information processor via data communications. Their common feature, which places them in this category, is that they are not designed to allow interaction between the terminal operator and the information-processing system. In fact, many of the devices described here under noninteractive I/O are also used as remote batch terminals. Detailed terminal descriptions are part of the definition of network processing and so they are not included here.

5-5 SWITCHING

The final Level IV function is Switching, which has only two Level V elements. These are shown in Figure 5-10.

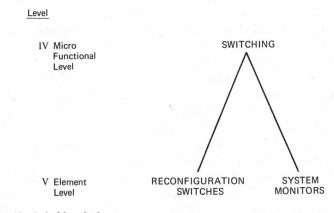

Figure 5-10   Switching devices.

Switching is the process of changing information paths, generally by changing the pattern of connections between devices or components of the information-processing system.

Reconfiguration Switches

The first Level V entry consists of Reconfiguration Switches which are devices used to change hardware connections. For example, a peripheral such as a card reader may be switched between two information processors for load-leveling purposes. Reconfiguration switches used to change peripheral connections are generally called peripheral switches. This is the most common type of reconfiguration switch.

Other similar switches may be used to change the configuration of the main system, either for load leveling or, more often, to provide fail-soft capability. Occasionally a central system component, such as a processor, may be switchable for load leveling just as peripherals are. This capability is not very common in present day equipment, as most hardware is not sufficiently modular to allow this type of switching. However, there are trends developing in this direction; future systems are much more likely to have these features.

Processors and main memory are more often reconfigured for fail-soft purposes than for load leveling, although this capability is also fairly rare today. For example, a processor failure in a multiprocessor system should not be fatal to the entire system. To make continued operation possible, it may be necessary to modify the configuration so that the surviving processor performs all vital functions such as interrupt handling. Some computers provide only manually operated reconfiguration switches for this purpose. Others provide both manual and programmable switches so that dynamic reconfiguration can take place under software control. In high availability systems, this type of reconfiguration is very important.

Main-memory failures may make similar reconfiguration necessary so that unusable memory is configured out of the system, and remaining memory presents a sequential address range. The latter may be unnecessary, but it gives better utilization than discontiguously addressable blocks. If the reconfiguration is performed entirely by software, memory addresses will be discontinuous.

Central system reconfiguration is often handled entirely by software if the necessary hardware support is not provided. For example, if a memory area cannot be reconfigured mechanically, it can be left connected but marked unusable via software. The ability to mechanically reconfigure components is preferable since it includes the capability to decouple a failing component from the main system, decreasing the chance that it will cause a system crash. The software aspects of reconfiguration are discussed in Chapter 12, Integrity.

System Monitors

The other Level V entry consists of System Monitors. Although these might be considered a special type of reconfiguration switch, they usually perform a separate and distinct function related to switching.

System monitors, or watchdog timers, or deadman timers, as they are also called, are independent devices used to monitor an information processor's performance. In the simplest case, the monitor is a device connected to some significant information-processor hardware component in such a way that if the information-processor hardware fails, the monitor will detect this fact. This variety of monitor device is often called a deadman timer, for obvious reasons.

The basic monitor detection of hardware failure may be expanded to catch at least some processor software failures. This can be done by adding a timer to the monitor and providing a way for the information-processor software to reset the timer. If the timer is not reset within the required interval, this triggers the same action as if the monitor detected a hardware failure. By proper planning in the processor software, resetting the timer can indicate that the main-line processing routines are executing correctly.

Monitors of this type are most often used in redundant, fail-soft or fail-safe configurations, so that a failure is detected rapidly and causes reconfiguration. The watchdog timer may be connected directly to the reconfiguration switches and automatically cause the required switchover, or it may be provided with some type of output printer, terminal, or alarm by means of which it can notify control personnel that switchover is needed. If the monitor is connected between two information processors in a fail-safe configuration, as shown in Figure

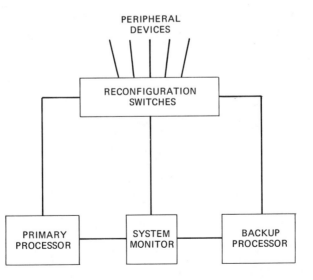

Figure 5-11   Fail-safe configuration.

5-11, it may cause the backup system to take over on failure of the prime system.

Monitor hardware ranges all the way from very simple mechanisms to general-purpose minicomputers used for very sophisticated monitoring of a large information processor or processors. When a computer is used for this purpose, it can of course perform other logical checks to determine that the monitored system or systems are operating correctly.

SUMMARY

When considering the hardware functions and devices needed in an information-processing system, the most important point to be analyzed is the relationship between hardware and software. Does the software take advantage of hardware features? Or does it limit the hardware by not making use of available capabilities? Does the hardware make programming difficult, so that features may not be used because they are poorly implemented in the hardware? These, and many other similar questions, should be asked continually in the analysis procedure. A lengthy iterative process is generally required to consider and properly evaluate the relationships between hardware and software as applied to a particular information-processing system. Only in this way can a well-matched set of hardware and software be obtained.

SECTION **IV**

Software
Functions

CHAPTER 6

Languages

The first of the Software Level IV functions to be discussed is Languages. The term language can be used, in this case, in its dictionary definition as the vocabulary or set of technical expressions used in a specific business, science, etc. Computer languages are similar to human languages in that each provides a vocabulary by means of which certain procedures, structures, functions, and so on can be expressed. Languages are effective tools for translating problems from some external form (flow charts, narrative definitions) to computer executable form.

The relationship between languages and the next software function, applications, is an important one. Languages provide the vocabulary in which the procedures which form applications can be expressed. It is of course equally true that languages are the medium by which all other functions, as well as applications, are implemented. However, the relationship between languages and applications is particularly close, especially because of the heavy use of higher-level languages in applications. Certain languages have been created because of specific application needs not met in other languages. In fact, the original compiler languages were created to meet fairly specific application needs. The ties between languages and applications have always been close.

The whole evolution of computer programming languages has been a process of continually reduced complexity, thus opening up the use of computers to an ever wider group of people. The first computers were programmed in machine language; the actual binary, octal, or decimal codes which activated the processor circuitry were provided by the programmer.

Assemblers provided a quantum decrease in programming complexity making it much easier to learn to program, and also making it possible to program much more rapidly.

Compilers afforded another enormous decrease in complexity, and they opened up programming to a vast new group of people. Programming efficiency (output per man hour) increased greatly.

The latest decrease in complexity is still incomplete, but it dates from the introduction of data management languages. These have greatly extended the programmer's ability to handle complex data structures without great difficulty.

Figure 6-1 shows how this decrease in complexity and increase in effectiveness have taken place over time. The dates shown are not the date of invention or introduction of the particular type of language, but the date at which it came into relatively common use.

The Languages function is subdivided into Level V elements and Level VI techniques as shown in Figure 6-2. Each of these items is discussed in the following pages.

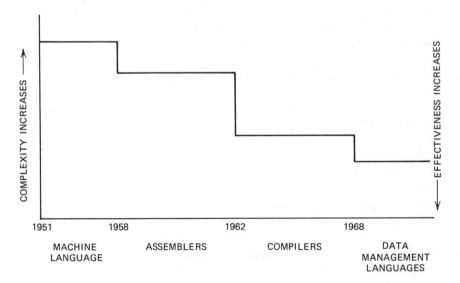

Figure 6-1 Language evolution.

I Network
Level

II Processing
Level

III Macro
Functional
Level

IV Micro
Functional
Level

V Element
Level

VI Device/
Technique
Level

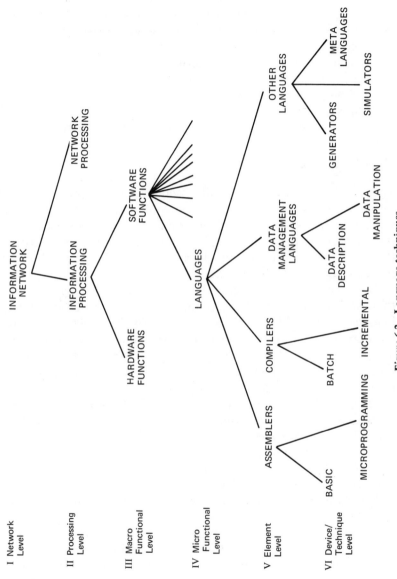

Figure 6-2 Language techniques.

6-1   ASSEMBLERS

The assembler is the language most nearly related to direct machine coding. There is generally a one-for-one relationship between assembly-level and machine-level instructions in the simplest form of assemblers. Each assembly language is therefore very closely tied to a specific computer, and it can be used only with that hardware.

There are two types of assemblers, each of which forms a Level VI entry. One is the basic assembler, the form with which many programmers are familiar. The other is the assembler which operates on microcoded hardware; this is a relatively recent addition to languages.

Basic Assemblers

This Level VI entry includes all Assemblers which provide a certain set of services to assist the computer programmer. The first of these services is support of mnemonic instruction or operation codes, so that the programmer can code LDA, for example, rather than directly using the octal or hexadecimal equivalent of the machine instruction which causes a "Load A" to be executed.

The second general service is the ability to use symbolic rather than actual addresses when coding. It is probably difficult today to imagine coding without this feature, but in the 1950s it was normal for a programmer to know the exact absolute address of every item in his program and to code using those addresses. Using assemblers today, any location can be referred to symbolically (by name), and the address is provided by the assemblers.

The third service provided by assemblers is the ability to use pseudo operation codes. Pseudo ops are mnemonic operation codes which have no equivalent in the computer's instruction repertoire but are instead instructions to the assembler itself. Pseudo ops can be used to generate constants needed in the program, to control assembler output (listing and/or cards, error notes, etc.), to break up the coding into address segments or blocks, and many other similar functions.

Finally, most assemblers provide macro instruction capabilities. Macro, as the name implies, stands for a large instruction, or one made up of many smaller instructions. This capability allows the user to define a macro instruction consisting of any sequence of assembly-level instructions. After definition, the user can call on that macro by the symbolic name he assigned, and his defined sequence of coding will be generated by the assembler. Often used coding sequences can be defined as macros with great savings in programmer time, although sometimes at a cost in execution time and/or memory space.

The basic form of macro simply defines an unchanging set of code which is generated each time the macro is used. To be really useful, the macro must also be able to accept variable parameters so that different data can be inserted each time the macro is used.

This can be shown most easily by example. Figure 6-3 shows a macro prototype which is the skeleton or outline of a macro as defined by the programmer. This particular macro compares one data field, in the computer's A register, to another data field in memory. The name of the macro is COMP.

```
COMP            MACRO
                LDA         #1
                CMPA        #2
                TZE         #3
                ENDM
```

Figure 6-3   Macro prototype.

Each of the "#" items shown in the macro prototype is a variable to be replaced by a parameter supplied at assembly time. When assembling a program, the COMP macro might be used as shown in Figure 6-4, which also shows the macro expansion. The variables PAY, LIMIT, and CHECK correspond to the variables #1, #2, and #3, respectively, in the macro prototype.

```
COMP        (PAY, LIMIT, CHECK)


            WHICH EXPANDS TO:


            LDA                 PAY
            CMPA                LIMIT
            TZE                 CHECK
                        •
                        •
                        •
        CHECK  — — — — — — — —
```

Figure 6-4   Macro use.

The features and capabilities provided by different assemblers vary widely. This is particularly true of the macro facility, which is so extensive in some assemblers that it overlaps into the area normally covered by the compilers.

Microprogramming Assemblers

The Microprogramming Assemblers, which are a fairly recent development, form the other Level VI category. These assemblers are being developed in conjunction with the completely or partially microcoded processors described in Section 5-1. This type of assembler may have all of the features described earlier for basic assemblers plus the additional features described here.

Microprogramming differs from normal assembly-level coding in its ability to control micro processor functions. These are basic hardware functions, such as opening a control gate, setting a flip-flop, or opening a path between a register and an adder. In nonmicrocoded computers, these micro functions are already combined into hardwired patterns to form assembly-level operations.

The microprogram which controls such a system is most often loaded in ROS and is not alterable except by physically replacing that ROS with a new version. Microprogramming is used in this case to create the pattern to be loaded into ROS, and it is basically a one-time process for each version of ROS.

Other computers have a writable control store, which means that the microprogram can be written from the computer, rather than being recreated via hardware manufacture as is the case with ROS. Writable control store requires the same type of program as ROS, but it is applied in a less permanent manner. This technique makes it possible to consider customizing an information processor for specific applications.

Because the technology of microprogramming is still developing rapidly and is almost entirely confined to use by computer hardware manufacturers, it will not be discussed further here. For an in-depth description of microprogramming, the reader is referred to the excellent book on this subject, already mentioned in Chapter 5, by Semir S. Huson.[1]

---

[1] *Microprogramming: Principles and Practices,* Prentice-Hall, Englewood Cliffs, New Jersey, 1971.

6-2 COMPILERS

The second Level V element of Languages consists of Compilers. These languages have the goal of independence from any specific computer. In this respect they are unlike assemblers, each of which is closely related to a particular computer's hardware characteristics. Rather than being computer-oriented, compiler languages are generally said to be problem- or procedure-oriented. Complete machine independence is seldom achieved in a compiler language, but a very high degree of independence is common. To some extent, independence is paid for in reduced performance, which leads to some trade-offs being made in practice between efficiency and complete machine independence.

Compilers evolved as the result of attempts to solve two problems. One problem is the difficulty of programming in assembly language, particularly as computers grow larger and more complex. The other problem is the inability to transfer programs from one computer to another.

Programming complexity is considerable, even on relatively small and simple computers, when assembly language is used. It is impossible to ignore the way the computer works; the programmer must keep track of word sizes, signs (if any), the system's addressing structure, etc. This difficulty originally interfered with the general use of information processors by making it unlikely that anyone except a professional programmer would write programs. A programmer came to be generally needed as an intermediary between the user who has a problem and the computer which can solve the problem. Even worse, a programmer requires considerable training and experience to program well in assembly language, and he must go through a new learning cycle each time he begins to program a different type of computer.

Program transferability, like programmer transferability, is minimal using assembly language. In theory, a program's logic should be transferable from one computer to another, but in practice even this proves illusory in assembly-level programs. This type of coding is so heavily dependent on computer characteristics that the logic often requires rework to be moved to a computer with different features.

Compilers were created to attack these problems. In fact, the first compiler language, Fortran, was developed to make it possible for mathematicians and engineers to write programs in a language similar to the arithmetic expressions with which they are familiar. The approach was a spectacularly successful one; Fortran does in fact lend itself to use by nonprogrammers. It also greatly eases the programming tasks of professional programmers who must work in mathematical terms. For an in-depth description of the Fortran language, see *Fortran Programming* by F. Stuart.[1]

The other most commonly used compiler language is COBOL, which was designed to ease the programming burden of business data processing applications. COBOL was developed under the auspices of the Department of Defense with the avowed goal of standardization and hence transferability. This goal was certainly not realized in early COBOL compilers. Computer manufacturers each implemented a different subset of the language and then often added special features to enhance performance on their particular machine.

Even with this diversity, the use of COBOL significantly reduced the difficulty of converting programs from one computer to another. Today, COBOL is being standardized and subdivided into logical subsets for implementation. The day seems relatively close when conversion of COBOL programs from one type of computer to another will be a trivial process. Fortran is undergoing similar standardization, and so transferability is improving in that language also.

Ideally, transfer of a compiler language program from use on one computer to use on another should require only recompilation on the new system. However, even when this is not the case, transferability is significantly better when using compilers than when using assembly language. Compilers tend to be procedure-oriented, while assemblers are computer-oriented. A program written in any compiler language can generally be transferred to another compiler, even perhaps a compiler for a different language, without procedural reorganization. Thus, transferability is improved even without compiler standardization. With the additional advances in standardization, true transferability may be achieved eventually.

There are a great number of other compiler languages available today, in addition to Fortran and COBOL. Many have particular areas of specialty; for example, JOVIAL is well suited to command and control applications and is used by the armed forces for that purpose. LISP is adapted to list processing applications; BASIC (developed at Dartmouth) is a simple terminal-oriented computation language well suited to time-sharing use. The only general-purpose compiler language other than Fortran and COBOL being used fairly extensively is PL/I.

PL/I was originated (and called by a variety of other names) by SHARE, the association of IBM large-scale system users. PL/I is felt

[1] John Wiley and Sons, New York, 1969.

by some to provide a language rich and flexible enough to use as the only compiler, replacing both COBOL and Fortran. The complete language is extremely rich and complex but is well suited to subsetting. Subsets can be used to give substantially the same features as other simpler languages, such as COBOL or Fortran, while the full set remains available to solve more complex problems. A description of PL/I can be found in *A Guide to PL/I* by Seymour V. Pollack and Theodor D. Sterling.[1]

It will be interesting to observe the future evolution and use of PL/I. Its development represents an effort to standardize and reduce the total number of languages, while the many special purpose languages being developed concurrently represent an opposing trend of language specialization. It may well be that both trends will survive and prosper, each in the appropriate areas of use.

Batch Compilers

The first of the Level VI subdivisions of Compilers includes Batch Compilers. This most common, or batch, compilation method consists of reading in the entire source program, then starting analysis and code generation. Batch compilation requires one or more phases for completion, and the number of phases is sometimes used as an adjective to characterize the compiler. Two- and three-phase compilers are the most common. The book, *Anatomy of a Compiler* by John A. N. Lee, gives a good description of how compilers operate.[2]

The compliation process generally consists, first, of a phase called lexical analysis. This phase translates input statements into characterstrings acceptable to the next compilation phase. Lexical analysis determines that the statements received form "grammatically" correct sentences within the structure of the particular language.

The next phase is called syntax analysis. This consists of a parsing process which determines whether or not the string produced by lexical analysis is correct. This process may produce object code directly. More often it produces a structural representation from which code is generated in still another compilation phase.

In some compilers, actual code generation takes place separately in the system's assembler. The compiler's final phase simply turns out assembly language which is handled normally as assembler input. This method is not very often used, as it is slower than direct code generation. Its only advantage is the generation, as a byproduct, of an

---

[1] Holt, Reinhart and Winston, New York, 1969.
[2] Reinhold, New York, 1967.

assembly-level equivalent of the compiler statements. However, the trend among programmers seems to be in favor of compiler-level debugging, so the need for this assembly code is diminishing.

Incremental Compilers

The other Level VI technique used under Compilers is Incremental Compilers. These differ from batch compilers by performing the compilation process incrementally, processing each source statement individually as it is input. These compilers are used in time sharing and other interactive environments. Their purpose is to make the compilation process directly interactive with the user at the terminal. The incremental mode of operation would be meaningless in a batch environment where no user is available to converse with the compiler.

The extent of the processing done incrementally varies in compilers of this type. Some process each statement completely, including code generation, to the degree possible. This approach may place some restrictions on the user; for example, he may be required to define data formats and variables at the beginning of his process so that these are available when reference to them occurs. More complex incremental compilers may, instead, compile conditionally, going back later to fill in undefined references.

Other compilers perform only lexical analysis incrementally, so that most input errors are noted at once, and then leave the remainder of the compilation process until the entire source has been accumulated. This approach is an attempt to compromise between the user's desire for rapid error notification and the difficulty and increased overhead involved in incremental code generation.

Of course not all compilers used in interactive systems are incremental; many are batch compilers even though they receive their input incrementally. This mode is often satisfactory, particularly where simple languages (BASIC, for example) and short programs are the rule. The various types of compilers are discussed in "Batch, Conversational, and Incremental Compilers" by Harry Katzen, Jr.[1]

6-3 DATA MANAGEMENT LANGUAGES

The third Level V element under Languages is Data Management Languages. Included in this category are languages developed for the

---

[1] *AFIPS Conference Proceedings*, **34**, 1969 Spring Joint Computer Conference, New Jersey, 1969, pp. 47–56.

specific purpose of defining and using files or data bases. Data management functions may be implemented in the form of extensions to compiler-level languages. They may also take the form of generators (see Section 6-4). In these, the user fills out forms describing files and file use; these forms are input to a program generator; and the output is a program, programs, or subroutines specifically tailored to the file(s) and processing described.

Although data management languages have come into general use quite recently, some languages of this type have existed for a number of years. At the present time, a number are marketed by hardware and software vendors. For example, MARK IV[1] is a very popular data management software package, marketed by Informatics Inc. IBM provides a data management package titled IMS,[2] while Honeywell furnishes the I-D-S[3] (Integrated Data Store) data management language. In its original form, I-D-S was developed by General Electric in 1962; it is therefore one of the earliest languages of this type still in use.

Data management languages have been developed to meet a need not filled by the general-purpose compilers. When Fortran and COBOL were first developed, the main file media were punched cards and magnetic tape. Mass storage was not really being widely used at that time, and so it was largely ignored by the compiler developers. This has seldom proved to be a major handicap in Fortran; however, COBOL presents quite a different picture.

COBOL was developed for business data processing, and it is in this area that the use of randomly-accessible mass storage has proven so important. However, COBOL originally had no mass-storage handling ability, and when one was added it was totally inadequate to the average user's needs. Only now (in the 1970s) is a serious attempt being made to add useful mass-storage management features.

The lack of COBOL features for data management on mass storage has been felt by many installations, and it has led to the creation of the present set of data management languages. The area of data management is too important to many users to be left unfilled. In the future, as data management features become more generally available within compiler languages, data management software as a unique category may diminish in importance.

---

[1] *MARK IV File Management System*, MK IV SD02 5M968, Informatics, Inc., Sherman Oaks, California.
[2] *Information Management System/360, Version 2*, Form GH20-0765, International Business Machines Corporation, White Plains, New York.
[3] *Integrated Data Store (I-D-S) Reference Manual*, Order No. BR69, Honeywell Information Systems, Waltham, Massachusetts.

Data management is very closely related to file management, which is described in Chapter 9, but it is also distinct from it. File management handles each file as an entity, providing space for it on mass storage or other media, cataloging it, and providing access control via catalogs. File organization and file format are unknown to the file management functions.

Data management, on the other hand, deals with data organization within the space provided by file management. Data management must be aware of data formats within the file, but it is not concerned with how or where the file is physically stored or how to access it physically. These distinctions are important, and the separation of function is important to define properly both the data and file management functions.

Data Description

The first of the two Level VI techniques under Data Management Languages is Data Description. This function provides the means to define the organization and format of a file or data base. Format description consists of defining how large fields are, what their sequence is within the record, and sometimes what type of data representation is used—packed numeric, alphanumeric, binary, etc.

The file organization is described by defining how records are stored within the file space. They may be stored sequentially, in which case the field(s) on which sequence is established must be defined. If records are stored randomly, some method of retrieval must be specified; that is, what key field(s) makes each record unique? Some data management schemes store records partially or entirely at random but also link them together so that they can be accessed sequentially, perhaps in a variety of sequences. There are many ways of organizing data, and either the user must define the one(s) required, or the data management software must provide default conditions.

The process of data description requires that the file definer fill out a set of descriptions. These may take the same form as COBOL data definitions, or the description may be accomplished by filling in blanks in a set of special purpose definition forms provided by the originator of the data management package. In either case, the two basic items to be provided are exact record formats and record-to-record relationships (file organization).

Conceptually, the definition of a data base is a one-time task. However, in practice a data base is defined, created, and then used.

Although the manual definition process may take place only once, it is necessary to make those definitions available when the actual data base is created and at every subsequent use. There are two quite different ways in which this can be done.

In the simplest way, the data description is embedded in every program which uses the data, including the program(s) originally used to create it. This method is familiar to all COBOL programmers; if the same data is used by many programs, identical data descriptions are required in all of the programs. The definitions may be used during program generation or compilation to tailor the coding for the exact data formats involved. Alternatively, the definitions may be present in the program and used by coding which adapts interpretively to the data definitions. These code generation and interpretive approaches are not mutually exclusive; sometimes the code is partially tailored but also adapts interpretively during execution.

As an alternative to including the data description with all programs, the definition may be stored with the file data, either in the same file space or in a separate area. This is known as the schema approach; the definitions are the schema by which the file data itself can be deciphered. This approach is well defined in the *Data Base Task Group Report to the CODASYL Programming Language Committee.*"[1]

Creating a schema is then the heart of the data description process. It consists of filling out a set of definitions for fields, records, and inter-record relationships. These definitions then make up the source form schema, and from them an object form schema can be created by compilation, generation, or other similar process.

Once the schema has been created, it can then be used by programs accessing the data. This generally requires that the schema be available when these programs are compiled and again when they are executed. Although in the schema approach the data definition is not embedded in the compiled program, it is generally used at compilation time to determine what type of working storage is needed in the program.

The data management system generally relies on the file management system to create a place to store the schema, and it uses file management to retrieve the schema whenever it is needed.

One of the attributes of the schema approach, in some cases, is the ability to define and use subschemata. A subschema is a logical subset of a schema and may differ from it in certain respects. A sub-

---

[1] Association for Computing Machinery, New York, April, 1971.

schema, in the simplest case, can be used to define a portion of the entire file described by the schema. This technique can save memory, since the schema or subschema must be in memory when in use. Subsetting can also be used as a security measure; a program can be restricted to specific file segments by defining a subschema including only the area that program is authorized to access.

One of the advantages of the schema approach is that it is easier than in the conventional data definition approach to change data formats. When the file definition is included in each program which accesses the file, any significant change requires that all programs be changed accordingly. Since the schema is separate from accessing programs, it is often possible to change only the file and schema and let the programs adjust dynamically to the new format.

Data base format changes have always been very troublesome, particularly when programs are data format dependent, which almost all are. Using the schema approach, it is possible to make many changes to a file's data format and organization without any program changes. This is, of course, only true within reasonable limits. A complete redefinition of the file's format and organization cannot easily be handled by any method.

Using schemata, simple changes can be made as follows. It may be necessary, for example, to expand a record by adding another field. First, a new schema showing the new record format is required. To add the field, a program can be executed which reads via the old schema, provides the data for the added field, then writes via the new schema. It is not necessary to do this in a single pass, although in practice this may be the most convenient method. Programs which refer to the record during conversion from old to new format may need both schemata, although this is not always the case. After the new field is added to some or all of the records, programs using the old schema will not be able to use the new field, but they will not be bothered by its presence. If a program uses the new schema before the field is added, the field content will simply be presented to the program as null.

It can be imagined that a great deal of complex data management software is required to provide these features. However, the payoff in simplification of the applications involved is generally very great.

The distinction between data description and file creation is a real one. Data description only sets the stage for creation of the actual data in the assigned file space. Data creation usually involves execution of a special task, which uses as input the data definitions and sometimes the actual data. Formatting of the data takes place, guided by the definitions. The data is also organized and placed within the file area as specified in the definitions. If no data is input, the space is simply initialized as necessary, perhaps with block identifiers and other similar data. Data creation is in fact only one form of the data manipulation described next.

Data Manipulation

The other Level VI technique under Data Management Languages is Data Manipulation. This includes features provided to allow access to and modification of the data described via the preceding technique.

The language for data manipulation, like that for data description, may be implemented in different ways. It may consist of statements to be used at compiler level, either in one compiler or in several. It may instead consist of parameters input to a generation process which produces object (or possibly compiler/assembler source) coding to execute the desired functions.

Data manipulation always requires some means of accessing the data descriptions. The methods for achieving this access were discussed in the preceding section. In the schema mode, the schema or subschema must be available both during code generation and at execution time. At generation time the schema is needed to determine working storage layouts, etc. which are tailored to the data format. At execution time the schema is needed again so that the interpretive routines which handle data and file formats can tailor themselves to the specific schema.

Although the use of schemata in data management is very attractive, it is rare as yet. This concept seems to hold considerable promise of improvement in data management techniques. In particular, the ability to change formats with reasonable ease will be of great assistance.

Data manipulation consists of the ability to perform basic functions concerned with the content of a file or part of a file. These functions are READ, WRITE, MODIFY, and also STORE and DELETE. The first three functions apply to data already in the file, while the two latter allow records to be added to or removed from the file.

Perhaps the most variability in data management systems exists in the ways in which data access can be expressed. When a record is to be read from the file, it must be uniquely identified. There are, in general, two ways this can be done.

One of the most common methods of identifying a record to be accessed is to specify its position relative to some other record, or to the start or end of the file. This is of course the way one progresses through a sequential file. Access starts with the first record in the file, then continues by accessing the "next" record until all are exhausted.

Data structures which are not, strictly speaking, sequential can also be accessed via positional relationships. A structure may consist of sets of records, in which each set has one master record and n detail records, all linked together. Figure 6-5 shows such a record set. (Figures 6-5 and 6-6 are drawn from the Honeywell Integrated Data Store

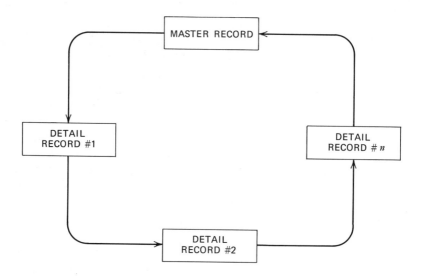

Figure 6-5   Linked data structure.

(I-D-S) data management system, and they also represent structures defined in the Data Base Task Group report referenced on p. 89.)

In this type of structure, the master record can be accessed (often randomly), then each of its associated details can be accessed by requesting the next record. The relationship in this case is not achieved by storing the records sequentially, but by providing a linkage pointer(s) in each, chaining them together. This method is extremely flexible since the pointers may go both forward and backward if necessary, making it possible to traverse the chain of records in either direction.

Very complex data structures can be created via this chaining technique. A detail in one chain can be a master in another. Figure 6-6 shows an example of this type of structure.

In this example, there is one chain consisting of a master record of all customers, and n detail records, each representing an individual customer. In the other type of chain, each of the customer records is the master of a chain containing that customer's orders as details.

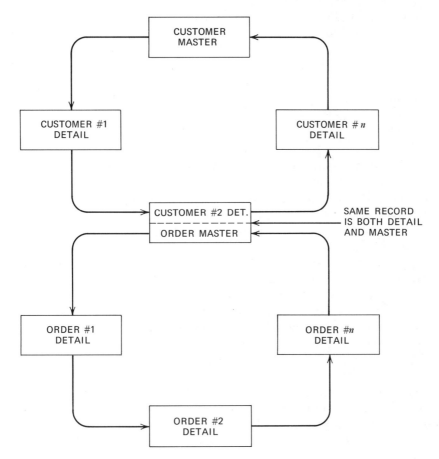

Figure 6-6 Complex linked data structure.

This structure could easily extend to other levels; the next might be a chain in which the order record is the master and each line in the order is a detail.

Still another often used access method is purely random; records are referred to by some identifier which is, or can be converted to, the item's position in the file. In the best case, the record is accessed directly using this information. When multiple records have an identifier which converts to the same file position, some may be stored in overflow locations, and a search (or seek down the overflow chain) is required to find them. Generally the data management software hides this process from the user.

Data management may allow multiple concurrent accesses to the same data. If this is done, File Management (Chapter 9) and data management work together to control such access.

First, the allowable combinations of accesses must be specified. There are the following basic types of access to file content:

- READ
- WRITE
- APPEND
- EXECUTE
- PURGE

There are many possible combinations of access types, but in general only innocuous combinations are allowed. Two concurrent accesses in READ mode, for example, cannot interfere with each other. READ and EXECUTE modes generate no interference. However, any combination which includes one of the other three modes will cause potential interference.

Here, as in other areas, file management can be considered to work in cooperation with data management. The concurrent access control function of file management (see Section 9-2) processes each initial request for file access. By keeping track of accesses in process, it can check each new request and accept only those which would not cause interference. For generality, the file management routines require a list of acceptable access combinations for each file and/or each data management language. The simpler data management packages do not allow concurrent access except in READ or EXECUTE (if supported) modes. More complex data management systems allow a variety of concurrent access types. In this case file management checks for allowable combinations prior to the start of access, and data management must then furnish all necessary interference control while access is in process.

Let us then consider the complications inherent in the various possible combinations of access modes. As noted earlier, multiple READS, multiple EXECUTES (assuming reentrant code being executed), and a combination of READ and EXECUTE do not cause interference, and they are therefore almost universally supported.

The PURGE mode can also be eliminated from consideration. PURGE means to destroy the file content, and so it cannot be done while there are active users of the file.

The most interesting types of concurrent access are those which include at least one WRITE user. Allowing one or more WRITE accesses concurrently with READ access(es) can cause potentially disastrous results.

For example, consider the following sequence of events:

Program A reads Record 1
Program B modifies Record 1

.

.

.

time passes

.

.

.

Program A reads Record 1 again

This is a classic example of what is called the "shifting data base." Program A reads the same record twice, at different points in its processing, and it sees a different version each time. Programs which are not written to run in a concurrent access environment often become confused and malfunction in situations of this type. On the other hand, a carefully designed program should be able to handle this successfully.

Another example of this same type is also interesting:

Program A reads Record 2
Program B deletes Record 2

.

.

.

Program A attempts to read Record 2

This is simply an aggravated case of the example shown earlier, but it is even more likely to cause Program A to feel nervous because of the shifting data.

In each of the above examples, Program A was reading only, while Program B was updating (reading and writing). Consider the much more complex case where both A and B are updating the same file:

Program A reads Record 1
Program B reads Record 1
Program B updates Record 1
Program A updates Record 1

If update is performed by replacing fields rather than by incrementally changing them, the above case will result in the loss of Program B's update. Program A read the record and performed some kind of computation using record content. When it was ready to write the record, it simply wrote back the result of its computation, ignoring the fact that Program B had changed the record during the time intervening between A's read and A's update. In the best case, if the two programs did not use any of the same fields within the record (and only updated fields were written back), no harm would be done. In the worst case, all of B's processing would be lost.

Notice that in the earlier example of one READ and one WRITE user, only the reading program was adversely affected by concurrent access. In the multiple WRITE example, the data base itself was damaged because only part of the executed updates appeared in it. In many cases, data management routines do not try to prevent the first case, but they *do* prevent the second so that data integrity is preserved.

In general, there are two approaches possible to the solution of this problem. One is to place the responsibility on the application programmer to include all of the logic necessary to handle concurrent access, with some help from data management. The other method is to hide the consequences of concurrent access from the programmer and handle it entirely within data management. Both of these approaches are discussed in the following pages.

If the programmer is given the responsibility, he is generally also given commands by means of which he can lock and unlock specified segments of the data base. While an area is locked, data management prevents any other access to that area. A sample program sequence might be as follows:

Program A locks File Segment 1
Program A reads Record 1-1
Program A updates Record 1-1
Program A unlocks File Segment 1

If another program attempts to access within the locked area, data management delays it until the preceding program unlocks or completes execution. End of execution is always an implied unlock of any areas locked by the completed program.

This type of lock can be applied at any of several levels. If it is at the file level, the concurrent access effectiveness is reduced, but locking and unlocking are easy to implement. More often, some logical or physical segment of the file can be locked, which reduces the chance that other programs will be stopped by the lock.

A variation of this approach allows the program to symbolically reserve a file area. This does not prevent others from entering the area, but if any do so and modify data, the reserving program is informed on its next access attempt. This can be shown in the example:

Program A reserves File Segment 2
Program A reads Record 2-2

Program B reads Record 2-2
Program B updates Record 2-2
*Program A updates Record 2-2

At the point starred, the update is not performed, and instead Program A is notified that the record he is trying to update has been changed since his last access. He can choose to ignore this, or more likely, he can loop back through his logic and reread the record. In this situation, one can visualize a possibly endless loop for Program A. In practice, of course, this is very unlikely to happen.

There is one other aspect having to do with the concurrent update control being placed on the programmer. Often it is felt that programs which only read should allow for a shifting data base, so that they can run with concurrent WRITE users without difficulty. This is generally feasible, with one exception. Structural changes to the data should be (but sometimes are not) hidden from the program. For example, such a program traversing a chain that is being modified should not be allowed by data management to "fall off" the end of a partially-linked chain. This is shown in Figure 6-7.

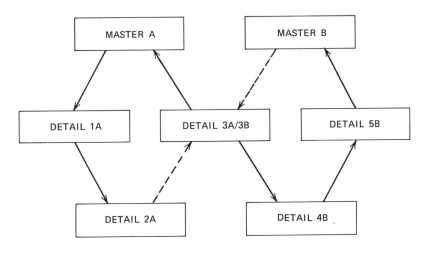

Figure 6-7   Data structure modification.

The example shows Detail 3 in the process of being unlinked from Chain A, thus losing its identity as Detail 3A. It is then being linked into Chain B, where it will become Detail 3B. During the transition, a program progressing from Detail 1A to Detail 2A, and then to Detail 3A may find a broken chain. The data management system should lock all such areas automatically while change is going on.

Some data management systems, instead of placing any of the concurrent access control burden on the programmer, assume it all. This approach makes the problems transparent to the user program, but of course it complicates data management considerably.

Either of two ways can be chosen to accomplish this end. Data management may prevent a program from accessing anything which may change, or it may allow access and later rollback and restart the program if change occurs. Both of these methods rely heavily on the existence of a good rollback capability; see Chapter 12, Integrity, for a complete discussion of this feature.

If the method chosen is to prevent incompatible accesses, data management must monitor each access to the data base. Using a rather complex set of rules, it must analyze each access to determine if interference could result. For example, consider the following sequence:

Program A (WRITE mode) reads Record 1
Program A updates Record 1
Program A reads Record 2
Program B (READ mode) reads Record 1

In this case, Program B is prevented from reading Record 1 until Program A completes successfully. This prevents B from seeing an erroneous version of the record if A subsequently fails and its updates are rolled back.

The next example is very similar to the above:

Program A (WRITE mode) reads Record 1
Program A reads Record 2
Program B (READ mode) reads Record 1

Even though, in this case, Program A has not updated Record 1, Program B may still be prevented from accessing it. The assumption would be that A may well update Record 1 later, since A is a WRITE mode program. If the syntax of the data access language is such that "retrieve for update" can be distinguished from "retrieve," then interference can result only from the former. In many cases, unfortunately, the language is not this explicit and so the intent to update must be assumed.

It can be seen that this approach involves considerable overhead, since the data management routines must monitor and record all accesses which cause potential interference. As the number of accessed records increases, the overhead also increases. This method is well suited to transaction processing where large numbers of short-running jobs may require access to the same data base.

A slightly different approach to this problem requires the same overhead of monitoring and recording, but it does not delay a program to prevent access to a record used by another program. Instead, the access is allowed and noted, and a "dependency" relationship is established. This can be shown in terms of the example:

Program A reads and updates Record 6
Program B reads Record 6

At this point, B is said to be dependent on A, because it has used the results of A's update to Record 6. If Program A subsequently fails and its updates are wiped out, Program B must also be rolled back and restarted.

This method is superior to the one described earlier, in that delays are not as prevalent. If one assumes that the majority of jobs complete successfully, this approach may be a good one. It does, however, have certain other disadvantages inherent in the fact that a dependent job cannot complete until the job(s) on which it is dependent completes successfully.

This can be illustrated by the following example:

Program A updates Record 1
Program B reads Record 1
  Therefore Program B is dependent on Program A
Program B updates Record 2
Program C reads Record 2
  Therefore Program C is dependent on Program B
Program C updates Record 3
Program D reads Record 3
  Therefore Program D is dependent on Program C

In this example, the string of dependencies has grown very long. (In practice it could be even more complex.) None of the programs B, C, and D can complete until A does; C and D cannot complete until B does, etc. If A, for example, were a very long-running job, the delays might be substantial. As noted above, multiple concurrent update is most satisfactory when short-running jobs are involved.

These two methods, delay to prevent interference and dependency relating, both allow multiple concurrent update accesses. In each case, the result is exactly the same as if the jobs were run serially, except of course that they complete more rapidly.

There is still another, quite different, approach to the control of concurrent accesses. This uses the principle of "no update in place;" that is, the main file is not updated when a program issues a WRITE. Instead, the update is stored in a separate area uniquely assigned to that program. Each of that program's reads must be checked against its update area. If that program has updated the record earlier, it is given its updated copy; if not it is given the copy from the main file.

Two or more programs can be updating the same file concurrently using this technique. This is shown in Figure 6-8.

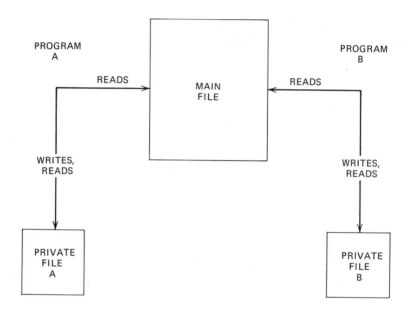

Figure 6-8 Delayed file update.

In the example, Program A's private file contains only the records it has updated, and Program B's file contains only its own updates.

Without any other supporting action by data management, this is a very useful way to allow test runs against a production file. If the jobs being tested cannot update the file, they cannot harm it. When used for test purposes, the private update file is usually printed or output in some other way, then destroyed.

If, instead, this technique is used to control multiple concurrent updates in a production environment, at some point the updates must be applied to the main file. This is done by periodically stopping access and moving the updates to the main file. Although simple in theory, this is not so in practice.

If only one set of updates exists, it can simply be written to the file. If there are two or more sets, they must be compared and combined while being written to the file. In some cases inconsistencies may arise, causing one of the jobs to be rolled back and rerun. For example, two programs might operate as shown in Figure 6-9.

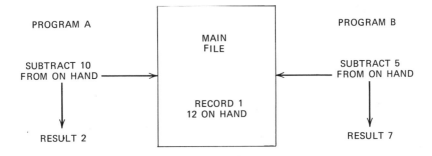

Figure 6-9   Results of delayed update.

By combining the two updates (-10 and -5) shown in the example, a negative balance is obtained. In some cases this may be acceptable, but more often it is not. Generally if these programs had been run sequentially, the second would not have subtracted its full amount from the balance.

This example points out one of the effects of this type of update. Each program produces output based on its view of the file, which may not be correct. This may or may not be acceptable, depending on the particular application. Some feel that this type of inconsistency is acceptable when a data base is being continually updated on-line. In this environment, *any* picture of file status can only represent it at the particular fleeting point in time when the snapshot is taken.

A rather limited type of concurrent access exists in the delta file configuration described in Section 5-2. Figure 6-10 shows an example of this configuration. A fully generalized concurrent access by two separate processors, while not impossible, is extremely complex to control. So, in practice, systems of this type control access by allowing only one processor to enter a given file at any time. While this is rather restrictive, it is usually satisfactory. The main purpose of the shared storage is to pass data from one system to the other, so there is seldom any real need for both to simultaneously access any area.

All of this very lengthy discussion of data management control over multiple concurrent update leads to the conclusion that it is a very complex subject. There are, in fact, very few data management systems which allow any form of concurrent update with WRITE user(s) involved. Those which allow free concurrent access to multiple WRITE users are even more rare. Some new techniques are needed to make concurrent access control less cumbersome and complex. Only when these are developed will this feature come into really general use.

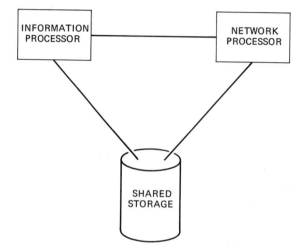

Figure 6-10   Delta configuration.

6-4   OTHER LANGUAGES

This final Level V entry under Languages is a sort of catch-all which accommodates the less generally used, and more specialized, types of languages. The preceding three Level V entries all covered basic and general purpose languages which are widely used. The entries under this heading are much more restricted in use, although each is very valuable in its particular area of specialization.

Generators

Generators, the first of the three Level VI entries, are very useful languages which cover a broad range of functions. The earliest, and still most common, form was the report generator. Section 6-3 pointed out that data management languages are sometimes implemented in the form of generators.

A generator is a software package which contains a number of routines to accomplish specific functions. These routines are capable of accepting input parameters and modifying themselves as the parameters indicate. For example, a general routine to extract data from a file and print a detailed report would include code to pick up fields from the file, code to edit the fields, and code to place them in a report format for output. The input parameters would determine where each field starts in the file, how long it is, what edit rules to use, and in what position of the print line to place it.

Report generators also include the ability to accumulate totals, often at various summary levels. In this case, parameters are required to specify which fields to accumulate, when to add or subtract, which fields are used to control total breaks, etc. Again, the report generator package contains basic code to perform these functions, which modifies itself as needed. The IBM System/3 RPG is a fairly typical example of report generators.[1]

There are actually several varieties of generators, one of which should probably not be called a generator in the purest sense. This is the type of software which actually executes interpretively, using the input parameters, rather than generating specific code. This approach is less efficient than code generation, but it may be perfectly acceptable for one-time jobs. Report generators are often used for seldom-run or one-time reports, and so efficiency is not the prime consideration.

More commonly, specific code is generated for the particular job defined by the input parameters. Sometimes code generation is an integral part of the execution process; again, this is appropriate for nonrecurring jobs. More often, generation is a separate operation. Parameters are fed to the generator which produces a set of tailored code. This code is output as an object file, and it can then be used as part of a job stack, just as any other object file can. Occasionally the generator output is in the form of compiler or assembly source language, rather than object code, but this is rare.

Generators are rather limited in scope because of the inherent complexity in parameterizing and tailoring code for general use. They also tend to turn out rather inefficient code. However, even with these failings they have considerable advantages. They are easier to use than any other language, in most cases, since the user simply fills out a set of parameter forms defining the job. A particular one-time report which falls within the capabilities of a generator can be produced very rapidly and with relatively little programmer effort. Generators are also used to great advantage in converting simple programs from one type of computer to another, again because of their ease and speed of use.

Simulators

The second Level VI entry for Other Languages covers Simulators. These languages provide methods to simulate sets of functions. There

---

[1] *IBM System/3 Disk System RPG II Reference Manual*, Form SC 21-7504, International Business Machines Corporation, White Plains, New York.

are simulators which allow programs written for one computer to be run on another computer; the computer's characteristics are simulated in this case. Other simulators allow noncomputer processes to be simulated on a computer.

Simulation of one computer on another computer, by software means alone, is generally very inefficient. This is particularly true if the two computers have radically different hardware characteristics. For example, simulating a character- or byte-oriented computer on a word-oriented system is very inefficient. (The reverse is less so.) Often simulations run slower than the system being simulated, even though the actual computer used is a much faster and more powerful system than the one simulated.

This inefficiency has led to the increasingly general use of hardware to aid or accomplish the simulation process. When hardware is used, the process is called emulation rather than simulation. Depending on the sophistication of the emulation hardware and whether or not it requires some simulation software in addition to the hardware, emulations generally perform at least as well as the emulated system, and often better. One example of a hardware emulator is described in *IBM/360 Conversion Aids: The 7074 Emulator Program for IBM System/360 Models 50 and 65.*[1]

The other class of simulators includes those used to model or otherwise simulate physical processes so that their actions can be observed and studied. For example, processes such as the operation of an oil refinery or of an electrical power plant are often simulated. The goal is generally to determine how much such processes will react to changes in their environment. Also, a new plant not yet built may be simulated, with the goal of determining the best way to construct it.

One of the types of processes which can be simulated is a computer application or set of applications forming a system. This technique can be very useful, not for simple systems, but for complex on-line and/or real-time information systems. In complex processes it may be very difficult to determine in advance of implementation whether or not the system design is adequate. In particular, the performance to be expected is difficult to predict.

By mathematically simulating the system, one can often observe design flaws early enough to modify them before implementation. Inadequate or adequate performance can usually be determined. However, it is also true that the simulation may not be as useful in itself

[1] Form No. C27-6908, International Business Machines Corporation, White Plains, New York.

as is the careful analysis required to set up the simulation. This in-depth review of the design may, in itself, point out flaws. If it does not, the simulation may do so by revealing that the results of the system's processing will not be as expected.

Although it is not worth simulating simple systems, a good simulation of an extremely complex system may also be impractically expensive. For example, a model of a multiprogramming on-line operating system may take almost as much effort to develop as the operating system itself. Generally, therefore, it is only practical to simulate broad functions rather than to try to model a system in depth. Occasionally this is worthwhile, but it is always time consuming and expensive.

Meta Languages

The third and final Level VI entry covers Meta Languages. These are languages which are extremely high-level, more so than the compilers, and which are also very generalized. Most frequently they are used to generate compilers or assemblers for lower-level languages.

One example of a meta language is a "compiler compiler," that is, a system which creates a compiler. The characteristics of the compiler, the input it is to receive and the output it is expected to produce, are all described in macro terms to the meta language processor. It then creates a compiler which, at least in theory, is equivalent to a hand-coded set of software routines to perform the same compilation functions. An example of this approach is described in *A Compiler Generator* by W. M. McKeenan, J. J. Horning, and D. B. Wortman.[1]

One of the interesting features of meta languages is that they are usually completely machine independent, not in their own execution form, but in terms of the output they can generate. The compiler compiler referred to above should be equally able to create a compiler for an IBM 370 system or for a Univac 1110 system (which are systems with quite different features). This is possible because all of the characteristics which distinguish one computer from another can be described explicitly to the meta language processor. This is in distinct contrast to the usual language processor which contains an implicit, rather than an explicit, description of the computer for which it is turning out code.

Meta languages are, at present, in the research and development stage, and so they are of little interest in the average information sys-

[1] Prentice-Hall, Englewood Cliffs, New Jersey, 1970.

tem. However, as the techniques involved become more generally understood and better developed, they may find broader use. For example, these languages may provide an approach to defining and generating entire application systems for a variety of computers, or they may make practical the use of very specialized programming languages for some applications, if these languages can be easily defined and if the compilers to process them can be produced easily. The progress of meta languages should therefore be watched carefully for developments of general interest.

SUMMARY

The various languages, particularly the assemblers, compilers, and data management languages, are the base on which all software rests. Software functionally will continue to expand because of new requirements in the total spectrum of information processing. Changes, expansions, and improvements in current languages can be expected. This is particularly true of data management, which is essential in the on-line transaction-processing systems now coming into broad use. New specialized languages will undoubtedly be created to serve particular application needs. The lack of time and competent programming personnel will continue to force the average installation toward the use of high-level languages. The use of assembly-level languages will no doubt diminish, even in complex software such as operating systems. The future lies with the easier-to-use, more standardized high-level languages.

CHAPTER 7

Applications

The second Level V entry under Software Functions is Applications. This entry includes all software written to perform functions associated directly with user problems. Typical applications are payroll, cost accounting, order entry, inventory control, and so on. The list is literally endless, since there are innumerable items which fall into this class. In fact, the majority of all software in existence falls into this category.

It is interesting to note how little real progress of a basic nature has been made in writing application programs. In the early days of computing every program was treated as a special case, and all of its code was newly created. If any common code was used in more than one program, this was done by an individual programmer reusing some of his own routines, or possibly obtaining and using another programmer's code for certain functions.

Some early advances in this respect occurred with the use of common subroutines, particularly in conjunction with the Fortran language. This provided a start toward the use of common code to perform standard functions in a wide variety of otherwise unrelated programs. Another step in this direction occurred with the use of standard I/O routines such as IOCS. (For a present day example of the use of IOCS, see the *UNIVAC Operating Systems IOCS Programmers Reference.*[1]

Many people believed that these beginning steps toward coding standardization would lead to greater degrees of commonality than they have in fact done. For example, at various times it has been stated that a single payroll program could be used (modified slightly as necessary) to compute *any* payroll. This ambitious idea proved impractical for several reasons.

First, significant differences in the same application used at different locations do in fact exist. To use payroll as an example again, hourly and salaried workers are paid quite differently. Hourly workers under union contracts must be paid in accordance with those contracts, which are often unique to a particular company or even to a particular plant. On the other hand, it is true that all payrolls require common computations of federal taxes, applicable state and local taxes, etc.

The second reason the desire for common-use application programs proved impractical in many cases is the so-called NIH (Not Invented Here) syndrome. System designers and programmers would generally rather create an application from scratch than to adapt a standard package to their needs. There is a fairly pervasive feeling that it takes as long to become familiar with a standard software package as it does to write a specialized one, and of course there is a certain amount of truth to this. It may in fact be easier to write a new program, particularly when documentation is inadequate, than to modify an existing one. When programs are large, however, this argument seldom holds water.

There has been quite an upsurge in the production, sale, and use of generalized application software in the last few years. The greatest reason for this is undoubtedly the rapidly growing cost associated with data processing installations. As designers' and programmers' salaries have increased (often out of all proportion to productivity), the cost of writing unique software has become unreasonable in many cases. This has led installations to look more carefully at the use of standardized packages. It has also often led them to the conclusion that a generalized package, even if it is not exactly what is desired, is worth using because of the greatly decreased cost.

This trend has of course been magnified by the unbundling of charges by some computer hardware manufacturers. When software vendors attempted to sell generalized software in competition with similar but free software from the computer vendors, they had little

---

[1] Form UP-7526, Sperry Rand Corporation, King of Prussia, Pennsylvania.

success even when their product was sometimes clearly superior. In the current situation where both products may be charged for, however, true competition comes into play. This tends to enhance the vendors' efforts to make their software really useful so that it is competitive. Computer users are therefore finding a wider range and higher quality of generalized software from which to choose.

Application programs are designed to process particular types of data for a specific purpose; they can therefore be said to be procedure sensitive. That is, the characteristics of each application program, or set of related programs, are determined by the process being programmed. It is also true, although less often recognized or admitted, that applications are sensitive both to the language(s) used and to the operating-system environment within which they exist. It is important to recognize these facts so that they can be minimized to the degree possible.

In considering the sensitivity of applications to languages, we must realize that a given program is of course dependent on the features (or lack of features) of the language in which it is written. When analyzing which language to use, we must consider the available features. Equally important, in many if not all cases, is the language's ability to support change and transferability. In the current state of the art, fewer and fewer applications can be found in which there is a valid reason for the use of assembly-level languages. (This is also coming to be true in the development of software such as operating systems.)

Application sensitivity to the operating-system environment varies widely, depending chiefly on the complexity of the application. An operating system should ideally be transparent to the programs which run under its control, but in practice this is never so. However, a program's dependence on the operating system will be less in some cases than in others.

The applications which are least likely to be sensitive are straightforward batch jobs written in higher-level languages. As soon as applications become more complex, they become more closely tied to a particular operating system. This is especially true of on-line applications. The support offered for these programs varies greatly, and of course the application will use the features provided by the operating system within which it is actually implemented.

This topic was not introduced in order to present solutions, since there are no real solutions at present. The best that can be done is to maintain continued awareness of the effect of the operating system on applications. This should lead to minimization of this effect whenever feasible without an unacceptable loss of performance. The dependence should also be thoroughly documented, in all of its aspects, so that it can be taken into account when the application is later changed or moved onto a different information processor.

The Applications function has only two Level V elements, and two Level VI entries, as shown in Figure 7-1. Each of these is discussed as follows.

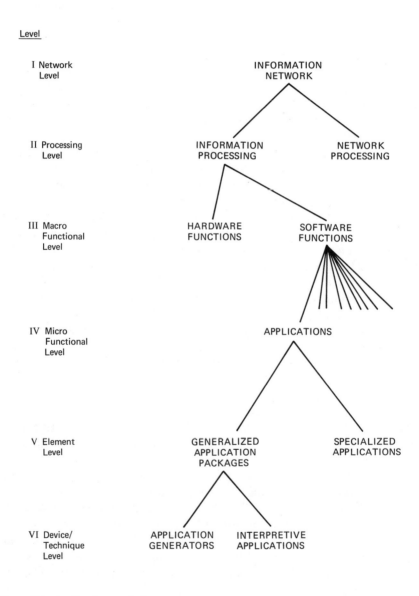

Level

I Network Level — INFORMATION NETWORK

II Processing Level — INFORMATION PROCESSING / NETWORK PROCESSING

III Macro Functional Level — HARDWARE FUNCTIONS / SOFTWARE FUNCTIONS

IV Micro Functional Level — APPLICATIONS

V Element Level — GENERALIZED APPLICATION PACKAGES / SPECIALIZED APPLICATIONS

VI Device/ Technique Level — APPLICATION GENERATORS / INTERPRETIVE APPLICATIONS

Figure 7-1   Applications techniques.

7-1   GENERALIZED APPLICATION PACKAGES

Generalized application packages are those in which a single application program is written to serve the needs of many users. In spite of differing ways of conducting business, many companies have similar needs for information-processing applications.

For example, all banks perform demand-deposit accounting (often called DDA). The basic functions of updating customer account records and producing statements and discrepancy reports are identical in all banks. Of course not all perform these functions in exactly the same way, but often the differences are caused by implementation methods rather than by functional distinctions. The other side of this similarity coin is that there are legitimate differences within functions at various banks. For example, service charge computations vary from bank to bank. Also, banks with branch locations need procedures to handle branch records, and they must be able to assign unique identifiers for each branch.

The idea of creating and using parameterized application packages is based on the concept of functional similarity combined with individuality of details which do not affect the main logic flow. These packages are written to perform a defined set of functions felt to be commonly required. When more than one way to perform a given function is in common use, a choice between them is made based on number of users, ease of implementation, or some other factor. Generally the vendors of these packages attempt to point out that alternative ways of performing functions should be acceptable as long as the results are equivalent to those obtained by another method. Frequently this can be done successfully if the results really are equivalent.

An application package written in this way may in a few instances be adequate for customer use without any modification. More often, however, parameterization is necessary so that each user can adjust the software to his exact needs.

There are three methods of adjusting a basic application software package to specific needs. The first method does not really belong in this section, as it consists of modifying the coding, by hand, to suit the customer. This results in a turnkey software system; this is discussed in Section 7-2.

The other two methods fall within the category of parameterization. The first of these uses the generator approach; the second consists of interpretive execution.

Application Generators

The first Level VI entry includes Application Generators. This technique consists of defining the application's modifiable features in terms of a set of parameters. Each user prepares a set of these parameters to define his own application, then inputs them to a code generation process. The generator uses as its other input the basic application code already provided.

The generation process consists of applying the user's parameters to the appropriate portions of the basic package and modifying it based on these parameters. The output from this process is a program specifically tailored as desired by the user.

We use the banking DDA example again. One of the sets of input parameters might be a definition of how to compute service charges. If the basic package is properly written, it should be possible to modify the computation all the way from a variety of formulas to a null condition (the latter for those banks which make no regular service charge).

Parameterizing ranges from simple to very complex. An example of the simplest type might be a parameter used to define a percentage figure needed for a specific calculation. It is more complex, from the user's point of view, to parameterize entire formulas. In this case the basic package simply contains a call to a calculation, and the parameters furnished completely define the computation to be made at that point.

Other parameters are often literals. For example, bank credit cards usually carry a bank identifier several digits in length. A generalized application to process credit card statements would require as a parameter the identifying number of the bank using the program.

Still other parameters may define which part of the total package is needed in the generated output. For example, an application may be written to produce two output reports, one in detail and one in summary form. Parameters can be used to define which one (or both) of these reports is needed.

Other parameters may be used to define report format if no standard is provided. In some generalized applications a variety of output data may be available for use in reports. The user may be allowed to define the format and content, within the limits of available data, of his output. Report definition is of course one of the most popular uses of the generator technique, and it is suitable for use in parameterized application packages.

Still another type of parameter is used to define file formats if these are not dictated by the package. Generalized application software sometimes accepts as input and produces as output files of any format, as long as they contain the necessary data. This is a very useful feature, and it adds to the value of the package.

This description assumed the use of generators; the actual technique need not be code generation. Sometimes a compilation process is used instead. In this case the parameters are created in the form of data descriptions and/or statements in a standard compiler language, and then are compiled as part of the basic application package, which in this case is furnished in compiler source form. The code produced by the compiler is tailored to the user's needs just as the generator output is.

Both the generator and compilation methods have advantages and off-setting drawbacks. Generators usually allow more detailed parameters to be specified, and more variability to be achieved during generation, than compiler methods. Since the generator is itself a program, it can do extensive analysis, computation, and manipulation using the parameters and basic code to produce the output. On the other hand, the parameters needed may be complex to prepare, and they will probably be unlike any other programming language. The efficiency of generator output is directly dependent on the skill of the implementor of the generator and cannot be predicted.

The compilation method is more limited in the variability which can be parameterized than the generator method, because a standard language must be used. However, parameters, including insertion of entire routines, are very easy to define since the standard compiler language is used. Efficiency can, to some degree, be predicted since it is dependent on the particular compiler used (plus the techniques used in the basic application program).

Each of these methods is a satisfactory way to customize a particular generalized software system for specific use. A wide range of variability can be achieved using a basic starting set of software depending on the ingenuity of the system implementor.

Interpretive Applications

The other Level VI entry under Generalized Application Packages consists of Interpretive Applications. These applications are not tailored for use by a generation or compilation process. Instead the parameters are provided and used when the application program is executed.

Interpretive execution involves writing code which can dynamically modify itself as necessary, based on the parameters presented to it. The most common interpretive method consists of using a basic set of code able to adapt itself to a variety of data structures. The code must be given a definition of the data structure at execution time rather than at generation or compilation time. Within the limits built into it, the interpretive software can handle any data structure defined to it.

The actual process of interpretive execution is much like the generation process. The interpretive package uses the input parameters to modify itself just as the generator modifies the basic code to produce specific coding. Depending on how it is implemented, the interpretive package may or may not remember and reuse the modifications it makes to its code. That is, the first time it encounters a particular parameter and modifies some of its routines to handle this, it may save the modified routines and reuse them as needed. On the other hand, it may be completely interpretive and treat each new condition as a special case.

The interpretive approach has certain advantages and disadvantages when compared with the generation/compilation approach. Interpretive software can adjust to different parameters, often including different data structures, dynamically. It is not necessary to generate or compile a version of the software for each specific case. Instead the same software can be used in a variety of situations with only dynamic parameterization.

The disadvantage is of course in performance. It is exceedingly rare for an interpretive system to approach the performance level of a noninterpretive software package. The difference varies, partly depending on complexity and degree of the modification needed interpretively and partly depending on whether the interpretive routines repetitively tailor themselves as needed or retain these modifications.

Therefore, if operating efficiency is important and the application is executed frequently, the generator approach is preferable. For seldom-run jobs, or in cases where the same application must process in a variety of situations (different inputs, etc.), the interpretive mode offers advantages.

7-2 SPECIALIZED APPLICATIONS

Specialized Applications, the second Level V entry, form the major part of all software in existence today. In spite of some increase in use of the parameterization methods just described, there is still an enormous amount of specialized application software in existence and continually being created. A specialized application is one written for a particular function within a particular environment. It may of course have limited ability to accept parameters and modify its operation based on these. However, the parameterization capabilities are much narrower in nature than those described in Section 7-1.

Acceptable parameters are often of the type that define which of two or more options built into the software are to be used. For example, a payroll program run each day may be able to output two reports: one a daily listing and one a weekly accumulation. The program will need an input parameter defining whether a daily or a weekly run is in process. Incidentally, this type of parameterization is equally applicable to the software described in Section 7-1, but it is at a different level than the major tailoring for a particular installation.

Similarly specialized applications are sometimes written to execute in an interpretive manner, so that they can be used for a variety of purposes. Again this variety is within the context of a given installation's work, and it is not designed to serve the needs of a number of customers.

One can say, in fact, that there is considerable overlap between generalized and specialized packages. The former usually have a wider range of variability than the latter, and they are designed to perform in a number of user installations whose needs are similar but not identical. The latter use many of the techniques of the former but are generally intended for fairly restricted use, and they are much less able to adapt to different circumstances.

One type of application package which falls into this overlap area was mentioned earlier. This is the package which is written for one purpose, then modified to suit another or others. In practice this technique is quite often used, particularly by software vendors.

For example, a vendor may have an application system which performs certain functions. Rather than making it variable by means of generation or interpretive execution, he may choose to modify it for each customer's needs. This method produces a specialized, unique set of software at lower cost than if no basic software had been available to build upon.

This method has certain advantages. Parameterization, by any method, requires considerable effort during software design and implementation. It must take into account all known cases where modification might be required. If a customer wishes to modify a portion of the system not designed to be parameterized, this either cannot be done or can be done only by specialized modification. Therefore, if a designer has guessed poorly at the items which need to be parameterized, custom modifications are inevitable. Although vendors are mentioned, specialized applications may also be built via modifications by the users of information systems. The beginning point may be a standardized or parameterized application package obtained from a vendor, or it may be a program obtained from another user with similar needs. Often user groups (associations of companies or other organizations who use the same type of computer equipment) exchange programs freely for this purpose.

In either case, the user can modify the software to do exactly what he wishes. If the basic package is suitable to his needs and well implemented and documented, his costs to modify it should be substantially lower than the cost of creating unique software from scratch. Software testing will also be easier than for a unique package, assuming that the original software was adequately tested. This mode therefore has many advantages whenever suitable software is available to build upon.

Although the many methods described earlier are used to obtain application software for a particular purpose, most of it is in practice written from scratch. If this is done by a software vendor or other contractor, the result is called a turnkey package. This differs from user-written software only in that a vendor and a contract are involved; otherwise the process is identical.

SUMMARY

It seems evident that the trend away from completely unique and specialized applications must continue, for strictly economic reasons if for none other. Software is an extremely large factor in any information-processing installation's budget. Fewer and fewer installations will, in the future, be able to afford large programming staffs which essentially duplicate much of the design and programming effort performed by vendors and at other installations.

This trend will reinforce, and be reinforced by, the improvements being made in application techniques. As generalized packages become easier to modify and use, they will come into ever wider use. New application-oriented languages and generators will aid in this process. Eventually specialized software may come to be the exception rather than the rule in the average business information-processing system.

CHAPTER 8

Utility

The next Level IV software function is Utility. The term "utility" has historically been used to group items not necessarily similar, which do not fit easily into other groups and are not of sufficient importance to form new categories. The items included here fit that definition.

It is interesting to note that, of the nine Level IV entries under Software Functions, only the first three are truly "user-oriented." User-oriented, in this case, means that they are of direct interest and use to application programmers. All of the other functions, while necessary and often used by programmers, are peripheral to the main task.

The user-programmer's main task is the creation of application systems. The bulk of his effort consists of using languages to write applications. While doing so, he will generally require at least some interfaces to the other functions, such as file management, resource management, and so on. But these latter functions are peripheral to his main effort, although of course they are also essential to it.

Utility routines fall into the gap between the strongly user-oriented pair of functions— languages and applications—and the rest of the functions. They are often used directly by programmers, but they are not as important as the language/application pair. On the other hand, some of the utility functions may also

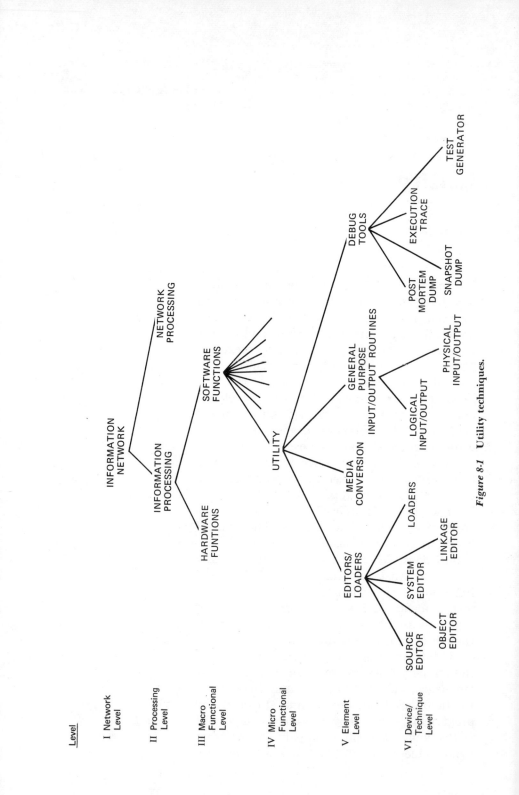

Figure 8-1 **Utility techniques.**

be used by the operating system, and/or they may be part of that system. They are therefore in a sort of "no man's land," functionally speaking.

This ambiguity is reflected in the variety of implementation methods for the items grouped here. Each of these items can be found as part of an operating system in some implementations. Each is also found in the form of computer-vendor-provided (but not operating-system) software in other implementations. There are also cases in which each of these items is specially created by users and is therefore outside of the vendor-software system.

In spite of this wide range of implementation and the ambiguous standing of these items in the software scheme, the utility functions are particularly important. No information-processing system can function effectively without an efficient and suitable set of these routines. Figure 8-1 shows the Level V and VI entries which make up the Utility function.

8-1 EDITORS/LOADERS

Editors and Loaders are grouped to form the first Level V entry, because they are so closely related. Editors must generally operate so as to produce data acceptable to the loaders. These, in turn, are often dependent on the editors and can only operate within the limits of the data provided as editor output. Both, of course, must operate within the framework of the computer hardware used and also within the constraints of the operating system.

Of all the utility functions, the loaders are most often part of the information processor's operating system. It is common practice for an operating system to contain one or more loaders, sometimes one for its own use and another for problem program use. However, even loaders are sometimes user provided to include nonstandard features and/or to improve performance.

There is an enormous variety of editors and loaders from which significant examples were chosen for inclusion here.

Source Editor

The first of the Level VI items is the Source Editor. A source editor is used to manipulate routines or programs in source form: that is, in compiler/assembler input language. Depending on its complexity and the environment in which it is used, a source editor may handle only one language as I/O, or it may handle a variety. The most useful editor is one which handles the full range of languages available on the particular information processor where it is used.

An editor is intended to aid in building and maintaining libraries of source routines. In editing, whether a given routine is a free-standing program or not is unimportant. To the editor, routines are simply identifiable, named blocks of source coding.

Building and maintaining libraries imply both the use of files for storage and the existence of catalogs to identify and describe those files. The editor makes use of File Management (Chapter 9) to establish the file space and catalogs for the libraries. Source form libraries are most often created on demountable media, since they need not be continually available to the information processor. Occasionally, as in some time-sharing systems, source libraries are kept on-line at all times for rapid access.

The source editor accepts as input source language statements and directives or command statements. The latter direct the action to be taken in processing the source statements.

The initial action required is to build a library of the source routines provided. The editor usually does so by defining a file or subfile for each routine and then writing the routine into the assigned file space. The more elegant editors perform content checking (unless directed not to) to determine that the input is valid in format for the language specified. More often, no checking is performed; data is simply stored.

Part of this building process may be line numbering. The editor will generally accept, and optionally check, line numbers according to the conventions of the language used. It may also provide a standard numbering discipline to be used in place of, or in addition to, the language standard. The user may wish to employ only the editor line numbers to manipulate his data and wait until edited data is output to apply language format numbers. The editor will also supply output line numbers.

The library must of course include a catalog identifying the routines which are included. Cataloging on mass storage is a very simple process, since the catalog can be a list of routine names and their starting locations on the device. Tape libraries sometimes need more complex cataloging to achieve efficiency. For example, it may be useful to insert a copy of the catalog preceding each routine on the tape. Searching for the next routine to be accessed is then in the correct direction, no matter how the tape is currently positioned. These techniques are unnecessary if the library and input are maintained in some logical sequence (alphabetically by routine name is common), but this is sometimes impractical.

When modifications to the routines are necessary, the source library is updated. Updating requires directives indicating the source language statements affected by the update. When the update is a deletion of a statement(s), only the directive is required. When additions or changes are needed, the directive must be accompanied by the new or modified source statements. Updating of magnetic tape libraries is accomplished by creating a completely new copy, while mass-storage update may require changing only the affected portion(s).

The source editor usually also provides directives which allow the data to be printed out, either selectively or completely, for manual analysis or for historical purposes.

The source editor also provides a link to the object editor (described next) by providing facilities to assemble/compile the source libraries to produce object code. The actual compilation or assembly process uses the appropriate language processor, which must be called by the editor. Directives are also required to specify which routines are involved in this process. The output from the assembly or compilation must be an object routine in a format acceptable to the object editor. In practice, the point at which assembly or compilation takes place is arbitrary; it may be initiated by either the source or the object editor.

Object Editor

The second Level VI item consists of Object Editors. These are directly linked to the source editor since the functions are performed using output from the source editor.

The object editor is very similar to the source editor, except that its purpose is to update object-level libraries. These may be maintained on either tape or mass storage, either off-line or on-line to the computer.

This editor normally updates only at the level of adding, replacing, or deleting entire routines, rather than at the individual statement level as the source editor does. There is seldom any need to update an object routine at the individual statement level. In fact, that would be opposed to one of the main objectives in maintaining source/object libraries. The intent, in general, is to encourage source-level corrections, so that the source version of each routine is always correct, and the object (and any other) version simply mirrors the current source.

If object libraries are updated in detail, the correspondence with the source libraries is soon lost.

Directives are needed in object updating just as they are in source editing. These directives describe the exact action the updating process is to take on each routine. Directives are also required to indicate what output should be provided—normally a listing of the changes made is provided and optionally a complete listing of the object-library catalog may be produced.

The object libraries maintained by the object editor are used as one form of input to the two editors described next, the system editor and the linkage editor. They may also, in some information-processing systems, be used as direct input to one of the loaders described later in this chapter.

System Editor

The next Level VI entry, the System Editor, is an editor which uses object code as input and transforms it into a specialized loading format. The format may be either core image or modified core image, depending on the computer hardware. This is called a system editor because the output format is tailored for operating-system routines rather than problem programs. This type of editor is unnecessary in some cases if both system and problem routines can be loaded identically. The Honeywell Series 6000 editor is a good example of this type of program. It is described in the *System Library Editor Reference Manual*.[1]

The input to this editor consists of object code plus directives. The object code may be obtained from a library maintained by the object editor, or it may be input in the form of cards or other media output by an assembler or compiler.

The system editor may also have facilities for maintaining libraries of data in its output format. In that case, its library maintenance features are similar to those described above for the object editor.

Ideally, a special editor should not be required to handle operating-system code, but reality is seldom ideal. When presented with a choice between consistency and efficiency, implementors will generally choose the latter. It is not unusual, therefore, to find specialized editors and loaders in some cases.

Linkage Editor

The next Level VI entry is the Linkage Editor, which is the final form of editor to be discussed. This editor uses object code as input,

[1] Order No. BS18, Honeywell Information Systems, Waltham, Massachusetts.

either from a library or from assembler/compiler output. Its output is a set of loadable code ready to be loaded into the information processor's memory. Probably the most widely used linkage editor is described in *IBM OS Linkage Editor and Loader*.[1]

The main feature of a linkage editor, which provides the name, is its ability to link together separately assembled routines. This editor can handle routines assembled and/or compiled in a variety of languages, as long as the object code produced in each case follows a standard format and complies with a set of conventions.

The most important of the common conventions is the method of handling global symbols. Global symbols are references within a routine to items not contanied within that routine. The programmer is usually required to flag these references as global, so that the compiler or assembler will not treat them as undefined symbol errors. However, the programmer cannot define them, and so the assembler simply keeps a list of these global references, assuming that they will be defined later.

The programmer must similarly flag global symbols, if any, which are defined in his routine and can be referenced from outside of it. Often, by convention, the entry point of every routine is automatically made a global symbol, regardless of any action by the programmer. The assembler also makes a list of these global symbols, in this case including the definition with the symbol.

The linkage editor is given one or more object routines as input. These routines will usually have undefined global symbol references which the editor must fill in. If two or more routines are being edited together, they will normally have global symbols to link to each other. In many information-processing systems they will also have global references to common routines which are part of libraries available to all problem programs. An example might be references to the general-purpose I/O routines described in Section 8-3.

It is important to be aware of the two types of common routines available within the framework of most operating systems. One type, although a standard routine maintained as part of a system object library, is combined with the problem program, either at editing or at loading time, and from that point on it is part of that program. The other type is not a part of the user program, but it is dynamically linked with or used by the user program when in execution.

Linkages to this latter type of routine are not expressed as unde-

---

[1] Order No. GC28-6538, International Business Machines Corporation, White Plains, New York.

fined global symbols since they are not editor/loader linkages. Instead, they are assembled as a call which, when executed, will produce an entry to the supervisor to obtain the desired service. These calls can be considered as predefined global symbols, known to the system assemblers and compilers. Since this call type of linkage is not part of the editor/loader function, it will not be discussed further here. It is covered in more detail under Fault Handling in Section 11-1.

The linkage editor must satisfy each undefined global reference found in the routines it is editing. It does this by searching available libraries according to some algorithm. This usually consists of first searching any user library or libraries defined to it via input directives. This allows the user to link current routines with previously assembled ones maintained in his own libraries. It also allows him to provide his own versions of commonly used routines contained in system libraries if this is necessary. If the user does not require these facilities, he need not define any libraries to the editor.

The next location to search, if undefined symbols remain, is the system library or libraries of general-use routines. These normally contain logical and physical I/O routines, debug routines, data manipulation routines etc. If the libraries are large, they may be separated for efficiency into high- and low-use routines and searched in that order.

As we have just mentioned, the sequence of the library search algorithm allows the user to substitute his own specialized routines for all or any part of the common library. This method is very useful when testing new versions of these routines since only the testing program uses the new version, while all other system users continue to access the older version. This technique is also useful for programs which have specialized requirements and need some modification of the standard routines.

During this library search undefined references are filled in as they are found. However, additional references may be found undefined in the routines obtained from the libraries. The same search is used to locate these, and the editor continues its process until all undefined references are resolved, or until all libraries have been exhausted without finding all references. The latter case represents an error and causes an abnormal termination of the linkage edit process.

The output from the linkage editor is a block of object coding with all references defined. It includes the original user routine(s) plus any routines obtained from libraries to satisfy global references. This output may be immediately presented to a loader or saved on a file for later loading.

Loaders

The fifth and final Level VI entry under Editors/Loaders covers Loaders. There are several different types of loaders, but they all perform the basic function of loading object-form code into the main memory of the computer. There are two basic types of loading: core-image and relocatable. To some degree these differences are caused by different hardware features in various computers.

Core-image loading is the fastest of the loading methods since it consists of reading in, sometimes in a single I/O operation, a block of code which is ready for use without any modification. Obviously this assumes a previous system edit process which assembled the object code into core-image format and wrote it out to secondary storage.

Core-image loading can be used only if the code is written so that no relocation is needed or so that any relocation is dynamically applied during execution. For example, if all references within the code are relative and modified by a base address register at execution, the code is said to be floatable since it can be executed anywhere in memory without modification. Problem programs are often written this way; supervisor state routines may not be affected by a base register in certain machine architectures and thus cannot be made floatable in the same way. In this case, special care must be taken to make these routines floatable. This is sometimes not really worthwhile for core-resident routines which are never moved except in case of major system reconfiguration.

Relocatable loading can be used in any computer with base address registers. Burroughs computers were among the first to use this technique. See the *Burroughs B5500 Information Processing Systems Reference Manual* for a description of relocatable addressing.[1]

The format for relocatable loading requires that each instruction be accompanied by information specifying how it is to be relocated. For example, addresses may be relocated relative to the starting address of loading. If multiple routines, not previously linked by a linkage editor, are loaded together, addresses in all except the first must be offset to compensate for the other code loaded into the same address space. Other instructions may contain data rather than addresses, so these are marked to bypass relocation.

Relocatable loaders sometimes take the form of linking loaders,

[1] Form 1021326, Burroughs Corporation, Detroit, Michigan.

which combine the features of a linkage editor (described earlier) and a relocatable loader.

In all versions, relocatable loaders can work from a variety of input sources. They may accept card-image object code either directly from cards or from a file or object library. They may also accept a special relocatable format produced by an editor or an operating-system module. This format consolidates coding into strings, rather than card images, and it accompanies each string with relocation data. This type of input can be loaded more rapidly than card image because fewer I/O operations are required. However, it is slower than core-image loading because of the relocation which must take place.

One final function must be discussed in relation to loaders. This is the swapping or roll-in/roll-out function used in some systems, particularly those which support interactive use. When it is necessary to replace some code in memory with other code, there is first a decision as to whether or not the resident code must be written out. Generally operating-system code need not be written out, since it does not modify itself; that is, it is in pure procedure form. Problem programs are seldom pure unless the entire system concept is built around this. Paged systems, for example, generally use pure procedure, and their compilers produce pure procedure, so it is unnecessary to swap out code in these systems.

When data must be written out, this is done either in core image or in relocatable format. Even in systems which do not normally use core-image loading, it may be possible to swap in this mode, as long as routines are always returned to their original locations when read back from swap storage. This is rather restrictive but represents a considerable time saving. More often data is written out and reread in relocatable format, so that it can be returned to any location in core. It was pointed out earlier that some code is floatable, in which case core image can be used regardless of whether or not it is reloaded in its original location.

This concludes the discussion of the Editors/Loaders entry. This is an important one since loading efficiency can have a significant effect on system performance. This is particularly true in transaction-processing systems, where actual processing of each input is often trivial but great numbers of inputs must be handled. Processing may in fact be less than load time, which then becomes a very significant factor. The editing and loading features and performance should therefore be thoroughly analyzed when investigating a software system for possible use.

8-2   MEDIA CONVERSION

Media Conversion, the next Level V element of Utility, is a function which has been present in computer systems since their early days. It is used in a variety of ways and is required, in some form, in almost every system.

The basic function of media conversion is to move data from one medium to another. The media most commonly used include punched cards, magnetic tape, mass storage, and printer/plotter/ COM. The first three are used as both input and output media, while the final group is output only.

Media conversion is performed for a variety of reasons. Input data required for job execution is often converted from punched cards to disc, drum, or tape as a first step. This allows actual job execution to use the data from high-speed media, rather than from the relatively slow-speed card reader. Similar reasoning applies to job output which is to be punched into cards, printed, plotted, or placed on microfilm. These output devices are slow in relation to processor speed. It is therefore more efficient to place data on a high-speed device, often mass storage, when it is created and then convert it later to its destination media.

These examples may fall into the specialized media conversion category called Task Input/Output (Section 10-2). If so, the functions are usually performed by the operating system. If not, and these functions are performed by individual users, they fall into the normal user software class.

There are many other reasons for media conversion. Often these have to do with information movement and/or storage. For example, it may be necessary to move data which exists on fixed mass storage in one computer to another computer for use there. The simplest way to do so may be to move the data to a tape reel or disc pack so that it can be physically transported to the other computer site.

This is an example of a media conversion which may be either a straightforward data copy or involve editing and formatting. If the two computers referred to in this example use identical software systems, a direct copy is probably sufficient. If they do not, it may be necessary to reformat the data so that it can be used by the other system. Reformatting may consist of code transliteration (ASCII to EBCDIC (Extended Binary Coded Decimal Interchange Code), for example), or it may involve moving and rearranging data fields and/or the volume labels to conform to the receiving machine's conventions.

There are some media-conversion packages which allow extensive modification during the data transfer from one medium to the other. These packages work on the parameterization principles described in Section 7-1. They allow the user to describe the input and output data formats and provide the processing necessary to perform the conversion. This is a very useful feature in media conversion.

Although rare, there are instances of remote media conversion which involve transmitting data to a remote batch terminal which performs the required reformatting, etc. Data can be transmitted in this way and placed on tape or disc pack (or possibly cards or paper tape) at the remote location. This serves the same purpose described earlier of moving and converting data, but in a more expeditious manner if the distances are great.

The desire to store data off-line from the information processor is another reason for using media conversion. File dumps of information on mass-storage devices are the most common example of this use. It is standard practice, in data base oriented installations, to perform periodic media conversions to move the data to magnetic tape. Since tape is the most inexpensive medium for long-term inactive data storage, it is generally used for this purpose. Although file dumps might not normally be thought of as media conversion, they are in fact a good example of this category.

8-3   GENERAL-PURPOSE INPUT/OUTPUT ROUTINES

The next Level V entry covers General Purpose Input/Output Routines. The ancestor of this type of routine was IOCS, the first of the general-purpose I/O packages. These routines continue to be important in today's systems, although often for a different reason than in the past. I/O routines were originally used in application programs so that each programmer did not have to write his own version. Today, as more applications are written in higher-level languages, fewer programmers have a need to use these I/O routines. However, now the coding generated by compilers can use these routines.

General-purpose I/O routines provide an interface with the hardware-level I/O performed by the operating system. In a few systems these routines are actually used to issue I/O commands, but in most multiprogramming systems only the operating system can do so. (This is described under Input/Output Control in Section 11-1.)

Normally the general purpose I/O routines interface with the I/O control portion of the operating system to issue I/O. This interface is at the physical I/O level; that is, it is in terms of a physical I/O transfer. This is also one of the levels at which the user or other software can interface with these routines.

There is another level of interface provided which is at the logical rather than the physical level. When the user interfaces at this level, the I/O routines work in terms of logical records and perform all of the necessary physical I/O without overt user requests.

At either the logical or physical level, these routines may provide additional options. For example, in a system which uses multiple code sets on various peripheral devices, code transliteration may be provided as part of the I/O process.

A variety of peripheral devices can usually be handled by these routines. Ideally all devices are handled, but occasionally devices such as graphics or plotters require special purpose I/O. The device independence which is a general goal of I/O support is improved if the same routines, with the same external interfaces, are used in every case. The user then does not have to be aware of device characteristics.

Logical Input/Output

The first of the two Level VI entries is Logical Input/Output. This is a logical level interface between the user and the general-purpose I/O routines. At this level the commands are usually GET and PUT, to read and write logical records. The user must define his file format, either in detail or by specifying that it is a standard format (possibly one of several) known to the routines.

Using this definition, the I/O routines can perform any operations necessary to provide the requested logical READ or WRITE. For example, if a GET is requested from a blocked file, the following actions are required. First, the appropriate block of records must be read into memory. This is done using the physical I/O functions described later. Using the file definition, the I/O routines then locate the correct record within the block. Depending on the options specified and conventions of the system, the record may be left in the buffer and the user given a pointer by which he can access it, or it may be moved to a location specified by the user. Normally options are provided to specify whether the I/O is to be single- or double-buffered. If the latter, the I/O routines will automatically keep the buffers filled in sequential file processing. (Double buffering is not normally used for random files.)

Similar actions take place as a result of the PUT command. In this case the user provides a record for input. The I/O routines insert this into an output block, write the block when full, and swap to an alternate buffer if one is available.

In addition to the GET and PUT interfaces, the user is required to OPEN each file before use and CLOSE it on completion. OPEN generally initializes the I/O routine's tables and sets up the necessary linkages between these and the user coding and/or the operating-system I/O control. For sequential files, OPEN also generally initiates I/O to fill the buffer(s), so that data will be available without delay when the first GET is issued. CLOSE performs any WRITES necessary to flush out the buffers and eliminates linkages set up by OPEN between the file and the problem program.

The logical I/O interface is the one most often used by system software, such as compilers, and also by most application software. Generally, however, the logical level is limited to use on files which are in relatively standard format. Nonstandard format files can sometimes be handled by the physical I/O routines which are described next.

An example of both logical and physical I/O routines can be found in the Honeywell Series 6000 system's *File and Record Control* routines.[1]

Physical Input/Output

The other Level VI entry consists of Physical Input/Output. At this level the interface commands are usually READ and WRITE, which act upon physical rather than logical records. Any record deblocking or blocking to obtain logical increments within the physical records must be done by the user.

As in the logical interface, the user is required to OPEN and CLOSE his files. These commands establish or destroy linkages as described earlier, but they have no effect on file buffers.

The physical I/O interface is seldom required except for nonstandard format files. However, it is often used indirectly since the GET and PUT functions are normally implemented to perform I/O via the physical I/O routines. When the GET routine needs another buffer full of input it reads by calling READ; similarly PUT writes full buffers via call to WRITE.

---

[1] Order No. BN85, Honeywell Information Systems, Waltham, Massachusetts.

8-4   DEBUG TOOLS

Debug Tools, the final Level V entry under Utility, are those features provided to assist in testing new software. Debug tools have existed in the batch environment for a number of years. A great deal of effort is now being spent on the development of similar and more advanced tools for interactive use. Interactive debugging is already proving to be a much more effective method than batch debugging, and its efficiency can be expected to increase as better tools are developed. For a description of an on-line debugging system, see the *Dynamic Debugging Techniques (DDT-10) Programmer's Reference Manual.*[1]

Post Mortem Dump

The first of the Level VI Debug Tools is the Post Mortem Dump, which is the one which has been in use for the longest period of time. This dump is produced after execution, generally because of an abnormal termination but also optionally after successful completion. It consists of a print-out of main memory used by the job. It may also include the contents of secondary storage, such as swap files, associated with the job.

This dump may be a complete or a selective one. For example, the user working at compiler language level may need only register and working storage contents, and he can use a selective dump to obtain this data. Users working at assembly level more often require complete dumps.

A very useful technique is to save a full dump in a file on mass storage or tape. Items can then be selectively printed as needed, and analyzed, without producing a complete dump. This is a useful tool for interactive debugging, where the dump can be selectively analyzed from a terminal. Full-memory dumps output to an interactive terminal are of course impractical.

Snapshot Dump

The second Level VI entry covers the Snapshot Dump. This is a picture of all or selected portions of memory taken at specified points during test execution. This method is used in both batch and interactive debugging.

---

[1] Order No. DEC-10-CDDD-D, Digital Equipment Corporation, Maynard, Massachusetts.

Snapshots require definition, within the program being tested, as to where and when they should occur. This definition may consist of instructions inserted while the program is being written. It may also be possible to define snapshot points externally and have them automatically inserted by the debug software.

Snapshots may be output immediately as they occur, or they may be saved on a file for later output. If saved, they can be selectively output or investigated as just described for post mortem dumps. Snapshots are very closely related to the next item.

Execution Trace

The next Level VI item is the Execution Trace. Snapshot dumps can be considered a form of trace, and they are often used in conjunction with the trace as a debug aid.

A trace consists of a record of the execution paths taken through the program being tested. In the most detailed case each instruction executed can be listed, but this is seldom necessary. It is more normal to print the path taken at each branch, which effectively traces execution flow. It is often helpful to use the snapshot dump to record the state of switches, working storage, buffers, or other meaningful items accompanying some or all of the trace entries.

The trace may be used interactively. Sometimes each branch in execution causes the user at the terminal to be informed and execution to halt at that point. The user can then investigate memory content at once, then continue execution or not based on his analysis. This approach gives great flexibility, which may be needed when debugging complex programs.

Test Generator

The final Level VI item under Debug Tools is the Test Generator. This is a software system which provides input data for program testing.

Generators may be programs which produce data according to a set of definitions. Normally a certain amount of randomness is introduced so that the test data will represent a reasonable range, or the data may simply be produced mechanically by providing one example of every possible data condition. This type of generator greatly reduces the programmer's effort since creating test data is a lengthy and tedious process when done manually.

Another type of test input is produced by a form of simulator. It is often necessary to test receipt and transmission of data from many remote terminals when testing on-line applications. Actually using large numbers of terminals is seldom practical, except possibly in the latest stages of testing. A program which simulates many terminals is therefore extremely useful. The simulator generates test messages dynamically, simulating the conditions which would exist if the messages had been transmitted from many terminals. The ability to modify its message generation algorithm dynamically is very useful.

Test generators and simulators are widely used for testing vendor-created software such as operating systems. The general user could frequently benefit from appropriate use of these tools and techniques.

SUMMARY

The utility function includes miscellaneous items necessary to complete the user's software system. Editors and loaders provide him with the means to maintain his routines and programs on a variety of libraries, in a variety of formats, and then load them into memory when ready for execution. Media conversion allows him to move data or files freely from device to device. General purpose I/O routines give him two levels of standard interfaces to the hardware I/O features. Debug tools assist him in testing his software prior to putting it into production use. All of these are necessary features in an information-processing system.

CHAPTER 9

File
Management

The fourth Level IV software function is File Management. It is important to make clear the distinction between file management and data management. File management includes those functions required to create, access, and delete a file as an entity. Data management includes those functions needed to create, use, and delete the file content.

File management generally does not require any knowledge of file format. For example, it need not know the size of blocks and/or records within the file. Neither does it require any knowledge of how data fields are arranged within individual records. Data management, on the other hand, is intimately concerned with these points. Data management may be optionally provided as part of the computer's operating system, or it may be left to the user to provide. A single file management system may support a great number of different data management methods, some widely used and others unique to a particular user or even to a particular problem program. Data management is discussed in detail under Data Management Languages in Section 6-3.

This distinction between the terms file management and data management is not as yet widely accepted. However, in the author's experience it greatly simplifies complex system descriptions. Data content of a file is independent of how a file is created, cataloged, and accessed at the file level. Blurring this distinction often leads to sloppy design. File management and data management are treated as two separate entities throughout this book.

The concept of a file is of course one of the most basic in an information-processing system. "An ordered collection of related information elements" is a good abstract definition of the term file. However, when it comes to applying that definition in practice, a wide range of opinions as to what constitutes a file exists within the computing community.

When referring to data on magnetic tape or mass storage, a fair degree of consistency is found; this is usually called a file. However, even this is not universally true. The MULTICS system, for example, has no concept of a file as a unique item; what would generally be called a file is simply another segment within the virtual-memory system. This concept is described in *The Multics System: An Examination of Its Structure* by Elliott T. Organick.[1]

Common usage is much less consistent in respect to data on media other than tape and mass storage. These may or may not be termed files. Sometimes, for example, a deck of cards is referred to as a file, while in other cases it is not. Similarly, output prepared for a printer may or may not be called a file. In general, the media is less important than the fact that the data has a relatively short life span. The tendency is to consider long retention data a file, while not applying that term to data which is retained for only a short time.

While retention may be one way to distinguish between files and nonfile data, another method sometimes used is based on incremental versus batch mode of data creation and use. Data created and consumed incrementally can be thought of as a message, rather than as a file, while data used as a logical entity or batch is termed a file.

As an example, consider the data input by a user at a time-sharing terminal during an interactive session (sign-on to sign-off). It is difficult to fit this into the normal concept of a file. The data is created incrementally as a series of commands and/or responses to requests exchanged between the user and the computer. Taken together, these do not form a logical accumulation of data. Each increment is received by the computer and processed independently, and it can be thought of as a message to the computer. Incremental computer output also falls into the same class of message, rather than file, data.

[1] The MIT Press, Cambridge, Massachusetts, 1972.

It is easy to point out that there are striking differences between this and a standard card reader input deck. Generally (not always, of course) a deck is read into the computer as an entity and stored as an entity before processing. There is usually a logical relationship between the separate cards which form the deck so that, taken together, they have some meaning. While such a deck may be retained only a short time, that is generally the only thing which distinguishes it from more permanent data bases.

This discussion simply serves to point out that there is no universally recognized definition for an information-processing-system file. Common usage varies between computer manufacturers and often even between installations. For purposes of this volume, therefore an arbitrary definition is used; i.e., a file is "a collection of related data elements which exists as a logical entity and is stored and referred to as an entity for some period of time within the computing system."

File management is structurally a simple function. It consists of the Level V and Level VI entries shown in Figure 9-1. Each of these items is described in the following pages.

9-1 FILE ESTABLISHMENT

File Establishment forms the first Level V element under File Management. This function might equally well be titled "file creation." However, to distinguish between the file management functions of defining and cataloging a file and the data management function of creating data within the file, the term "establishment" was chosen.

The two Level VI entries under this heading are Definition and Cataloging. File definition is the process of defining the file's attributes, assigning it a unique identity, and optionally reserving space for it. Cataloging creates and saves entries for the file in a catalog of all files within the system. It is through catalogs that the file can later be accessed. Neither file definition nor cataloging place any data in the file space; that is done via the data management function.

File Definition

The first of the two Level VI entries is Definition. This is the process by which the person or software component defines the attributes of the file to be established. Exact user interfaces to the file definition process vary widely, partly because of different system features and

Level

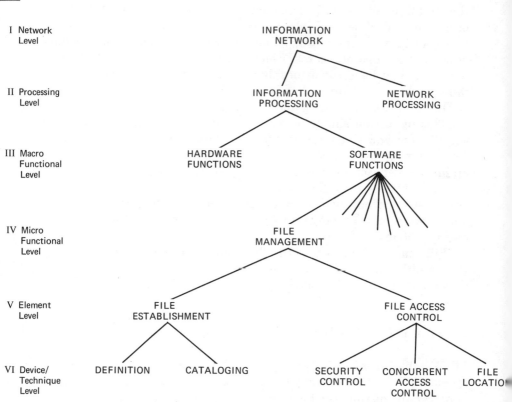

Figure 9-1   File management techniques.

partly because the user may be operating either interactively or in batch mode. Some of these differences and variations are pointed out in the following description.

File definition starts by assignment of a unique name to the file. File naming conventions vary widely. Early operating systems often required that each file be given a completely unique name; this presented a considerable problem if a number of different users were independently naming files.

Present day systems are usually more flexible. They require only that each user uniquely name all of the files he defines. His user name or identification is concatenated with file name to ensure that the correct file is accessed. Two different users can therefore assign identical names to their files without any resulting ambiguity.

In certain circumstances, file naming can also be accomplished by the system without any explicit action by the user. For example, in a time-sharing system the user may be able to enter the command SAVE to request that his current working file be retained. The system may require that the user furnish a name for the saved file; on the other hand it may provide a name automatically. If the system provides the file name, it will do so using some convention, such as combining the user's identification with the job or interaction identification he had in process when the SAVE was entered. The user must be aware of these file naming conventions so that he can later access the file by that name. (In some cases this may be unnecessary. The system may be able to retrieve the user's files without any explicit user request by file name, but this is not generally possible.)

In file definition, as in many other areas, it is important to remember that there are various categories or types of users. In cases where casual or clerical users are able to define files, the definition is almost always done implicitly. The user has little or no control over where or how the file is created, and he has no need for such control.

The system programmer or other expert user, on the other hand, may have a definite need to control files. He may wish, for example, to define a corporate data base. If he has a great deal of information about how the various parts of the data base are expected to be used, he can define it quite exactly. He may wish to place high activity sections on rapid-access mass storage, medium activity sections on slower-access storage, and still lower activity sections on demountable or archival storage devices. The ability to control file definition in this detail is totally unnecessary to the casual user, and in fact it would be inappropriate to give him such freedom.

There are other parameters which the user may be either required or allowed to optionally provide as part of the file definition process. One of these parameters is the amount of space needed for the file. In some systems this parameter is required so that the space requested can be compared against the resources reserved (charges allowed) for this user. If it exceeds his allowed resources, definition of the file may be refused until additional resources are provided by system control personnel. Other systems simply provide space dynamically as needed and notify the user, if necessary, when his resources are exhausted or are nearing that point.

Another file definition parameter which may be included is a description of where to place the file: that is, on what type of storage or on exactly which device. This information is generally not required because file management attempts to provide device independence for its users. That is, it hides from them the problems associated with space management, the differing characteristics of different storage devices, etc. However, complete device independence is not always appropriate.

If the user is allowed to specify where the file is to be placed, he may do this in a quite general or symbolic form. For example, the user may be allowed to specify "demountable" or "fixed" devices, and "high," "medium," or "low" access speed or other similar criteria. This specification may also be allowed at a very detailed level; for example "place the file on device n, accessible via channel m," or other similar instructions.

It should be noted again that many operating systems try to keep all user definitions at the more general level. Control is thereby kept in the operating system, which can presumably do a better job of file space management than the average user can. However, operating systems designed to support large on-line applications are generally forced to allow the more specific user control, because the degree of file access efficiency needed in these large-scale systems can seldom be achieved without direct and expert user control over file placement.

Even in cases where the system provides completely automatic file management requiring no eternal direction, the user must have a certain basic level of control over placement of his file. He must, for example, be able to specify that his file is to be placed on magnetic tape if this is important to him. It may be a requirement of his application that the file be on tape so that it can be used to drive an off-line printer, or perhaps be used on another information processor. This level of control is generally required, and it can be provided without significantly interfering with the system's ability to manage file space effectively.

Other attributes of the file may also be defined at this time. These include security control information and data needed to control concurrent access to the file. These attributes are discussed in more detail in Section 9-2, which follows.

The file definition function is the user's way of describing a file; cataloging is the system's way of remembering the file definition.

Cataloging

The second Level VI component of File Establishment is Cataloging. Every file system includes the concept of cataloging, since this is the means by which the system later locates files which have been defined to it. Some file management systems make the cataloging mechanism invisible to the user; he is not allowed to perceive it or to control it in any way.

The file management system's catalog is a set of entries describing all of the files known to it. Each file has one or more entries in the system's catalog. For convenience, it is general practice when speaking of a file's catalog entries to refer instead to the file's catalog; that practice is followed here.

A file catalog, in the simplest form, is simply a record of the file's identity and the location where the file content is stored. This record must be available to the system so that when access to a file is needed the file can be found. This is particularly true of files on demountable media such as magnetic tape and disc packs. If the system does not catalog these files, manual procedures to catalog them must be provided instead. In fact, most present day installations still rely heavily on manual cataloging procedures for demountable files, but this is often less desirable than automatic control.

Basic cataloging is usually performed without any explicit user action, and it takes place at file definition time. It consists of creating a catalog entry and storing it where it can always be located by the system. The catalog entry must contain, as a minimum, the file name, and it usually also contains the file owner's identity if this is not part of the file name.

If space has been assigned for the file, the location(s) provided is also stored in the catalog. If a maximum allowable file space has been defined, this is also stored in the catalog entry. Generally all information provided by the user or furnished by the system during file definition is stored in the file's catalog. The data contained in the catalog can be referred to as the file attributes.

Although this very simple cataloging is frequently adequate, more complex cataloging techniques may be made available. The user is then given a certain amount of control over how catalogs are formed. The user may gain one or both of these benefits: the ability to define relationships between otherwise independent files and/or the ability to more accurately control access to the file.

One file cataloging technique sometimes used is to form hierarchical tree structures consisting of catalogs and files. An example of such a structure is shown in Figure 9-2, where catalogs are represented by circles and files by squares, and the relationships between them are shown by the connecting lines.

In this example, the node labeled A is the root of the tree or the highest-level catalog. It is linked to two lower-level (hierarchical)

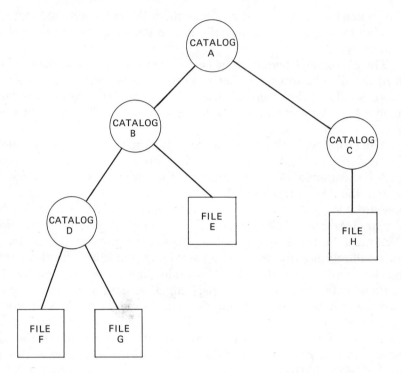

Figure 9-2 Catalog/file structure.

catalogs at nodes B and C. The node C catalog has one file, labeled H, attached. Down the other major branch, catalog node B has one file, E, and a subsidiary catalog, D, attached. Catalog D has two files, F and G, attached.

This type of catalog structure can only be created under user direction. The complex relationships between files represented by the above diagram cannot be known to the file system except through user input. Of course it is important to remember that files can often be defined by software components as well as by system users. Therefore, relationships between files defined and owned by the operating system can also be expressed in complex catalog structures.

Although there are cases where complex catalog schemes of this type are not only useful but necessary, many files need only the basic cataloging described earlier. A job stack input file, for example, requires cataloging, but only enough to identify and locate the file. The basic cataloging capability, sufficient for such uses, requires less overhead than the more complex schemes, and it is therefore recommended whenever adequate.

Two examples of diffrent cataloging schemes, one complex and one relatively simple, are found in the Honeywell File Management Supervisor[1] and the IBM Data Management System[2].

File definition and the creation of the required catalog(s) are sufficient to establish a file known to file management. Any attempt to access that file, including access for purposes of creating data to be stored in the file, must also be achieved via the file management function.

9-2   FILE ACCESS CONTROL

The other Level V entry under File Management is File Access Control. *All* access to file space known to the operating system via file establishment must be monitored by file management. This does not mean that each individual READ or WRITE of file content is monitored, but before reading and/or writing can take place the initial access to a file must be checked by file management. This control over file access is required for several reasons which are discussed in the remainder of this chapter.

A request for file access is made by a user or by another operating-system software component. Often the software makes an access request on behalf of a user so that he does not need to do so explicitly. Explicit requests may take the form of JCL statements in an input job stack. These specify the file to be accessed and the mode of access (READ, WRITE, etc.). The latter may be given an implied default value of "READ" if not specified.

Explicit access requests may also originate from an interactive user. Although the request form is different, the same information must be furnished.

Just how the file is identified in an access request depends on the file naming conventions used and on the cataloging method. (Both of these topics were discussed in Section 9-1.) In the simplest case the user furnishes the file name, and this is sufficient to identify the file in the system's catalog.

When complex cataloging schemes are used, as just described, the file identifier which must be furnished in an access request is also more complex. It generally consists of the concatenated catalog and

[1] *GCOS File System Reference Manual,* Order No. BR38, Honeywell Information Systems, Waltham, Massachusetts.
[2] *OS Data Management Services Guide,* Order No. GC26-3746, International Business Machines Corporation, White Plains, New York.

file names necessary to reach the desired file from the root of the tree structure. For example, in Figure 9-2 the identifier for File G would be "Catalog A/Catalog B/Catalog D/File G." With multilevel cataloging, the simple identifier "File G" has no meaning since the system cannot locate the file with only that information.

This first step of finding the appropriate entry or entries for the file in the file management catalog is basic to access control. Of course, if no entry matching the request can be found, the request is assumed to be in error and is refused. An interesting variation of this is found in one file management system; if the requested file cannot be found one is established. This is a very convenient way to define files, but it is also a little awkward. A simple spelling error in the access request will, in this system, result in the establishment of an unwanted file.

Security Control

The first of the three Level VI File Access Control entries is Security Control. One of the reasons that all file access is filtered through file management is so that file security is preserved. Security has two aspects: one is the protection of user privacy by preventing unauthorized access to his files; the other is the protection of his data's integrity by preventing unauthorized change to its files. These subjects are discussed in the context of the broad aspects of system integrity in Section 12-3.

Security control is achieved by associating some set of passwords and/or permissions with a file. Access to the file is then allowed only by a user who can present the required passwords and/or who has the correct permissions. Generally, but not always, the file owner (whose identity was associated with the file at time of establishment) is exempted from these checks.

Passwords are set up as part of the file attributes when the file is established; they must be input as part of the file definition. If an hierarchical catalog structure is created, a different set of passwords can be defined at each level. This makes it progressively more difficult to achieve access, since the entire cumulative set must be presented to obtain access at the lowest level. Figure 9-3 shows multiple passwords used in a multilevel catalog structure.

In the example shown, an access to File D is allowed only if the passwords for Catalogs A, B, and C and File D are given. Access to File E requires the passwords for Catalogs A, B, G, and R plus File E. File H has no password itself, but access to it is controlled by the

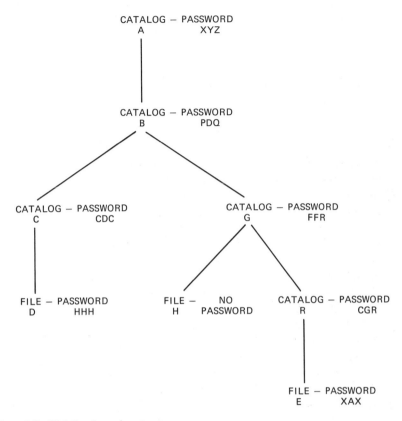

Figure 9-3   Multilevel catalog structure.

requirements for passwords associated with Catalogs A, B, and G.

Passwords can usually be changed at any time by the file owner and possibly also by others specifically authorized by the owner. Control can therefore be retained by changing passwords if they have been disclosed to unauthorized personnel.

Permissions are also used to control access. Permissions are the means by which the file owner defines who is allowed to access his file data, and in what mode. For example, if the file owner gives "general READ permission," anyone can read the file. Notice, however, that he can restrict this by appending one or more passwords to the file. This reduces the general permission, so that effectively anyone who knows the password can read the file.

Specific permissions can also be used to define exactly which individual(s) can perform certain functions. Generally a file owner will allow only a few (if any) people to write in his file, modifying its content. These people will be given specific permission; "John Doe, Jane Smith, and Sam Jones" are allowed to write. This can also be further restricted via password, although this usually accomplishes nothing; presumably the owner wishes these people to access the file so he will give them the necessary password(s).

Security control therefore consists of checking each access request to determine that it has been either generally or specifically allowed by the file owner. At each catalog level, a password is checked for, and if one is present the input access request must have a matching password or it is rejected. When access is requested from an interactive terminal, the user may be asked for the necessary password(s) by file access control. He may also be given more than one chance to enter them to compensate for typing errors, etc.

If the file level is reached successfully via the password checks, the requestor's permission is also tested. The access request must define mode of access, and the permission check is against that specific mode. If the requestor does not have specific or general permission in the mode requested, the access is denied.

If security is important in a particular installation, it may be desirable to have attempted but refused access requests reported by file access control. The file owner can be notified, but this is often difficult unless he is always accessible at a known terminal location. It is generally more practical to notify the computer console operator or a system control terminal which is always manned. This allows an immediate investigation of the access attempt, if this is important.

Concurrent Access Control

The second Level VI entry is Concurrent Access Control. This subject is covered in so much detail in Section 6-3, Data Management Languages, that it is only briefly sketched here.

File access control must include all necessary checks for incompatible concurrent accesses to the same file. Beyond identifying the file, an access request must include the mode of access needed. The mode indicates whether the requestor intends to read from the file, to write to the file, read plus write, execute the code contained in the file, or possibly only append new information to the end of the file.

The access mode is used when the access request is checked for compatibility with any other access already in process. Of course this may be unnecessary if the file owner does not allow anyone else to access his files; however, this is seldom the case. An information-processing system will generally include at least some public or semi-public files, such as accounting files, order files, etc. These files are accessed by a variety of programs designed to read, update, etc. Access control is required to prevent interference between these jobs.

Concurrent access control consists of checking each access request against accesses already in process for the same file. If none is in process, any type of request can be granted. The allowed access is then noted as in process (often in the file catalog), so that future access requests can be checked against it.

If any access is in process, its type and the requested type must be checked for compatibility. The ability to support concurrent access to the same file is usually a characteristic of the data management method used rather than of the file management function. The type of shared access(es) allowed must be known to the file management routines, either from information stored in the file catalog or via dynamic interface with the data management routines to be used.

The role of file management is simply to check access requests against the rules supplied by data management. If the request is allowed according to these rules, it is granted. File management remembers what is is process, so that further access requests can be checked against current use. Beyond this, all control over concurrent access is accomplished by the data management function.

File Location

The third and final Level VI entry is File Location, which is the function of finding where the file content is. It was noted in Section 9-1 that file location is one of the items kept in the file's catalog. This information defines the device or devices on which the file resides as well as the relative location or locations within each device. For example, if the file is on a reel of magnetic tape, the location information is usually the volume label of the tape. This is also required if the file is on disc pack, and in this case the file's location within the pack is also required if it does not fill the pack.

When the file's location shows it to be on demountable medium and the specific reel or pack is not mounted, this information is used to request the operator to obtain and mount the file. There is, of course, a pause while this is done, since manual intervention is very slow in comparison with computer speeds. The access request is not complete until the device is available on-line.

Regardless of where the file is located, the location is generally furnished as part of the response to an access request. This information will be required for use by the Input/Output Control function (see Section 11-1) when actual reading or writing of file data begins. By keeping this information in the catalog and obtaining it via file management, this function is consolidated into a single place. This is quite important because it makes relocation of file data feasible. For example, Section 12-2 describes how data is sometimes moved because the storage area it formerly occupied has been damaged. As long as the information mapping logical file data to storage devices is kept only in the catalog, data can be moved by changing only that record. This is a very useful feature since it allows considerable flexibility in moving all or part of any file's data as needed.

There is one other aspect of locating file content. It is possible, using the same cataloging described, to control the parts of a geographically distributed data base.

A distributed data base is a file or set of files which form a logical whole, but which are separated and attached to two or more information processors. The company files of a large corporation might be established as a distributed data base for several reasons. First, they might be too large to reasonably attach to a single information processor. Second, the majority of accesses might be geographically distributed.

Figure 9-4 shows an example of a distributed data base, owned by a company with headquarters in City A. The same company has three divisions, located in Cities B, C, and D. These cities are widely separated; they may in fact span the United States.

It is easy to imagine that most of Division X's processing will be accomplished in City B, using its own files. Divisions Y and Z will

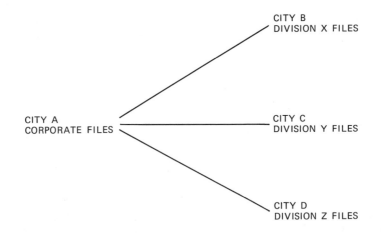

Figure 9-4 Distributed data base.

operate in a similar manner. Because of data transmission costs, this is often more economical than locating all files at City A and doing all processing there.

In a case of this type, summary data may be transmitted from the division locations to headquarters periodically and combined with corporate file data. Similarly, each division may sometimes need to obtain data from corporate files for use in local processing. If the file catalog at each location contains the names and locations of all files at all locations, this is a first step at data interchange.

In the simplest case this catalog information allows a job entered at any one of the locations, but requiring files at another, to be identified and transmitted to the remote location. This is very similar to Load Leveling described in Section 10-3. The job can execute remotely and transmit back the data it obtains if necessary.

It is amusing, but not of very general interest, to speculate on the more complex modes of file access in a distributed data base. It is theoretically possible, for example, for a job executing in one location to request file access and obtain data (or even update it) in a remote location. The software to handle such complexity is by no means current state of the art; it is rather something to be expected as a future development. The entire topic of distributed data bases was brought up simply to point out that current trends toward data-base-oriented, remote-processing information systems will force further exploration of techniques such as these.

SUMMARY

File management allows the user to establish files by assigning each an identity and a set of attributes. It provides him a cataloging mechanism by which he can express file relationships and control access. Although the preceding discussion of file establishment did not cover the aspect of file deletion, this must of course also be provided. Just as users can establish files, the owner of a file can later delete it when it is no longer needed.

During the file's life, all access to it is filtered through file management. This is the central focus for security control, concurrent access control at the file level, and knowledge of where the file is located. All other functions having to do with files, i.e., creation, manipulation, and deletion of file content are handled by the data management function.

CHAPTER 10

Task
Management

The fifth Level IV software function is Task Management. Task management controls all processes or tasks to be executed within the computer. The term task, as used here, refers to any uniquely identifiable unit of work to be executed. A task is commonly thought of as being the execution of a user problem program or some subset of a problem program. However, in the more general sense it can equally well be an execution path within an operating system.

A task is therefore an execution sequence which has a starting point and an ending point, and which may have significant events intervening between these two. Task management consists of the routines required to define the task, enter it into the system, cause its initiation, handle certain events during its execution, and finally handle its termination. Each of these is described in the following sections. Also described is the relationship between task management and the JCL.

Figure 10-1 shows the Level V and Level VI entries which make up the Task Management function.

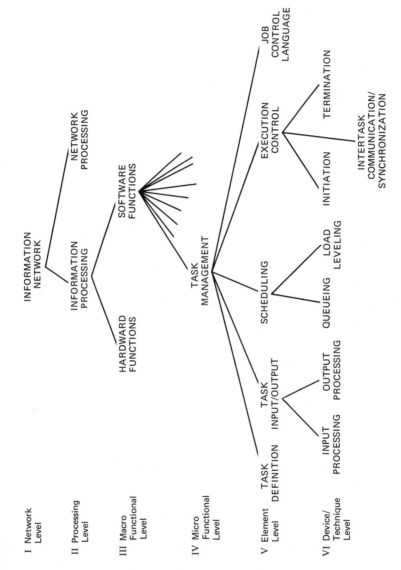

Figure 10-1 Task management techniques.

10-1 TASK DEFINITION

A function common to all information processing systems is Task Definition, the first of the Level V elements. It is seldom referred to by this title, and often it is not explicitly named or described at all. It is, however, essential to all systems. Task definition is the process of describing a task: that is, providing the code to be executed, describing resources needed for execution, and in some cases providing input data to be used. Task definition is a function separate from the request for task initiation, although in many cases the latter is inferred from the former. However, it is important to retain the distinction for purposes of this discussion.

A task, a series of related tasks organized into a job step, and/or multiple job steps forming a job can be defined in one or more of three ways. The first method is implied definition, which operates as follows. Batch operating systems allow (and indeed expect) a job with its component tasks to be defined at the time it is submitted for execution. This is the familiar function of creating a job stack formed of control cards (JCL statements), program decks, and data cards. The term "card" is not meant literally, since it may equally well refer to a card image stored on tape or created at some remote device. In this method the user defines his task and simultaneously requests execution.

The second task definition method occurs prior to the first time of execution. In this method, the task definition is created by the user and stored within the information-processing system. It is then referred to whenever that person or some other user wishes to execute the task. The stored definition is called a "catalog procedure" in some operating systems. This method is widely used in transaction-processing systems, because users of these systems are normally not programmers: i.e., clerks who input transactions which cause execution of prestored task definitions.

The third method of task definition is dynamic definition of a new task already in execution. Once defined, the new task may be executed immediately in parallel with the originating task, queued for later execution, or saved for execution at some later, but as yet undefined, time.

In each of these modes, task definition must include an indication of the program(s) and/or subroutine(s) to be executed and a list of the resources needed for execution. Sometimes other items are included in the definition, but these two are always required. Sometimes task definition parameters are implicit or inferred rather than furnished explicitly.

In defining the code to be executed, the user generally has several options. The simplest method is to include the code itself as part of the definition. This is often the case when task definition accompanies the task initiation request, i.e., when a onetime job is defined and executed.

Alternatively, the user may store his programs and/or subroutines in files (usually on disc or drum) and then simply include a pointer to the storage area(s) in a task definition. The operating system may also store programs and subroutines such as compilers, utility routines, etc., and if so the user can include pointers to those routines in his task definition.

Generally, the user is able to input his own program(s) in either source or object form, or in a mixture of the two. If the program is in source form, the operating system may immediately compile or assemble it, or this may be done later as part of execution of the defined task. In the latter case, an additional compilation task would be defined by the operating system so that this task could produce the object code required in execution of the basic task.

The other major requirement of task definition is to specify the resources needed to execute the task. This consists of listing the files, peripherals, etc. which will be used when the task is executed. It may also include a definition of memory space needed, estimated processing time to be used, and similar items.

The user may be required to include all or only part of this information in his definition. The operating system will usually provide the resource definition if the task involves the execution of routines, such as compilers, known to the system. Also, a standard or default resource requirement list for user tasks may be provided and applied to all task definitions unless the user provides overriding information. Often, therefore, no resource definition is required unless the user wishes to define a nonstandard task.

As mentioned earlier, the system may permit other entries in a task definition. These generally fall into the category of optional actions to be taken during task execution. For example, the user may be able to specify the action to be taken in case the task terminates abnormally. Other similar options might be the definition of alternate execution paths in a multiple task definition, and specification of the criteria by which the operating system should select a path during execution.

10-2   TASK INPUT/OUTPUT

Task Input/Output is the second Level V entry under Task Management. It includes the functions required to read task input into the computer and to write out data (reports, etc.) produced by that execution. Several operating systems refer to these functions, respectively, as SYSIN (system input) and SYSOUT (system output). As these titles imply, the functions are generally part of the operating-system services provided to the user.

Task input and output are really a specialized form of Media Conversion (see Section 8-2). They are described separately because of their unique features which are closely dependent on operating-system task management.

Task Input

The first of the two Level VI entries is Task Input, which is basically a media conversion process. It reads input from cards, tape, files, or remote devices and stores this in a system input file. It differs from other media conversions in the editing and formatting it performs.

Input editing involves analyzing the job or task data and checking for completeness, logical consistency, and so on. Editing as early as possible in the task execution cycle saves unnecessary processing of an invalid task.

Input formatting is performed to compress the task text into a compact internal format. This saves both storage space and processing time in later references to the data. Input data in batch systems, for example, is usually in 80 column card images. Many blank columns or data positions can be compressed into very small areas. The saving is even more pronounced when processing JCL statements which can often be reduced, via encoding, to a relatively few bits representing each statement.

Task Output

The second Level VI entry, Task Output, is also a form of media conversion. It moves data from the system output file to printers, punches, plotters, or remote devices. It also formats data appropriately for the specified devices.

Output formatting is almost the reverse of input formatting. Data (reports, messages) produced by task execution may be stored in compressed and encoded form to save space. When output is performed, the data may retain this format if it is transmitted to another computer (which can decode and reformat it). More generally, the output is destined for a printer, punch, or other similar devices.

Formatting then consists of decoding the format in which output is stored and modifying that format as required by the output device.

Output to a printer, for example, may require the insertion of forms control codes, causing the paper to be vertically spaced when appropriate. If the same data is output to a plotter, it will require different control codes appropriate to that device.

Creating output data in canonical form and converting that to device format only at time of output greatly increases the system's effective degree of device independence. Output destination(s) can be determined and/or changed at any point prior to actual output processing without affecting anything except the SYSOUT function.

10-3   SCHEDULING

The third Level V entry under Task Management is Scheduling. This includes two Level VI techniques, Queueing and Load Leveling.

Queueing

The first Level VI entry covers Queueing of tasks waiting to be executed. This is required whenever the system load exceeds its instantaneous execution capability. Generally, the only type of information-processing system which requires no queueing is one completely dedicated to some special purpose application in which demand is unvarying. In the majority of all systems, peak loads can be expected. These must be handled by queueing tasks and jobs until system resources are available to work on them.

In general, an information-processing system should be designed to smooth out peak-load demand via queueing. Input is usually generated by people who tend to work only part of the 24 hour day. A computer system, on the other hand, frequently operates all, or nearly all, of the 24 hours. It therefore may accept work which it cannot execute during the day and use that work to fill the night hours when no further input is available.

Queues are simply ordered lists of tasks to be executed. Queue size and arrangement vary widely among systems.

In some systems, usually of small scale, queues are fixed in size, and additional tasks cannot be accepted if the queues are full. Large and/or on-line systems more often provide queues of unlimited size. Some special purpose information-processing systems can limit queue size because there are other controlling factors. For example, a time-sharing system with the hardware capacity to simultaneously connect 50 lines need not have unlimited queues, since a maximum of 50 users can be active at any one time. (The number of tasks each user can have outstanding may vary, but it can be computed.)

A priority method of queueing is generally used. Operating-system tasks may have higher priority than any user task, and within user tasks there may be quite complex queueing methods. The simplest queues are arranged FIFO (First In First Out) and allow no priority to be externally specified. Even in this scheme priorities may be applied internally in order to obtain peripherals and/or other resources for a task which is difficult to allocate. (These points are discussed in Chapter 11.) Most systems allow the users to attach priorities to their tasks and then arrange the queue entries in priority sequence. In this method, also, priorities may be altered internally during allocation.

An example of simple priority queueing is shown in Figure 10-2. Jobs are queued waiting for execution FIFO within priority; in the example shown, priority zero is the most urgent, priority one is the next level, etc. Each new job received is examined for priority, then linked into the queue in its appropriate position.

NEXT TO EXECUTE   → JOB A — PRIORITY 0

JOB G — PRIORITY 0

JOB B — PRIORITY 1

JOB C — PRIORITY 1

JOB E — PRIORITY 1

JOB F — PRIORITY 1

JOB D — PRIORITY 2

JOB H — PRIORITY 2

JOB J RECEIVED, PRIORITY 0,
WILL BE LINKED HERE

Figure 10-2   Simple priority queueing.

Another queueing scheme sometimes used is to schedule each task to be executed at a particular time and to arrange queues in time sequence. As an example, the user might specify that a certain task was to be executed at 5:00 p.m. daily, and it would be given a queue entry corresponding to that time. When queueing by specified time, the user must also define whether or not the job must be executed no earlier than the defined time; that is, whether or not it is acceptable to execute it earlier. Often a "may-start" (or "run-no-earlier-than") time is necessary because the task must wait for input which will arrive by the specified time. If no may-start restriction is given, the task may be run earlier than scheduled if the system's processing load is light.

Another form of time-based queueing uses relative rather than actual time. A task can be scheduled to be run a specified time interval after receipt or to provide a specified turn-around time. In the latter case, the operating system must be provided with some method for estimating execution time. It can then compute the start time needed in order to finish soon enough to provide the desired response. This type of calculation is difficult at best, because execution times are so hard to estimate in multiprogramming systems. Although the calculation for relative time is different from that for actual time, the former results in queueing by time sequence exactly as does the actual-time method.

Figure 10-3 shows an example of a time-ordered queue spanning a 10 minute interval. The time given is the time at which the job is scheduled to start. Notice that one entry, for Job 19, has a may-start time specifying that it must not start before 1305. If its position in the queue is reached prior to that time, Job 19 will be bypassed until the specified time arrives.

NEXT TO EXECUTE   → JOB 4 — TIME 1301

JOB 27 — TIME 1302

JOB 12 — TIME 1303

JOB 15 — TIME 1303

JOB 6 — TIME 1304

JOB 7 — TIME 1306

JOB 17 — TIME 1306

JOB 19 — TIME 1306

(MAY-START = 1305)

JOB 23 — TIME 1309

JOB 3 — TIME 1310

Figure 10-3   Time-oriented queueing.

It is also fairly common to combine priority and time queueing so that major queue sequence is by time, and entries are ordered by priority within each time increment.

Regardless of how the queues are maintained, a queue entry is made for only one reason; task initiation has been requested. This request can be made in any of several ways.

Initiation is often requested implicitly rather than explicitly. As an example, input of a one-time task definition may implicitly request execution of the task. Input of a particular type of transaction data may imply execution of the task(s) required to process that data (this is generally true of transaction processing systems), or system users may be required and/or allowed to explicitly request execution of a task previously defined by the user or by the system.

We consider several examples. Task initiation may be made via job control statement, for example the command EXECUTE. (One can imagine that a job stack input without an EXECUTE statement will cause only task definition, while the inclusion of the EXECUTE statement in an otherwise identical job stack will cause task definition followed by execution.) When task definition and execution are simultaneous, the task to be executed is the one defined in the job control statements accompanying the EXECUTE statement.

Transaction-oriented systems or subsystems have as a primary characteristic the separation of task definition and initiation. Transaction-processing systems are built to allow the input of data only, without any accompanying task definition. The advent of the data causes execution of some predefined task or tasks. One example of a transaction-oriented subsystem is the IBM *Customer Information Control System*.[1]

All transaction types may initiate the same task, or each may initiate a different task, depending on how such a system is designed. If a single task is always initiated, it can then analyze the input data and, if necessary, call other subsidiary tasks to process specific data types.

Most often each unique transaction type contains a key identifying the task to be initiated for that particular type of data. The key may be manually inserted by the person preparing the input, it may be furnished automatically by the user's terminal, or it may be determined by analysis of the transaction data. A cross-reference table relating keys to tasks must be included as part of the task definition.

---

[1] Order No. GS20-0318, International Business Machines Corporation, White Plains, New York.

Transaction input causes a lookup to be made, the appropriate task definition located, and an EXECUTE request for that task to be processed. Obviously invalid input with an unrecognizable key is rejected because there is no match.

Finally, the last major type of request for task initiation is one in which a previously defined task is invoked explicitly via job control statement. The statement may be identical to that used in a self-contained task, except that the statement exists independently and refers (by some task/file name or label) to a task already defined and cataloged. For example, an EXECUTE statement for a COBOL compiler might refer to a complete task definition of compiler execution. In this case the EXECUTE request would be accompanied either by input data or by a pointer to filed data to be used as input to the compilation process.

One problem encountered in executing predefined tasks is that it is sometimes necessary to make minor changes to the definition. For example, a task which uses a magnetic tape as input may require a different definition of the specific tape (label identification, etc.) to be used each time the task is executed, or a task may be able to process input and output from/to a variety of media, with the exact one(s) to be specified at each execution.

To handle these situations, we must be able to modify some or all of the stored task definition parameters at execution time. This is usually acomplished by inputting the substitute parameters with the execution request. Depending upon the system, the user may be able to alter only a limited number of items, frequently only the identity of I/O files. In more sophisticated systems, he may have complete freedom to alter any items in the task definition.

Load Leveling

The other Level VI entry under Scheduling is Load Leveling. This is the function of exchanging jobs between information processors to even out workload peaks. This function only exists in information networks which include two or more compatible processors. The processors need not be identical, but they must be able to execute at least some of each other's tasks. For example, two computers which are not compatible at the object-code level may be able to exchange compilations or compilation/execution tasks if they have compatible compilers.

Load leveling between identical information processors is of course much simpler. However, even in this case jobs must be analyzed carefully to determine whether or not they can be exchanged. A job which uses a data base generally cannot be exchanged unless the file data required is transmitted with the job. This becomes quite complex since, if the file data is changed, the updated version must be returned to its original location. Meanwhile, other changes to that file area must be suspended, or the two sets of updated data must later be merged. Generally, therefore, load leveling is limited to those jobs which do not use a data base, or which only read and do not update it.

The load-leveling function is a subset of scheduling because this is the logical point to notice that the system is overloaded. It is possible to make this decision manually, rather than automatically, and simply input a notice to the scheduling function that load leveling is required. The degree of overload at which job exchange starts is quite important. Because of the extra overhead involved in transmitting jobs between processors, this should not be done unless a serious overload exists.

When it is determined that an overload exists, it is then necessary to determine which jobs should be sent to another information processor. The criteria for doing so were described earlier. Actual transmission to the other information processor takes place via the communication network. Special procedures are required to acknowledge receipt so that no data is lost in transit between the systems.

Automatic load leveling is very rare today, but as information networks continue to grow it will undoubtedly come into more general use.

10-4 EXECUTION CONTROL

The next entry in Level V is Execution Control. This includes all actions necessary to initiate task execution, to control communication and/or synchronization among tasks during execution, and to cause termination. Each of these Level VI entries is discussed in the following pages.

Initiation

The first Level VI entry is Initiation, which consists of selecting a task to be executed from the available queue(s). Selection depends on queue position (hence priority), but it must also take into account the resources required for execution compared to the currently available resources. To make this comparison possible, the task definition must include a description of the resources necessary to execute the task. Resources needed may consist only of main memory (the use of a processor is always assumed), or they may include a wide range of peripherals and secondary storage.

Task initiation interfaces with the subfunctions of Logical Resource Management (see Section 11-2) to obtain the necessary resources. If all resources can be obtained, task initiation is completed. If not, the attempt at initiation is discontinued, another task is chosen for execution, and allocation for it is attempted.

When resources have been obtained, task initiation concludes by loading the appropriate code into assigned memory locations and making the task a candidate for processor allocation. The loading process is accomplished through interface with a program loader (see Editors/Loaders, Section 8-1).

Intertask Communication/Synchronization

The next Level VI entry under Execution Control is Intertask Communication/Synchronization. This feature is required to allow multitasking, also called asynchronous processing.

The ability of a task, while in execution, to communicate with another task or tasks is a relatively new development. Earlier operating systems allowed this only indirectly, if at all. For example, it might be necessary for one task to create a file which could then be read by the other task. This indirect method is unsatisfactory when asynchronous task execution is required.

The need for intertask communication arises when a single program or job is separated into two or more tasks which can execute in parallel. Operating systems usually process in this manner, but application programs seldom do so. However, users sometimes need this capability which is particularly useful in a multiprocessor system. Execution of multiple tasks in parallel, if properly handled, can decrease the total time required to complete a job.

Parallel task execution requires operating-system support in two areas: communication and synchronization.

When related tasks executing asynchronously need to exchange data, they cannot communicate directly with one another; they are prevented from doing so by the protection methods used to keep tasks (related or unrelated) from interfering with each other. Therefore, to allow controlled communication, we provide the task with an operating-system interface in the form of command language statements. By using the appropriate statements, the task can specify which other task(s) it wishes to communicate with and what information, if any, it wishes to pass on. Operating systems vary in this respect; some allow great flexibility in the amount and type of data exchanged, while others limit interchange to the ability to set and test switches.

Task synchronization is also necessary. When two or more related tasks have been executing asynchronously, there must be a point at which the parallelism stops and single-task execution proceeds (or all tasks terminate). Depending on the implementation, synchronization may be controlled by any of the tasks, or control may be exercised only by a task specifically designated as the dominant one.

Synchronization requires a command language interface by which the task can request synchronization and specify the other task(s) involved. The control routines in the operating system then take the other task(s) out of execution and return control to the dominant task. Synchronization is equivalent to task termination for all but one of the tasks.

A multitasking language interface for COBOL has been under development for some time. The current status of this interface is documented in the *Asynchronous Task Group Report to the Programming Language Committee of CODASYL.*

Termination

The final Level VI entry under Execution Control is Termination. Task termination consists mainly of releasing resources used, which is done via interfaces with Logical Resource Management (see Section 11-2). If a task is allowed to pass resources on to another related execution, termination must be aware of the distinction between resources to be retained and those to be released.

There are two types of termination: normal and abnormal. Normal termination occurs when the task signals its completion to the operating system, and therefore it is presumed to have executed successfully. (Obviously this does not mean that it made no errors during its execution, but only that it made no errors detectable by itself or by the operating system.)

Abnormal termination occurs when an error prevents the task from completing execution successfully. Abnormal terminations most often occur when a problem program attempts to execute some sequence not allowed by the operating system. For example, the program may try to access memory or files it does not own, execute privileged instructions, execute invalid (nonexistent) instructions, etc. Any illegal act of this type causes the operating system to force the offending task into an abnormal termination, so it cannot damage any other tasks or the system.

A user task may also, of its own accord, request an abnormal termination because it has reached a point where it cannot proceed further. A task may do this if it detects a flaw in its own logic. More often, it will do so if an external error, such as an unrecoverable peripheral failure, makes continuation impossible.

Normal termination requires the release, or marking for retention and reuse, of resources which had been allocated to the task. Termination is followed by an attempt to select and start execution of a new task or tasks, since termination always makes resources available.

Abnormal terminations generally require some additional processing. If the system provides for file recovery via rollback, this may take place automatically whenever a task performing file update terminates abnormally. The rollback takes place as part of the termination process because the files used were part of the task's resources. If a file must be rolled back, it cannot be released for use by other tasks until rollback is complete. File protection and recovery techniques, including rollback, are described under Integrity, Chapter 12.

In addition to file rollback, abnormal termination may cause some special action to be taken in regard to the original task input. Normal termination usually releases the input job stack or input transaction data associated with the task. Abnormal termination may also do so, or it may do so only conditionally. In some circumstances it may be advantageous to retain the task input, in a special queue, until manual action can be taken to determine the cause of the abnormal termination. Often the error, when found, can be corrected by changing part of the task definition or part of the input. Saving the input is generally more efficient than asking the original input location to correct the problem and reenter the entire task. This is particularly true of remote input, especially in transaction processing systems.

10-5 JOB CONTROL LANGUAGE

The fifth and final Level V element of Task Management is the Job Control Language (JCL). JCL is listed under the task management function because it is most closely associated with that purpose, although it has features which are related to other information-processing functions.

A JCL consists of statements by which users can define the work to be executed and control executions in process to whatever degree the particular operating system allows. Each of the functions described earlier in this chapter is activated because of a job control statement or statements. The JCL is therefore the user's most direct interface with the task management function and its subfunctions.

For example, there must be a JCL statement or statements causing a task to be defined. Other statements are required to provide the definition itself. Similarly, JCL statements are needed to initiate task execution and to provide any parameters needed to define that execution.

The JCL is, in present day information-processing systems, part of the operating system. It is an extremely important part, since it is the user's means of controlling the system's actions.

User in this context includes all individuals who submit tasks to the information processor, and to some degree the operations (computer center) staff who interface with the system to direct its actions. Individuals who submit work to the system can be categorized as follows:

- Casual Users
- Managers
- Engineers and other similar professional personnel
- Clerical Users
- Programmers:
    Application
    System

Generally speaking, people in each of these categories wish to use the computer in a different way. The casual user knows little or nothing about how to operate the system, but he wants to use it for some purpose. At the other extreme, the system programmer may know a great deal about the hardware and operating system. The range of features available to each class of user is generally proportional to the user's level of knowledge. Quite frequently, different JCL facilities are provided for each class of user.

An operating system may also have a different form of JCL for each major mode of operation. For example, time-sharing users often have a different way of requesting program execution than batch users have. The computer operations staff (see Supervisory Control, Chapter 14) seldom has any language commonality with other types of users. This is to some degree unavoidable since different types of users have different needs. Generally, however, differences are caused by peculiarities of implementation rather than by substantial requirements.

To more graphically illustrate JCL principles, the following examples are presented. They are taken from the GCOS[1] operating system used on Honeywell Series 6000 and Series 600 computers, and they show the differences between batch and interactive control languages.

Figure 10-4 shows a batch job stack set up to request two Fortran COMPILE and EXECUTE sequences. The "$" character on the sample statements indicates to the operating system that these are JCL constituents and are to be analyzed for the commands they present. The meaning of each numbered entry on the example is given in the following pages.

STATEMENT
  NUMBER

1	$	SNUMB	JOBID, URGENCY
2	$	USERID	USER/PASSWORD
3	$	FORTRAN	LSTIN, DECK, DUMP
4		FORTRAN STATEMENTS	
5	$	EXECUTE	
6		DATA TO BE USED IN THE EXECUTION	
7	$	IF	ABORT, ENDJOB
8	$	FORTRAN	LSTOU, NDECK
9		FORTRAN STATEMENTS	
10	$	EXECUTE	
11	$	ENDJOB	

Figure 10-4   Sample batch job stack.

Statement 1 assigns an identity and priority (urgency) to the job defined here. This identity is required if the user later wishes to inquire about the status of the job.

Statement 2 defines the identity of the user submitting the job, and it may include a password for further security protection. This data is validity checked before the job is accepted for execution.

Statement 3 requests use of the Fortran compiler with the options specified: in this case a listing of the source input (LSTIN), an

[1] *Comprehensive Operating Supervisor (GCOS) Reference Manual,* Order No. BR43, Honeywell Information Systems, Waltham, Massachusetts.

output object deck (DECK), and a memory dump if the subsequent execution does not terminate successfully.

Statement 4 is the Fortran source program.

Statement 5 defines the next job step, which is execution of the compiled code. In the GCOS system, fatal errors during compilation will cause this step to be bypassed.

Statement 6 consists of the data to be used as input to this execution.

Statement 7 is a conditional statement, controlling whether or not Statements 8 through 10 are used. Statement 7 translates into a command to go to the end of this job stack, bypassing Statements 8 through 10 if the execution defined in Statement 6 aborts: that is, terminates abnormally. If it terminates successfully, processing will continue normally through the rest of the job stack.

Statements 8 through 10 define a second Fortran COMPILE-AND-GO, with different compilation options.

Statement 11 defines the end of the job stack.

Figure 10-5 shows a somewhat similar set of statements, arranged for use of time-sharing Fortran under GCOS. Since this is an interactive exchange, system outputs are shown underlined; user responses are not.

STATEMENT
  NUMBER

1	USER ID	USERID-x
2	PASSWORD	PASSWORD-y
3	SYSTEM?	FORTRAN
4	OLD OR NEW	OLD Filename
5	READY FOR INPUT	
6		FORTRAN STATEMENT CHANGES
7	?	LIST
8	?	RUN
9		DATA FOR EXECUTION, AS REQUESTED
10	?	RESAVE
11	?	DONE
12	SYSTEM?	BYE

Figure 10-5   Interactive job execution.

Statement 1 is a request from the system for the user's identity, and this is supplied. As in Statement 2 of the batch example, this data is checked for validity before the conversation proceeds.

Statement 2 is a similar request for the user's password, followed by his response, which is also checked.

Statement 3 is a question asking which time-sharing system the user requires, to which he responds FORTRAN, requesting the use of that compiler.

Statement 4 asks if his source input is already stored on a file or if he wishes to input it entirely from the terminal. His response of OLD, followed by the name of a file, causes the compiler to locate this file and set it up as the compilation input file.

Statement 5 is a comment that the system is ready for any changes or additions to the specified file.

Statement 6 consists of the user's Fortran statements representing modifications. Using the line numbers he supplies, the system merges these changes with the old file.

Statement 7 is actually repeated after each input line from the user. As long as he responds with source statements the file modification process continues. In Statement 7 he has responded instead with the command LIST, which causes his updated file to be printed out for his inspection. He could also choose to selectively list parts, rather than all, of the file.

Statement 8, after the LIST is complete, asks again for the next input or command. The user's response RUN requests execution of the program he has just modified. This RUN command is equivalent to the EXECUTE statement in Statement 5 of Figure 10-4. During execution, the program will request data entry to which the user will respond in Statement 9.

Following execution, Statement 10 again asks for the next command, and the user responds RESAVE. This causes his modified source file to be saved in place of the previous version. He can also respond SAVE and provide a new file name, so that both the prior and new versions of the program are saved.

Statement 11 again queries, and this time the user responds DONE, indicating that he is through with the system he has been using, in this case Fortran.

The system responds, in Statement 12, with a query as to the next system he wishes to use. Instead of requesting another, the user responds BYE, which signs him off of time sharing. (He could also have responded BYE at Statement 11, eliminating this last interaction.)

In comparing these two examples, one from the batch environment and the other from time sharing, the differences are apparent. These differences seem unavoidable because of the substantial diffrences in the batch and interactive modes of operation. The IF statement in the batch job, for example, is unnecessary in the time-sharing system. It gives the batch user a way to specify alternate actions to be taken based on occurrences during job execution. The interactive user is there personally during execution, and he can modify the commands he enters based on events. These simply point out some of the difficulties inherent in any attempt to use a common JCL for all purposes.

Examples of the use of two other JCL's can be found in the *Burroughs B5500 Electronics Information Processing System Operation Manual*[1] and in *OS/360 Job Control Language* by Harry W. Cadow.[2]

SUMMARY

Task management consists of the four functions used to process tasks through the system and the JCL used to control these functions. Emphasis on the individual functions will differ depending on the type of information-processing system. Task definition, for example, is very important in transaction-processing systems but less so in batch systems. Queueing and load leveling may be nonexistent or unimportant in small systems, while of great importance in larger ones. In every information-processing system the components of task management play an important role.

[1] Form 1024916, Burroughs Corporation, Detroit, Michigan.
[2] Prentice-Hall, Englewood Cliffs, New Jersey, 1970.

CHAPTER **11**

Resource Management

The next Level IV software function to be discussed is Resource Management. This is perhaps the most basic function of any information-processing system, and it is almost universally included in the operating system (except in very small computers). This is appropriate because of the complexity of resource management and its close relationship with the hardware characteristics of the computer system used. Figure 11-1 shows the Level V and Level VI subdivisions of Resource Management.

11-1 HARDWARE MANAGEMENT

Hardware Management is the first of the two Level V entries. It covers the most basic operating-system function, the control of the computer hardware. There are few, if any, conditions in which a problem program within a multiprogramming system is allowed to access the hardware directly rather than via the operating system.

There are, in general, two reasons why this access must be via the operating system. First, it isolates system users from the peculiarities of the hardware. In many computers, particu-

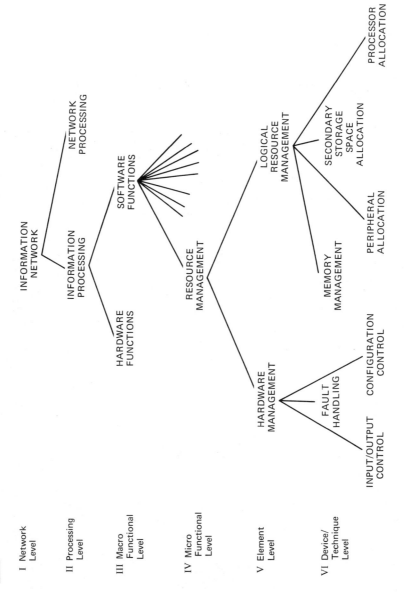

Figure 11-1 Resource management techniques.

eues. When device queues are used, the operating system maintains
eparate list of I/O requests for each device, even though multiple
vices may be accessed via the same I/O channel. When channel
eueing is used, all requests for devices accessed via a particular
annel are queued together.

Each of these queueing techniques has advantages and disadvan-
ges. Generally device queueing is useful, even on multiple device
annels, if the devices can perform some level of overlap. For example,
two disc devices share a single channel, it is often possible to send a
EK command to one device and then, while that is being executed,
e the channel for a READ or WRITE on the other device. Tape
ndlers have similar capabilities; a REWIND on one device can
ually be overlapped with reading or writing on another.

If device queueing is used, the operating system must in some way
k the queues to the channel, so that it is aware of the common
annel and will not attempt to execute incompatible I/O commands.
is not unusual for a single disc or tape subsystem to share two or
re common I/O channels which can be used interchangeably and si-
ltaneously. An example of this type of configuration is shown in Fig-
11-3. In that case, the system must link the queues to all connected
annels, and it can then issue as many concurrent commands as there
free channels as long as these do not conflict at the device level.
O control becomes quite complicated in arrangements of this type.

The queueing of I/O requests may involve priority ranking. Some
stems do not queue in priority order and simply handle all I/O on
FIFO basis. Others allow I/O to be ranked in two or more priority
els as part of the queueing process, causing high-priority I/O to be
viced sooner than lower-priority requests.

Priority schemes are useful when the I/O requests generated
eed the instantaneous capacity of the I/O channels and/or devices.
though this imbalance obviously cannot exist continuously in a suc-
ssful system, it will exist periodically for almost any device in any
stem. If such an overload never exists, the actual computer capacity
obably greatly exceeds the required capacity. These overload or
ak-demand periods are the reason priority schemes are needed.

One of the situations in which use of a high-priority I/O request
extremely useful is in the execution of tasks which consist mainly of
dia conversion. System-output processing, where problem-program
put accumulated on mass storage is converted to print, punch,
gnetic tape, or remote media, is such a task. This operation requires
y little processor time, but it must be able to issue timely I/O
uests in order to keep its peripheral and/or terminal devices oper-

larly in large-scale systems, very complex programming is required to
handle hardware functions such as I/O initiation, termination, and
exception processing. Each peripheral device or class of devices requires the use of techniques tailored to its specific characteristics. As
hardware devices have developed greater and greater capabilities,
their use has continually increased in complexity.

In addition to the level of difficulty associated with hardware-level
programming, its use almost always destroys program transferability:
that is, the ability to execute the program on another type of machine
or in some manner convert it to another type of system. A program
written at hardware interface level for one type of computer must be
heavily revised, or possibly completely rewritten, if it is to be executed
on a different type of computer. This fact has also helped to eliminate
direct hardware interfaces from application or problem programs.

The second reason why user access to the hardware is normally
denied is to prevent programs from damaging the system, either accidentally or maliciously. Possible damage may take two forms: destruction of the operating system and/or damage to other programs
and/or other users' files.

In summary, the existence of the hardware management function
protects user programmers from the complexities of the hardware,
while protecting the system and its other users from problem-program
malfunctions.

Hardware management is divided into three Level VI techniques,
each of which is described in the following pages.

Input/Output Control

The first of the Level VI entries is Input/Output Control. Although
the major function performed is issuing I/O commands, a number of
other functions are required to support I/O.

The control of remote devices (terminals) also falls into this
category, either directly or indirectly. Computers which use a multiline or single-line controller as interface to the communications facilities tend to handle remotes much as they do local peripherals, subject
of course to the physical differences involved. Computers which are
instead provided with one or more front-end network processors to
control the remote environment deal with terminals only indirectly.
In the latter case, interface between the information and network
processors is usually via an I/O channel (sometimes a specialized
one). Control of this interface also falls into the category of I/O control. The bulk of this chapter will discuss I/O control of local periph-

eral devices and ignore remote terminal control. That subject is properly part of network processing, rather than information processing, as explained in Chapter 1.

When an I/O operation is performed, a series of events similar to the following occurs (actual events vary in different systems):

- A problem or operating-system program requests I/O via call to the appropriate portion of the supervisor.
- If the request cannot be initiated at once, it is queued.
- When the requested device and channel are free, the I/O command is issued.
- Completion (or failure) of the I/O causes an interrupt, which is handled by the operating system.
- Knowledge that the request is complete is returned to the original requesting program.

The detection of an error or exception condition complicates this I/O event sequence. Errors generally add another step to the sequence, consisting of attempted error recovery. Error Detection/Correction is part of the integrity function, and it is described in Section 12-1.

Each of the events in this list is described briefly in the following paragraphs.

Request Queueing includes the receipt and queueing of I/O requests. A peripheral I/O operation originates with an I/O request. Some operating systems, and/or their accompanying support software, provide a number of levels at which an I/O request can be made. These levels may range from extremely symbolic to extremely exact, and they generally represent a range of flexibility inversely proportional to complexity; e.g., a user making high-level symbolic I/O requests has fewer options and exercises less control than one using low-level requests very close to machine language.

Even prior to queueing an I/O request, the operating system may process it to convert it from the language used by the requestor to the form of an I/O command. This processing is said to be device-dependent, because the logic used differs according to the type of peripheral being addressed. Operating systems try, with more or less success, to shield the user from these differences. Such systems are said to provide the user with device independence, since he does not have to be concerned with detailed device charactristics.

A typical I/O might involve a request for a record to be read from mass storage. The user presents a symbolic record address which is translated by other operating-system routines to a relative position

within a particular file. The I/O request is issued as of the data at that relative position. The queueing rou mine what device the file is stored on, where the file that device, and finally compute the actual hardwa record requested. This absolute address is then che of access by the requestor to be sure that it is wit which he is allowed access. If so, the I/O comman address is entered in the I/O request queue. The a involved in this sequence is shown in Figure 11-2.

USER REQUEST

"READ NEXT RECORD OF FILE

LOGICAL I/O ROUTINES

"READ BLOCK #44 OF FILE A"

I/O CONTROL

"READ DISC SECTORS #14-18
FROM DEVICE 4"

Figure 11-2 Input/output request sequence.

The operating system must generally provide which waiting I/O requests can be held until compl always required for shared devices such as mass st device is one which can be used by two or more pr concurrently.) Queues may or may not be needed for such as magnetic tape handlers, printers, etc.

Queues for unshared devices are necessary only are able to issue multiple I/O requests. This is som look-ahead purposes. In the look-ahead mode, one p multiple consecutive I/O requests for a single unshar waiting for completion of any. Some operating sy others do not. If look-ahead is not allowed, this effe the need for request queues for unshared devices.

Request queues may be separated into device

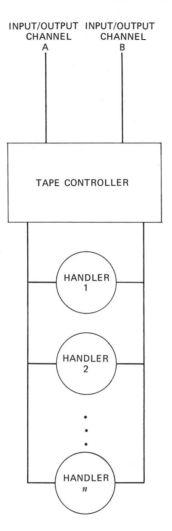

Figure 11-3   Multiple channel devices.

ating at full speed. The operating system may provide special features by which such a task is effectively guaranteed access to a processor at the appropriate times (for long enough to issue another I/O) and assured high priority for such I/O.

Another factor which may have an effect on I/O request queueing is the use of latency reduction techniques on rotating storage devices. Since rotational delay time is generally in the order of milliseconds, which is a very long time in today's nanosecond-cycle time processors, the incentive to reduce this delay is considerable. Latency reduction techniques attempt to eliminate delay by issuing the optimum I/O request available based on the device's current position.

Many mass-storage devices manufactured today assist the operating system's latency reduction procedures by providing information indicating where the read/write (access) mechanism is at a given point in time. This information may be available to the software in response to a status query, and/or it may be furnished automatically each time an I/O on the device terminates. The IBM 3330 disk system (mentioned on p. 58), for example, can furnish rotational positioning information to the software.

Position status information is used to determine which I/O can best be issued next. The normal request sequence may be modified to take advantage of this knowledge. The rationale is that total throughput will be improved by this technique, even though a particular I/O may not be given the priority expected by its originator.

Issuing I/O consists of taking an entry from an I/O request queue, performing any transformation necessary to convert the queue entry into a hardware-acceptable command, and then executing that command. In systems which maintain multiple request queues for a single channel and/or device, logic is also necessary to determine which queue to select from next.

Issuing a new I/O usually follows completion of a previous I/O; the sequence is as follows. First, I/O termination causes an interrupt. The interrupt handler passes control to the appropriate device-handling routine. This routine can then issue I/O for the free device or channel as rapidly as possible, so that no available I/O time is wasted. This sequence may be modified if the previous I/O terminated with an error condition, and therefore it may require retry.

Interrupt Handling is the next item in the I/O sequence, and it includes basic analysis of the status resulting from the I/O completion. Interrupt handling is one of the most interesting and important areas in modern information-processing systems. Since substantially all general-purpose information processors are interrupt driven today, it should be apparent that interrupt handling is basic to such systems.

In general, an interrupt results from the occurrence of any one of a number of possible events. For purposes of this discussion, an interrupt-triggering event is considered to be external to the central processor. Internal events which are logically equivalent to interrupts are called "faults" rather than interrupts. (Fault handling is discussed later in this chapter.)

The interrupt itself is a hardware-initiated transfer of control, causing the processor to stop current instruction execution and branch to a location previously defined by hardware and/or software. This location is generally called an interrupt vector, and it consists of a short sequence of instructions, or a single transfer instruction, leading to an interrupt-processing routine. An interrupt generally causes the processor to be put into the master or supervisory state, so that interrupt handling is performed by a privileged routine.

The specific events which cause interrupts and the interrupt-handling techniques used vary in different computers. Some computers provide interrupts for events not associated with I/O. However, the use of such an interrupt capability is not general, and it will not be discussed here.

The handling for all types of interrupts has certain common features. Because interrupts occur at unpredictable times, and in random sequence, the system must handle them whenever they occur. In general, this adds to the complexity of the software structure.

It is normally important that I/O interrupts be handled as rapidly as possible. The importance of this varies in different types of systems, being less evident in processing-oriented (scientific) systems and more evident in I/O-oriented (business) systems. If an interrupt is not handled efficiently, the result is the loss of potential I/O time because an I/O device or channel which could be used is idle. If the system's total I/O load is light, this loss may be unimportant. However, even with a light load, lost I/O time may result in noticeably slower response if the system is servicing interactive users. Great importance must therefore be placed on the speed and efficiency with which interrupt processing is handled.

It is usually possible to suppress the occurrence of interrupts, either completely or selectively. Most operating systems use this ability to protect themselves against unlimited levels of recursive interrupt processing. For example, if the operating system is processing an interrupt when another interrupt of the same type occurs, this is a recursive interrupt. The software would have to store the information associated with the earlier interrupt, process the later one, then remember to return to the first and complete its processing. This situation could become very complicated. Suppose, for example, that the second interrupt was not completed when a third occurred; the third was incomplete when a fourth occurred, etc.

To prevent this type of nested interrupt processing, the interrupt-handling routines usually inhibit all or part of the interrupts which can occur. The most common practice is to inhibit interrupts of the same or lower-priority levels during interrupt handling. If a higher-priority event occurs, an interrupt will be caused, but if any inhibited level occurs it will be remembered by the hardware until the inhibition is removed. A few systems inhibit all interrupts during interrupt handling.

A variety of interrupt types occurs in most computer systems. Considering only those interrupts associated with I/O, perhaps the most important one is caused by I/O termination. A terminate interrupt signals I/O completion, although it may indicate either successful or unsuccessful completion, and it is basic to I/O processing in any interrupt-driven system.

A successful termination interrupt indicates that the I/O command was executed to completion, and that no error or exception condition was encountered. Unsuccessful, or abnormal, termination interrupts are usually accompanied by additional status information, such as the type of error, whether or not the I/O function was started and/or completed, and other pertinent facts.

Another broad category of interrupts might be called "manual intervention" or "special" interrupts. This type of interrupt indicates a change in status, usually resulting from operator action. As an example, the operator might mount a disc pack or tape reel on a drive or handler, triggering an interrupt signaling the change from unready to ready status.

Some peripherals, such as consoles, have an "attention" key which can be activated by the operator, indicating his desire to interact with the operating system. Depressing the attention key causes this same manual intervention interrupt.

Status return analysis completes the interrupt processing. Status information obtained with the interrupt consists of data describing, often in considerable detail, the condition which exists. In the case of an abnormal terminate interrupt, status indicates the error(s) involved.

Status returns can also indicate other information, even when the interrupt results from successful I/O termination. Mass-storage subsystems may return the current actuator (read/write mechanism) position as status with each termination. This information is necessary for the latency reduction techniques described earlier in this chapter.

Status return analysis therefore falls into two major categories: that of deciphering error types on an abnormal interrupt and that of processing positioning data on certain types of normal interrupt. The subject of error detection, analysis, and correction is associated with I/O control, but logically it belongs to the integrity function. It is therefore discussed in detail in Chapter 12.

Fault Handling

The second of the three Level VI entries under Hardware Management is Fault Handling. The hardware implementation of a fault is very similar or identical to an interrupt. A fault occurs as the result of some event which requires immediate handling by the software. The distinction used here between faults and interrupts is that the former result from events occurring within the processor, while the latter result from events external to the processor (most often I/O-related events). In practice, some computer vendors refer to both types as interrupts, but the distinctions between them are easier to make plain if different names are used.

When a fault occurs, the normal sequence of instruction execution is halted, and a hardware-controlled transfer to a predefined memory location takes place. A different location is usually associated with each type or class of fault, and these locations are referred to as fault vectors. Each fault vector consists of an instruction or instructions to give control to the appropriate fault-processing routine. The occurrence of a fault may also cause the processor to be set to the master or supervisory state, so that the fault is processed in privileged mode.

Faults fall into two categories: those caused by the deliberate execution of fault-producing instructions and those caused when the processor recognizes some abnormal condition.

The deliberately produced, or programmed, faults are quite important in multiprogramming systems. Computers which have two or more processor states, for example supervisory and problem or master and slave, may provide a programmed fault. The most common use of this fault is to allow programs executing in the problem or slave state to enter the supervisory or master state and obtain services, such as I/O execution, from the operating system. Such entry must be tightly controlled to prevent the problem program from damaging the system. Use of the fault mechanism allows the transfer to supervisory state, but it gives control to an operating-system routine which can interrogate the request accompanying the fault and perform the required processing. The transfer of control from supervisory to problem state does not require similar protection, and it can be made directly rather than via fault. Only privileged routines can execute in the supervisory state, so they are allowed to enter problem state at any point they choose.

The other fault category consists of abnormal condition faults. The faults in this category all represent errors or possible errors, and they can be further subdivided into those caused by the hardware and those caused by the software. There is generally some overlap of cause; some can indicate either hardware or software error.

The fault caused by detection of a parity error in main memory is typical of the hardware-caused faults. Another example of this type is a fault caused because the processor fails to complete the execution of an instruction correctly and this is detected by its error circuitry.

Software-caused faults include arithmetic overflow, attempt to access memory outside of base address register limits, and many similar faults.

In the ambiguous fault category, faults which appear to be hardware-caused can sometimes be software-caused. Occasionally what appears to be a software fault may be hardware-caused. For practical purposes, ambiguity of this type is ignored while the information processor is operational. These cases can, however, cause problems in attempting to diagnose system errors.

Abnormal condition faults, whether hardware- or software-caused, can be separated into two groups for fault-handling purposes. The first handling method is used for faults which a problem program may be able to process itself. For example, a fault generated on arithmetic overflow may or may not represent an error in a particular program. The other type of fault handling is used for faults which a problem program cannot handle. These are discussed later.

Faults which can be handled by the problem program may be treated by the operating system as a user optional fault. That is, if the problem program wishes to handle a specific type of fault, it is allowed to do so. It must furnish the operating system with an address (within the problem program) to which transfer will occur when a particular type of fault is sensed. The program can then do anything it likes, including ignoring the fault. On the other hand, if a particular type of fault represents an unrecoverable error in the program, it can simply fail to furnish a fault-handling routine address and allow the operating system to do the normal processing. This approach allows considerable flexibility to problem programs, since they can separate those hardware fault conditions which should be handled in the standard manner from those which require specialized handling.

Abnormal condition faults which are not in the user optional class represent either a hardware failure, a problem-program failure, or perhaps an operating-system software error. Each type requires different handling, in detail, but all are approached in a common manner.

Generally speaking, each of these types of faults requires some type of error analysis to determine the reason for the fault. This may be followed by an attempt to correct the problem, or it may result in a failure of the faulting process. This may be a hardware component, a user task, a system task, or in the worst case, the entire system.

Since this type of fault analysis and correction falls under the integrity function, it is discussed in more detail in Chapter 12.

Configuration Control

The third and final Level VI entry under Hardware Management is Configuration Control. This includes the routines which keep track of the physical hardware configuration of the information processor. It also includes the linkage between the physical configuration and the logical or symbolic configuration seen by system users. This entry is in fact a bridge to the next Level V element, Logical Resource Management.

Physically existing hardware and the symbolic hardware perceived by system users are seldom identical. When this condition does exist, it is usually on very small-scale systems. On some large systems the separation is absolute. Each user or problem program may "see" a virtual machine, which may be totally unlike the actual hardware, and also totally unlike the virtual machine seen by other concurrent executions. General-purpose systems do not go this far in separating physical and logical hardware, but it is common to substitute a symbolic for an actual system configuration, and these differ to some degree.

The first task of configuration control is the establishment of the physical hardware complement. There usually exists a theoretical maximum configuration definition, as well as a current actual configuration definition.

Software systems are set up to handle some maximum set of hardware. This maximum set is formed from the list of permissible components (i.e., how many different types of printers, disc drives, etc. are handled as standard attachments) and a definition of how many of each specific type of component can be attached.

Since an installation almost never consists of the maximum set, software customization or tailoring is necessary to adjust the software to the physical hardware actually present. In small systems this may be unnecessary, because the spread between minimum and maximum configurations is not great. Excess coding may simply be unused without unduly damaging throughput or response. In large-scale systems this is seldom the case. The extent to which the software must be tailored varies, but some degree of tailoring is required.

There are two major methods by which software tailoring is accomplished. One is assembly-time tailoring, and the other is load-time tailoring. Some operating systems use both methods.

Assembly-time (or compilation) tailoring consists of assembling a software version for a specific hardware configuration. The hardware to be used is defined as input to the assembly process. That is, the types and numbers of peripheral devices, number of I/O channels, memory size, etc. are entered as assembly parameters. An example of this method is the system generation (SYSGEN) operation used on most IBM systems.[1]

The other major method used to tailor software to a specific hardware configuration is to include only the required code when the operating system is being loaded onto the hardware. This loading process may be a two-phase operation, and tailoring may take place in one or both of the phases. An example of this method is found in the startup procedures of the Honeywell Series 6000.[2]

The first loading phase consists of transferring the operating-system code from long-term storage medium (usually tape reel or disc pack) to operating storage. In this phase, tailoring may take place so that only routines which will be used are moved to operating storage. Unused modules are not moved. However, if the same disc pack is used for both long-term and operating storage, no tailoring is possible at this point since the first loading phase does not exist.

The second loading phase moves the permanently resident portion of the operating system from operating storage to main memory. Even paged operating systems require that some portion of the code be instantly available for execution. Tailoring is particularly important in this phase, because any extra operating-system code loaded unnecessarily reduces the space left in main memory for other uses.

The operations described above serve to define the physical hardware configuration. It is also necessary to relate this to the symbolic configuration. One of the operations which usually takes place at load time is the assignment of symbolic names or functions to hardware devices. For example, the operating system may require a definition of which mass-storage space and/or peripheral device(s) it can use for its own working area, as opposed to space and devices reserved for system users. There may be external public device names known to system users; these must generally be cross-referenced to the actual

[1] *IBM System 360 Operating System System Generation,* Order No. GC28-6554, International Business Machines Corporation, White Plains, New York.
[2] *System Startup and Operation Reference Manual,* Order No. DA06, Honeywell Information Systems, Waltham, Massachusetts.

hardware. By this method, hardware devices can be changed or reassigned while the user-known symbolic labels remain the same.

Once the symbolic configuration is defined we have the devices which can be referred to by problem programs and job control statements. Requests from users for data movement to/from symbolic devices cause the operating system to cross-reference between the user's symbolic labels and actual physical addresses.

Some systems include the ability to change the configuration during operation: that is, to reconfigure the system. Reconfiguration may simply change the physical hardware layout; in that case the symbolic configuration must be modified accordingly. It may also be possible to perform only a symbolic reconfiguration which does not affect the hardware, but which changes the symbolic names assigned to devices. Since reconfiguration is most often associated with Restart/Recovery, it is discussed in Section 12-2.

11-2   LOGICAL RESOURCE MANAGEMENT

Logical Resource Management is the second Level V element under Resource Management. It is separated into four Level VI items, each of which is described in this section.

This function includes the routines which determine how best to use available resources. Unlike hardware management, it is not concerned directly with hardware characteristics. Instead, it deals with hardware from a logical point of view, considering the hardware as consisting of allocatable resources. This may require some knowledge of the hardware, but at a much less detailed level than in the hardware management function.

In multiprogramming operating systems, the resources to be managed include peripherals, secondary storage space, main-memory space, and processor(s). Resources are needed to accomplish anything, whether the execution of an application problem program or execution of operating-system code. Sometimes different methods are applied to user and operating-system resource management; in other systems the same methods are used for both purposes. Since the differences generally arise not from logical dissimilarities, but from implementation methods, they are ignored in the following discussion.

Memory Management

The first Level VI entry is Memory Management. It can be described generally as the function of assigning main-memory space to tasks or processes in active execution status. In practice there are a large number of different memory-management methods, which vary greatly in their complexity.

The way in which memory is managed is frequently used to describe the operating system itself. For example, we speak of paged systems, MFT (Multiple Fixed Tasks) or MVT (Multiple Variable Tasks) systems, etc., where the description really refers to the memory-management method employed by the operating system. This general practice reflects the fact that memory management is one of the most fundamental characteristics of any operating system and to some degree determines what its other basic features will be.

The following paragraphs discuss the memory-management schemes used in each of several types of systems. The examples chosen do not form an all-inclusive list but are a set of interesting and representative samples. The types described are:

- Uniprogramming
- Multiprogramming, including:
  —Foreground/Background
  —Swapping
  —Multiple Fixed Tasks
  —Multiple Variable Tasks
- Paged

Uniprogramming System memory management is generally very simple; it might almost be said to be nonexistent. In the simplest form, it consists of checking each problem program to determine that it will fit into the available space (memory not allocated to the operating system). Memory management in uniprogramming operating systems is not very interesting, and it will not be discussed further.

Multiprogramming Systems are those systems in which two or more different tasks, processes, or programs are allowed to execute concurrently. Concurrent execution often, but not always, requires that multiple blocks of code be simultaneously resident in main memory.

Multiprogramming of course increases the complexity of memory management. This degree of complexity varies among the following schemes; they are presented in order of increasing complexity.

Foreground/Background Multiprogramming is the simplest method of multiprogramming, in that it allows only two tasks to share the computer memory; one is known as the foreground task and the other as the background task. The form of foreground/background processing called spooling was one of the earliest forms of multiprogramming.

Often, in these systems, the foreground program is time-dependent or peripheral bound; occasionally it processes remote data. The background task is apt to be processor bound and cannot have time dependencies; it is simply there to use up system capacity not needed by the forground task.

Memory management in this type of system is quite simple because there are only two memory areas and the size of each is fixed. Tasks are simply loaded into the specified area as necessary. Swapping (discussion follows) is sometimes performed within one or both of the memory areas, although this is unusual. Figure 11-4 shows a typical memory layout for this type of system.

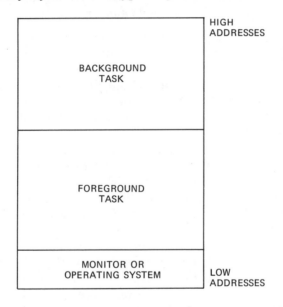

Figure 11-4   Foreground/background multiprogramming.

Swapping Multiprogramming is another often used memory-management technique. This is sometimes also called roll-in/roll out. Swapping is the process of writing some part of the contents of main memory to secondary storage and replacing that contents with other data. The data swapped is usually the content of the memory area assigned to a task or process; when this is written out the task is said to be swapped. The terms "unswapping" or "roll-in" are used to refer to the function of loading a swapped task back into memory from secondary storage.

Swapping is used in certain operating systems which do not allow multiple tasks to be in main memory concurrently. Instead, multi-programming is provided by the sequential loading and execution of multiple tasks. Swapping in this type of system consists of loading one user program into memory, allowing it to execute for some period of time (see Processor Allocation, following), writing that program to secondary storage, then loading a different user program and continuing the cycle. Any program smaller than the available memory simply leaves unused space. Obviously no user program can be larger than total available memory.

This mode of memory management is frequently used in small-scale, time-sharing systems. It is relatively simple and can result in satisfactory response to a reasonable number of users.

Multiple Fixed Tasks Multiprogramming extends the foreground/background concept to allow a larger, but still fixed, number of tasks to reside in memory concurrently. Main memory is partitioned by the user into some number of areas, the size of which is also defined by the user. The maximum number of areas allowed depends on the operating system, and within any one system it usually varies with the configured memory size.

Memory management in this type of system consists of handling each memory partition separately, loading tasks into each as necessary. Swapping may also take place within one or more of the partitions. The best known example of this type of system is the MFT version of OS/360. Figure 11-5 shows an example of a memory layout for this type of system.

Memory management is relatively uncomplicated in both the foreground/background and MFT systems, because the user is responsible for fitting his tasks into the memory partitions. He must generally also specify in which partition each task belongs. This is far simpler for the operating system to handle than the variable memory-use schemes which are discussed next.

Multiple Variable Tasks Multiprogramming is a far more complex memory-management technique. There are several systems which fit into the multiple variable task category; the best known is the MVT version of OS/360; however, the Honeywell GCOS operating system is probably a better example of this type of system. The operating system provides all control necessary to allow a variable number of tasks to occupy memory and share execution concurrently. The user, or problem-program author, has no responsibility for memory management except to insure that task size does not exceed total user-allocatable memory size.

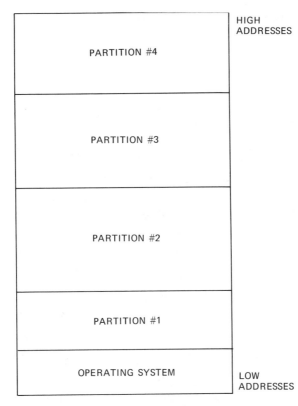

HIGH
ADDRESSES

PARTITION #4

PARTITION #3

PARTITION #2

PARTITION #1

OPERATING SYSTEM

LOW
ADDRESSES

Figure 11-5   **Multiple fixed tasks (MFT) multiprogramming.**

No memory areas, or partitions, are set aside. Memory management consists of comparing available tasks to available memory space
and choosing tasks to load which can best fit into the space. It can
easily be seen that this is a complex process, particularly if the average task is large in comparison with memory size. There is considerable danger that a task which is difficult to fit into memory may wait
for a long time before it is able to get into execution. A variety of
schemes are used to minimize this problem, the most common of
which involve some type of escalating priority to eventually force
allocation, sometimes by forcing other tasks to swap out temporarily.
Figure 11-6 shows memory as it might appear at a given instant of
time in this kind of system.

Generally speaking, this method of memory management is more
efficient if tasks to be loaded can be kept relatively small in comparison to total memory size, and/or a fairly large queue of tasks is
always available for execution. Both of these conditions can be

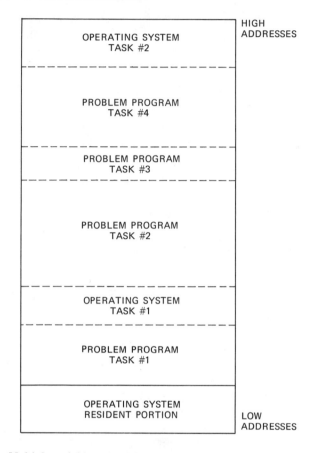

Figure 11-6 Multiple variable tasks (MVT) multiprogramming.

achieved but may require some user cooperation. For example, if a good overlay scheme is provided, users can be encouraged to cut basic program size and use overlays as needed. The fact that these strategies are unnecessary is one of the advantages of the paged systems described later in this chapter.

Memory management in systems of this type is usually limited to providing contiguous memory space for loading each task. That is, if a task requires 16K bytes of memory, a contiguous area at least that large must be located before the task can be loaded. The technique called memory compaction is used to minimize the effect of this limitation.

Memory compaction is used when sufficient space is available to load a specific task but is fragmented into two or more noncontiguous areas. In compaction, other memory-resident tasks are moved as necessary to obtain a single contiguous open area. The waiting task is then loaded into that space.

Some computer systems are organized so that contiguous loading is not required. However, there are few if any systems except those described next, under Paged Systems, which allow noncontiguous loading in a totally free manner. Hardware support in the form of multiple base address registers, or some similar mechanism, is necessary to allow noncontiguous loading.

Paged Systems form the final major memory-management method. Paged systems are very complex, and relatively few (compared to other types) exist today. Although paging could theoretically be implemented entirely in software, specialized hardware is necessary to achieve a reasonable level of performance.

In a paged system, main memory is divided into a number of "pages," usually all of the same size, or in some cases a limited number of multiples of a base size. A basic premise in paged systems is that an entire task need never be simultaneously core resident. Instead, only the page or pages actually being used are in memory, while the others remain on secondary storage. A reference from a memory-resident page to one not resident causes the referenced page to be brought into main memory. Memory management in this case consists of finding an available space into which the new page can be loaded.

Noncontiguous loading is the normal case in paged systems. Since each page is independent and must be uniquely linked to every other page it references, there is neither a need for, nor an advantage in, contiguous loading. Figure 11-7 shows an example of memory content at a point in time in a paged system.

One of the most difficult and important decisions required when creating a paged system is definition of the page size or sizes. The ideal size should be large enough to contain a reasonable amount of coding and to include most program loops within a single page. If the page size selected is too small so that execution loops tend to span pages, additional overhead results. If the page size is too large, memory is poorly used since fewer tasks can be accommodated concurrently than would otherwise be the case. At the present time, page size determination remains an art; it is not yet a science.

Paged systems are generally built around the use of reentrant coding, so that data and executable code are placed in separate pages. This makes it easy to mark each page to indicate whether or not it

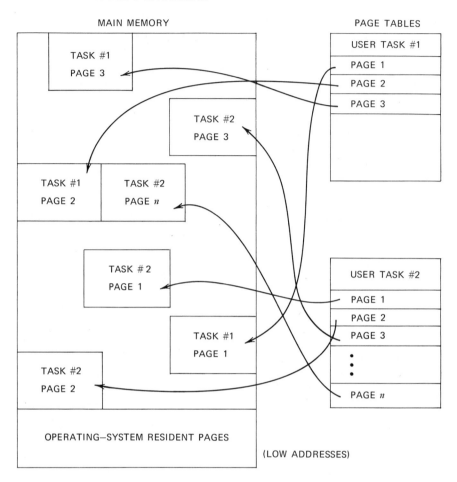

Figure 11-7   Paged system memory map.

has been altered while in main memory. When space is required, any area containing code or unaltered data, and not in active use, can be overwritten without being copied to secondary storage. If space cannot be found except in an inactive but altered data page, that page is written to secondary storage before its space is reused. This is important; inefficient paging systems can be very bad indeed, while good ones can be very good.

One of the considerable advantages of paged systems is that a task can be of unlimited size. (Some systems do impose a maximum size limit, based on the computer's maximum addressing ability, but such limits are so very large as to be equivalent to unlimited for practical purposes.) Further, the application programmer never has to worry about program size, overlays, etc. He can code without any concern for these items, and the operating system will fragment his code into pages and manage them for him as necessary.

An interesting example of the use of paging occurs in the formerly RCA, now Univac 70/46 TSOS (Time Sharing Operating System). In this system only interactive tasks are paged, while any concurrently executing batch jobs remain core resident continuously. It is thus a partially paged system.

Peripheral Allocation

The next Level VI entry is Peripheral Allocation, which deals only with unshared peripherals. Unshared peripherals are those devices which can be used by only one task at a time. Examples are card readers, punches, and magnetic tape handlers. Shared peripherals can be used concurrently by two or more processes; all mass-storage devices are potentially shared.

The need to use an unshared peripheral may be indicated explicitly by a system user. For example, the operating-system command language usually includes statements for requesting use of each of the various types of peripherals. The user may be able to state the need in his job definition, to be processed prior to execution, and/or state it while he is in execution in response to a need arising dynamically.

In some cases the user may receive allocation of peripherals without an explicit request on his part. For example, the user may request compilation of a source program. If the compiler in question requires peripheral allocation (for example, it may need a working tape), the user's request for the compilation may generate an implicit peripheral allocation request.

Although in theory the allocation of unshared peripheral devices is very simple, in practice it becomes quite complex. This is because of the conflicts generated by multiple users' peripheral needs in a multiprogramming system. This can be illustrated by the following example:

> Task A needs 4 tapes and 1 printer.
> Task B needs 1 card reader and 1 tape.

In a system with a total of 4 pages configured, Task A will obtain all of them. Task B may be able to obtain the card reader it needs, but it will be unable to obtain a tape and will have to wait until A terminates.

A more complex situation may arise in a system which allows jobs to obtain resources dynamically, and/or to retain allocated peripherals from one job step to a later job step. A potential "deadly embrace" condition may arise, as shown in this example:

Task A has obtained 1 tape and needs 3 more.
Task B has obtained 1 tape and needs 3 more.

In a system with only 4 tapes this causes a deadlock, since neither task can obtain the tapes it needs and therefore neither will terminate. The operating system must recognize this type of situation and resolve the conflict. This is usually done by terminating one of the tasks and restarting it for execution later.

Various systems handle this situation by different means. Some do so by not allowing dynamic allocation, some do so by not allowing allocation to be carried from one job step to another, some do so by look-ahead techniques, and some do so by logic to detect and resolve conflicts which arise. Some systems allocate resources by job, rather than by job step. If no dynamic resource allocation is allowed, deadlocks cannot occur in such systems.

In any case, peripheral allocation requires a series of tests for each attempted allocation, particularly when more than one type of peripheral is needed. First, a test is made to determine if the required number of peripherals of a type exceeds the total number of peripherals of that type configured. Any attempt to obtain more peripherals than are configured is rejected at once, since it can never be satisfied.

When multiple peripheral types are requested, each must be checked individually for availability. When a type is found to be available, the required number of devices is allocated conditionally while other availability checks are made. A discovery that a particular need cannot be filled causes any conditional allocations to be released, and the entire sequence must be attempted again later.

With this type of allocation procedure, there is the danger that jobs or tasks which are difficult to allocate will never be allocated. For example, a task which requires use of all of the tape handlers attached to the computer will be difficult to allocate, because one or more of the tapes will almost always be in use by other tasks.

This can be compensated for by marking tasks which are difficult to allocate, so that they have a better than average chance to obtain allocation. This may involve a priority scheme, in which difficult allocations are given a higher priority and are thus attempted more often. Some systems allow for an extreme case of difficulty by suspending all other allocations until the problem case can be completed. This is not recommended, as it is seldom workable. In some operating systems, manual intervention is relied on to handle these extreme (and presumably rare) cases of difficult allocation.

Secondary Storage Space Management

The third Level VI entry under Logical Resource Management is Secondary Storage Space Management. It controls space on shared peripherals: i.e., mass-storage devices. In general, there is some overlap between the shared and unshared use of mass storage.

In many systems, demountable mass-storage devices such as disc packs can be used in either shared (also called public) or unshared (also called private) mode. When unshared, a specific disc pack is assigned to one user. He can create one or more files on the pack(s), but no other user is allowed to use any of the space even if some is available. In this mode, a disc pack has many of the characteristics of a reel of magnetic tape, except of course that it consists of directly accessible rather than sequentially accessible storage. When a disc pack is used as a shared device, it is simply part of the total available storage with the added characteristic of demountability. However, use of space on the pack is controlled by the operating system, and files for several users may be entirely or partially resident on a single pack.

When a mass-storage device is used as an unshared peripheral, its allocation is controlled as described in the preceding section, Peripheral Allocation. The remainder of this section discusses mass storage only as used in shared mode. However, shared storage space management does have many similarities with pheripheral allocation since the same functions are required in each case. An inventory of total resources must be maintained, requests for allocation must be processed, and resources must be returned to inventory when no longer in use.

The first function required is the maintenance of an inventory of available space. If more than one type of storage is attached to the system, an inventory must be kept separately for each type. The operating system must maintain not only a record of the amount of available space, but sufficient data about each device or device type to allow it to match requests against available space characteristics. How much detail is required depends on how the user interfaces are defined.

The basic inputs to the space-management routines are requests for space allocation and notifications that allocated space is no longer needed and can be deallocated.

Requests for space may be generated by the application user, either explicitly via job control statement or implicitly via request for some other function which in turn creates a need for space allocation. The operating system will generally accept requests for a specified amount of space, without definition of the type of space needed. It may also allow the requestor to specify what type of space is required, either generally or in detail.

If the request states only that a specified amount of space is needed, space management allocates from the available inventory according to some standard pattern. A pattern is chosen to provide the best use of available space and the most efficient access. For example, the space-management scheme in a system with four disc devices might attempt to allocate space equally on all devices, thereby equalizing the load on I/O channels and devices.

Space-management schemes which do not depend on user input to determine where space should be allocated are generally not very efficient except in special purpose systems, for example time-sharing systems. Space requests in a general-purpose system may represent a very wide range of user needs. Perhaps the most complex example is an operating system which serves a large number of time-sharing users creating and using small private files, and which concurrently provides on-line and batch-mode access to a billion character data base by large numbers of users. The space allocation methods used for time-sharing files would almost certainly be unsatisfactory when allocating space for very large data bases.

Because of the difficulty of performing efficient space management under these conditions, operating systems take one or both of the following approaches. First, they may make initial allocation using some set of rules, then accumulate additional data concerning file use over a period of time, and if necessary modify the allocation using that data; and/or second, they may allow or request the user to furnish as much information as he has available about space use and perform allocation using that knowledge.

Many space-management routines accept the premise that complete external control is necessary in at least some cases. Knowledge of exactly how these files will be used is very important in determining how space should be allocated, particularly when we are creating large or long term files.

Consider, for example, a large integrated data base containing all of the records necessary to control a large corporation. Within such a data base there is usually a relatively small number of records or types of records which are accessed heavily. These records should be placed on rapid-access storage, while the remainder may be satisfactorily placed on slower storage. If no control is exercised over file placement, space allocation will probably be inefficient, and it may be quite a while before enough usage data is accumulated to correct the condition.

Processor Allocation

The final Level VI entry under Logical Resource Management is Processor Allocation. In simple uniprogramming systems, processor allocation consists of assigning the processor to the operating system or to the problem program in execution as needed. Multiprogramming systems require more complex processor allocation methods, and computers with multiple processor hardware have still more complicated methods of allocating the available processors. The following discussion first covers processor allocation in uniprocessor systems. Additional logic necessary to handle multiprocessor systems is then described.

Multiprogramming systems commonly use a time-slice scheme to give each concurrently executing task some processor time. A time slice is defined as consisting of some number of milliseconds or some other unit of measure. Each task in memory is given the processor in turn and allowed to execute for the duration of a time slice. At the end of that time, the processor is given to the next task waiting, etc.

This simple round-robin approach must of course take into account the fact that a task cannot always use its time slice. For example, if a task requests I/O, it can normally make no further use of the processor until that I/O is complete. Some systems prefer to leave the processor idle for any remaining portion of the user's current time increment, but most perform another processor allocation as soon as the task indicates it cannot proceed.

A task in a wait condition must either be taken out of the list of candidates for processor use or left in the list and marked ineligible. When the I/O request has been filled, the task can then be returned to the list or marked eligible, and it will then start receiving time slices as before. Most processor management routines maintain a list of eligible processor users, and one or more other lists of those not currently eligible, either separated by, or marked with, the reason for ineligibility.

The method by which the next task for processor allocation is selected varies in different operating systems. The simplest is the round-robin method, in which tasks are arranged in a single circular queue, and each is given its chance in turn.

Some systems expand this by maintaining two or more queues

rather than one. A priority level is associated with each queue. Processor time is allocated first to any task in the highest-priority queue. Only when there are no entries waiting in this queue is the next queue examined, and if multiple queues exist the process is continued down through the lowest-priority list.

This weighting scheme is sometimes used to provide better service to those routines which do not use the processor a great deal, but which need to obtain it rapidly when they do need it. An example is a task running a tape to printer (or any other similar peripheral bound) application. Such a task does little processing, but it needs to issue its I/O requests as rapidly as possible each time an I/O completes.

The potential drawback to priority schemes in processor allocation is that priorities must be carefully assigned. If too many tasks, or tasks which use a great deal of processor time, are allowed to have high priority, lower-priority tasks may receive too little processor time. In some cases this may be unimportant, but often lack of processor time will be externally noticeable in slow response to interactive users of the system.

Another method by which certain tasks can be given a higher priority is to increase the duration of their time slice. This means that priority tasks have the same chance as other tasks to obtain the processor, but they are allowed to retain it longer on each allocation.

Unlike problem-program tasks, some components of the operating system are by definition immune to the normal method of processor allocation. The routines which handle hardware interrupts and faults automatically obtain control of a processor whenever the interrupt or fault occurs. They usually retain control until they have completed the necessary processing. They are naturally set up to do this as rapidly as possible, and normal processor allocation can then resume.

Other noninterrupt handling components of the operating system generally obtain a processor in the same way that user tasks do. When a component needs a processor it makes, or has made for it, an entry in a queue, and when that entry is reached a processor is allocated for the task's use.

Allocation from this queue may differ in two ways from user task allocation. First, the operating-system queue may have a higher priority than any user queue(s), and it may be serviced first (although this is not always true). Second, no time limit is set; the component retains the processor until it completes whatever actions are necessary.

Allocating the processor for a fixed time has two aspects. User tasks are limited to a finite time slice to distribute processor time equitably. Also it is felt that such tasks cannot be trusted to relinquish control within a reasonable amount of time. Operating-system components, on the other hand, are assumed to be reliable and do only the necessary processing before relinquishing control.

The other aspect, which only applies to some computers, concerns the hardware timing mechanism itself. In the slave or task mode, it is always possible to take control from the process in execution via timer run-out. In the master or supervisory mode it may be impossible to take control away from an executing process, and so timing restraints are not physically possible with this type of hardware.

All of the discussion to this point applies to allocation in a uniprocessor system. However, a great deal of it is equally applicable, with slight modification, to multiprocessor systems.

There are two philosophies of processor allocation in multi-processor systems. One approach treats all available processors as equals, assigning any idle processor to any operating system or problem task which can use it. The other maintains a master/slave(s) relationship, assigning certain tasks only to the master processor.

The "equal-processor" philosophy requires no change in allocation methods from a uniprocessor system, except that two or more processors are available, so two or more tasks are usually in execution simultaneously. This approach has the significant advantage that failure of any processor makes no difference to system execution except in lowered throughput. The system is therefore inherently fail-soft with respect to the processors.

The master/slave philosophy usually requires some special handling in processor allocation. There may be a special queue of master processor tasks, or queue entries may be marked as to whether or not they can be executed by a slave processor. (The master processor is able to execute any task; only slave processors have limited abilities.) Thus if only master tasks are waiting, a slave processor may be idle. It is much more difficult to make such a system impervious to processor failure if the master processor is the one which fails.

Although the equal-processor philosophy is in many respects superior, it is not the one normally chosen in multiprocessor systems. There are in general two reasons why this is so.

Every multiprocessor system contains the inherent possibility of processor interference. This interference appears in various guises. As an example, two processors simultaneously attempting to execute the same code will physically interfere with each other in their attempts to obtain memory cycles to access the code in memory. When an interrupt occurs, only one processor is needed to handle it; if two or more try to do so they will simply interfere with each other. If there is a dependency relationship between any two tasks, simultaneous execution by different processors will produce different results than would sequential execution.

Hardware designed for multiprocessor use generally includes features to prevent some types of interference. For example, a particular processor may be designated in the hardware as the interrupt-handling processor, and it is the only one which responds to interrupts. To the extent that hardware has these characteristics, the operating system has no choice but to assign at least some master/slave processor relationships. It is probable that future hardware will be more flexible and allow software assignment of any processor to execute any function. Even at present these assignments, although made via hardware switch settings, are in some computers dynamically modifiable by software.

Even when no hardware restrictions exist, it is usually easier to code a master/slave relationship than an equal-partner control scheme. This is of course a generality, and as such it is open to argument. However, in the author's experience with both types of systems, the equal-processor scheme presented considerably more difficulty and complexity in design and implementation than the master/slave scheme.

SUMMARY

Resource management is undoubtedly the most basic, and also often the most important, function of an operating system. The control of basic functions, such as I/O, is extremely important, particularly because of its effect on the performance of the information processor. When analyzing an existing system, the elements of this function should be investigated in detail. When designing a new system, resource management must receive a great deal of in-depth attention.

CHAPTER 12

Integrity

Integrity is the next Level V entry under Software Functions. This includes features which improve the information-processing system's reliability and availability. Improvement includes preventing system failures when possible, recovering from those which do occur, and preventing data loss caused by hardware or software failure.

Integrity protection is one of the most important, and most often neglected, functions required in an information-processing system. In batch systems, integrity protection is often minimal. If the computer system fails, any jobs in process at time of failure must be rerun from the beginning. If the system supports mass-storage files, these files may require reload after a system or application-program failure.

This primitive mode of failure recovery cannot be tolerated in systems which are online or which are used to support critically important data bases. Probably the first information-processing systems to recognize the need for extensive integrity protection were those used in the manned spacecraft programs—Mercury, Gemini, and Apollo. These computer systems are literally vital to the astronauts' lives while a mission is in progress. Failure of the computer system itself, loss of the required data, or any serious error in computation can cause loss of life.

Another type of on-line system with a different requirement for integrity protection is the typical airline reservation system. Although no danger to human life is inherent in system error or failure, there is a very great potential monetary loss. An airline cannot operate for long without its mechanized reservation system. Extensive (and expensive) integrity-protection measures are therefore justified.

The average business today is moving closer to the airlines' mode. It is becoming more dependent upon its information-processing system, which is generally part of an information network. Protection of the business data base(s) is vital, as is assurance that the information network will be available for processing very close to 100% of the time.

Since the concept and techniques of integrity protection are not generally understood, they will be discussed in considerable detail. The integrity function separates into a number of Level V and Level VI items, as shown in Figure 12-1. Each of these items is discussed in the following Sections.

12-1 INFORMATION INTEGRITY

The first of the Level V elements is Information Integrity. This is an extremely important function which protects vital data against loss or damage (garbling, etc.) caused by detectable hardware or software failure.

There is one aspect of information integrity which is very difficult to control. This is the generation of incorrect data through problem-program errors. For example, if a file update program adds 2 to a record field when it should have added 3, that record will be incorrect. However, it is very difficult or impossible to detect such errors except by checks designed into the application itself.

This type of error is particularly hard to detect in transaction-processing systems. Batch updates frequently use batch total techniques, such as totaling all changes and comparing this with the difference between the old and new master file totals. Any errors such as the one described above would normally cause the control totals to be out of balance, resulting in a search for the error.

However, files updated on-line, one transaction at a time, cannot use these same types of checks. It may be necessary to save all transactions and also records of previous file status and to use these to audit the file content periodically. More often, the nature of on-line processing is used to advantage. If all program actions are reported

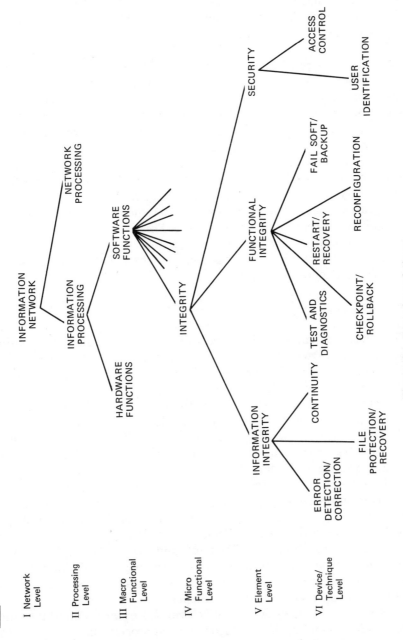

Figure 12-1 Integrity techniques.

Level

I Network
Level

II Processing
Level

III Macro
Functional
Level

IV Micro
Functional
Level

V Element
Level

VI Device/
Technique
Level

to the data input location, the terminal operator will generally notice an error in updating.

Other techniques can be used within application programs. Input data and updated file data can be analyzed for reasonableness, which will catch any serious errors in input or calculation. When these analysis routines are programmed separately and then inserted as required in problem programs, there is less likelihood that any one programmer's error will be serious. Of course checks of this type cannot detect an insignificant error, and in at least some applications a certain amount of error may be acceptable, particularly when compared to the high cost of eliminating all error.

The difficulty of determining that data is correctly processed by problem programs is an important aspect of information integrity. As vendors' operating systems offer increasingly sophisticated integrity-protection schemes, it is necessary to remember that these cannot control application-program accuracy. This is therefore an item of great importance in high-reliability systems.

Information integrity consists of the three Level VI items described in the following pages.

Error Detection/Correction

The first, and most basic, Level VI technique under Information Integrity is Error Detection/Correction. The first item which normally comes to mind here is peripheral error handling. However, there are two other classes of errors included in this category. One consists of hardware errors other than peripheral failures: for example, memory parity. The other includes software errors, either in problem programs or in system software, detected by the system. Both of these two latter types of errors were discussed briefly under Fault Handling in Section 11-1.

Peripheral error detection is present, at some level, in every information-processing system. Automatic error correction is less common, although much work is being done on the techniques necessary to correct data errors. Each information-processing system has an approach to handling I/O errors and other abnormal hardware conditions. The methods used vary partly because of differences in hardware and partly because of different system philosophies. These two points are to some degree interdependent.

System philosophy is usually determined by how important automatic error handling is felt to be. The approach may range all the way from the idea that errors seldom occur and can generally be handled manually, to the feeling that all errors should be handled automatically with the minimum manual intervention. Obviously, most systems fall somewhere between these two extremes. The trend, particularly in large systems, is toward automatic error handling wherever feasible.

The approach chosen is often determined by the specific computer's capabilities and the performance level it generally provides. Hardware which consistently performs in an error-free manner usually leads to minimum automatic exception processing in the software, which is undoubtedly appropriate. Another hardware characteristic which affects the philosophy of error handling is the amount of detailed status information provided by the hardware. If the hardware only indicates generally that an error exists, the software is forced to rely on manual intervention for more detailed error analysis and correction.

Hardware technology today is such that extremely low error rates can be achieved. This, however, is not enough. The applications now being developed make undetected errors intolerable, and they make manual error correction too slow to be acceptable. For example, the creation of corporate data bases on mass storage makes it extremely important that any data error is recognized and corrected, so that information used as the basis for control of a business can be depended upon. Increased use of interactive processing makes manual intervention in error processing, which was unnoticed in batch systems, appear intolerably long.

Peripheral error correction, at the most detailed level, consists of attempting to regenerate lost or altered data. The techniques used require that redundant data, which can be used to reconstruct any lost data, be carried. The degree of error which is correctable varies depending on the amount of redundancy provided. The most common hardware-error correction schemes, at the present time, are limited to correcting one lost or added bit within a physical record. A great many methods are available which make it possible to recover from more serious errors where multiple bits are affected.

Generally speaking, each added level of recovery capability increases the redundancy requirements proportionately. The redundancy needed rapidly becomes too expensive for any except the highest reliability systems. Complete duplication, the ultimate example of this approach, is described under File Protection/Recovery (following).

When redundancy is provided, error correction may either be accomplished by the hardware or by software. Which method is chosen depends on cost trade-offs between hardware and software implementations. Many different methods of error detection and correction are described in *Error Correcting Codes* edited by Henry B. Mann.[1]

Since automatic error correction is quite costly, hardware trends seem to be aiming toward reduced error rates while at the same time providing extensive error analysis capabilities. Special instructions are sometimes provided, intended for use only in test and diagnostic routines. The aim of these instructions is to allow software to pinpoint any error condition to the failing hardware component(s). When this goal is achieved, it will dramatically reduce the time required for hardware repair, since the majority of such time is spent in error diagnosis rather than in repair. Few, if any, present day general-purpose systems have the full range of such capabilities, but the need for such features is being recognized. Test and Diagnostics (T&D) are discussed in Section 12-2.

The category "hardware faults" covers hardware errors other than the peripheral failures just covered. This category includes memory parity, processor errors or failures, and major I/O-related failures such as of a multiplexor channel or other similar component.

Hardware-error faults may, in some operating systems, cause the entire system to fail. (Almost all systems fail on the occurrence of catastrophic faults, such as power failure.) More often, they cause T&D routines to be brought into execution, so that the error can be pinpointed while other activities (including problem programs not affected by the fault) continue processing normally.

Memory parities may be either transient or continuous. This is usually tested by retrying the instuction which detected the parity. If the retry is unsuccessful, that area of memory must be reconfigured out of active use. Reconfiguration is discussed in Section 12-2.

Some processor errors may also be correctable by software. Generally, the instruction is retried to determine if the error is an intermittent one. If it is not intermittent but is consistent, the software may elect to simulate the instruction, and/or to discontinue normal operation and enable T&D to test the processor. In a multiprocessor system other operations can continue normally while the faulty processor is tested.

In general, error detection is relatively well developed in current hardware and software. Error correction is much less well covered, and it requires many advances before being satisfactory in high-reliability systems.

The final category of errors covers software faults, which occur

---

[1] John Wiley and Sons, New York, 1968.

both in application programs and in operating-system software.

Problem-program failures may result in faults such as an attempt to access outside of assigned memory limits, an attempt to execute privileged or nonexistent instructions, or other similar errors. This type of fault usually causes a routine to be called to abnormally terminate the problem-program execution.

An error in the operating-system software itself may also cause a fault. This type of problem is very difficult to handle, since an erring software system may be unable to diagnose its own failures. Usually this type of fault causes transfer to a routine which tries to pinpoint the error which caused the fault. If this can be done, it determines whether or not it is reasonable to attempt to correct the condition by one of the following methods.

It may call in a new copy of the routine(s) which seems to be failing in the hope that this will eliminate the problem. It may cause certain routines, thus certain types of processes, to be suspended from further execution. For example, if the failure is connected with COBOL compilations, it may not schedule any more of these until the problem can be manually analyzed. Even though this is undesirable, the suspension of one type of processing may be more acceptable than failure of the entire system.

Another method of recovery is to cause one or more problem programs to be removed from execution. An operating-system failure is sometimes caused by a particular set of conditions associated with a specific program execution or executions; it is basically data-dependent. If this seems probable to the fault analysis routine, suspension of the suspected execution(s) is a logical step.

Only if none of these conditions can be successfully established does the operating system cease execution because of a software fault. Manual analysis, restart, and recovery are then required to resume operation. Restart/Recovery is described in Section 12-2.

File Protection/Recovery

The second Level VI entry is File Protection/Recovery. File protection is intended to prevent the loss of or damage to data contained in user or operating-system mass-storage file space and to repair damage when it does occur. Loss or damage may be caused by hardware failure, system software failure, or by action of an authorized user of the file. The latter is by far the most common failure in practice. This discussion focuses on mass-storage files because protection is most important for the information-processing system's data base, which is normally on mass storage. Protection of files on other media is seldom required, and if it is needed it can usually be provided simply by duplication. Large data bases are much more difficult to protect satisfactorily.

File integrity protection should allow the user to select the level of protection appropriate to each of his files, because the need for protection varies widely. The following file protection levels are typical of those most often defined (these examples are taken from the Honeywell File Management Supervisor referenced on p. 143).

- *Duplicated File*   A file with this protection level is created in dual copies, residing on different devices if the configuration permits. Both copies of the file are updated in parallel on any change. In case of a failure affecting one copy, access is switched to the surviving one, and the failed copy is then reconstructed. "Before" and "After" images (description follows) may be used to provide completely automatic recovery.
- *Automatically Protected File*   A single copy of this type of file is kept, but Before and After images are provided and used for any required recovery which is performed automatically by the system software. An alternative to the Before image protection is the use of delayed update, which is also described in this chapter.
- *Manually Protected File*   For this protection level only one copy is maintained, and the file is periodically dumped to demountable media, usually magnetic tape. Recovery is by user action, generally by reloading the file from the latest dump.
- *Unprotected File*   This type of file has no integrity protection; it is maintained in a single copy with no backup.

Three information integrity-protection tools were just mentioned, Before images, After images, and delayed update. Each of these is a different technique for providing file protection.

A Before image is a copy of a data increment prior to modification of that increment during a file update procedure. Depending on the technique used, a Before may be created for the exact increment of data changed (bit, byte, word, field, etc.) or, more generally, for a convenient logical increment within which the change occurred (record, block, page, etc.). The creation of a Before image just prior to update allows the update action to be canceled at a later time by restoring the data from the Before image. Befores are primarily a protection against software failure.

An After image is a copy of a data increment after modification of that increment. As with Befores, Afters may be written at different levels (field, record, page), although the most common increment is the unit written to mass storage. Afters are a duplicate of the latest image on mass storage, and they provide an alternate data source if the mass-storage image is destroyed. They are therefore primarily a protection against hardware failure. Figure 12-2 shows the sequence of events when creating a Before and After image for a file update.

A Before image is logically equivalent to the preceding After image of the same record. Befores are often used in addition to Afters because of the increased recovery speed they provide.

For example, the latest After for a particular record might have been written several days earlier. A long search through many Afters would be required to locate it. In contrast, the Before is always written during execution of the updating job. It is therefore quite readily available if needed.

Delayed update is another recovery technique which may be used instead of Before images. Delayed update is sometimes called "no update in place." Delayed update consists of writing any file updates

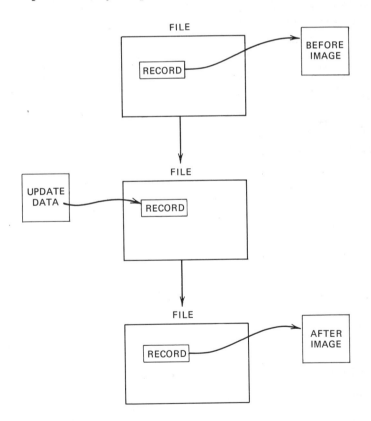

Figure 12-2 Protection techniques: Befores and Afters.

to a special update area, rather than back to the main file. Subsequent access to an updated record must retrieve the updated version. If the task or job terminates successfully, the changes are read from the update area and written to the main file. No rollback is required in case of software failure, because the file is not updated until failure is impossible.

A fourth integrity-protection tool which is generally necessary is the file dump. A dump is logically an extension of the After images, since it is an alternate copy of file data. However, the use of After images for all file recovery may be impractical. For example, if a record has not been updated recently, its latest After image may require a long search for retrieval. If dumps are taken periodically, retrieval need not go back farther than the latest dump.

Because it is impractical to dump very large data bases in a single operation, cyclic dumps are often required. Cyclic dumping consists of dumping a portion of the files each day, so that over a period of time, or a cycle, a complete dump is obtained. In this method, the time required each day for dumping does not become excessive. Figure 12-3 shows how a cyclic dump might be arranged.

In setting up a dump cycle, trade-offs must be considered between

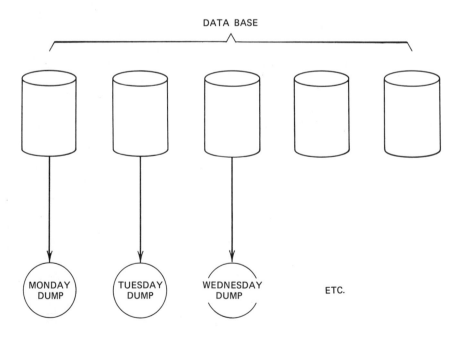

Figure 12-3   Cyclic dumping.

daily dump time and file reconstruction time. A rule of thumb some-times used is that a weekly cycle is satisfactory. The worst case of file reconstruction then involves going back less than one week. It may be necessary to make the cycle longer for extremely large data bases, or shorter if fast reconstruction time is considered important by con-trol personnel.

File recovery action depends on the protection method used and the type of error which occurs. The following are some of the most used recovery methods:

- *Information Move*   When an area of mass storage is expected to become unusable due to hardware failure, its contents can be moved to an alternate area if one is available. This of course depends on the hardware signaling expected failure, and/or software analysis of error histories to determine probable failure. The move requires either a hardware or software remapping so that access to the data is directed to the new location rather than to the original area.
- *Information Reconstruction*   When a mass-storage area has be-come unusable due to hardware failure, its contents can be recon-structed in an alternate area if one is available. This recovery involves locating the latest After image(s) or file dump(s) of the affected area. Once located, these are written in the alternate area. As in the information move method, remapping must take place. Figure 12-4 shows a schematic of information move and information reconstruction.
- *Rollback*   Rollback is the primary method of recovery from software failure. It consists of replacing current updated file content with the content prior to update, using Before images to do so. When an application or system software failure occurs, rollback can be used to restore file status as of the start of the interrupted execution(s). An alternate (but logically equivalent) form of rollback occurs when delayed updates simply are not posted, leaving the file in its original state.

Continuity

The final Level VI entry under Information Integrity is Continuity, which is intended to prevent loss or duplication of data passing into and out of the information-processing system. The basic technique used in continuity is sequence numbering. Numbering items sent to the information processor allows it to check for missing or duplicated numbers, thus detecting lost or duplicated input. When the informa-tion processor numbers its output, the receiver of that output can similarly check for loss or duplication.

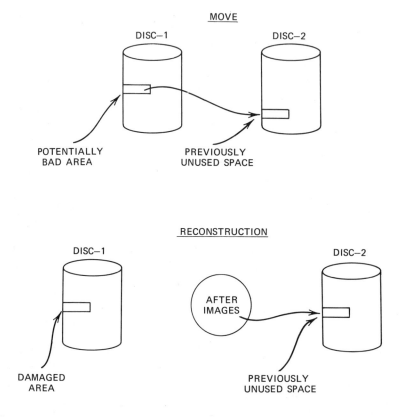

Figure 12-4 **Information move and reconstruction.**

Continuity requires that system users conform to certain disciplines for sequence numbering system input. This is easily accepted by some users but not by others.

Batch jobs input from a local device can be sequentially numbered, but computer personnel generally feel this to be irksome from an operational point of view. Their irritation is caused by the need to input jobs in exactly the correct sequence, and any disruption (such as that caused by a card jam) requires that jobs be renumbered.

Because of these objections, a compromise may be made by retaining a record, in the software, of local input actually in process within the computer and by taking steps to save this record if a system failure occurs. This technique detects input loss caused by system failure, but it does not detect input lost because an operator failed to enter it into the system.

Similar problems exist in sequence-numbering remote job entry items transmitted from remote batch terminals. As with local batch input, a compromise may be necessary between strict continuity controls and operating problems.

Sequence numbering is generally acceptable to system users when messages are transmitted from keyboard terminals. A sequence-number discipline has historically been used in message-switching systems, and it is equally applicable to data transmitted to an information processor. Strict continuity controls are important, because remote input can be lost due to communication line failure or network-processor failure, as well as because of operator error or information-processor failure.

Most message-switching systems enforce a sequence-numbering discipline because of the probability of a certain amount of data loss in transmission. When the information processor is an element of an information network which also includes message-switching capability, the processor may rely on the network processor's enforcement of this discipline for its check on input loss. Generally, in fact, it must do so. Otherwise, each terminal is forced to sequence number its computer message traffic and its other messages separately, which is awkward. This is an area in which information processing and network processing interface closely.

Although input loss is sometimes hard to detect, because of this kind of operating-procedure problem, input duplication is always detectable, assuming that no input terminal or local device is allowed to duplicate its message identifiers over a reasonable period of time. (Usually a day, or roughly 24 hours, is used.) By keeping a list of message identifiers previously received from each station the information processor can detect and reject any duplicates. However, it should be noted that certain kinds of input duplication are generally not detected in practice. Input of identical data text under two or more different message identifiers is generally not detected. Only the duplication of message identifiers is detected, which is usually sufficient. The detection of duplicate input is particularly important in data-base-oriented systems, where undetected duplicate input might cause duplicate data base updates.

Although message loss can be detected, this is not enough; the lost message must be recovered. For example, if input loss is detected, the sending computer or terminal is notified to transmit or retransmit the missing message. If the originator is a computer and has a copy stored, it can be programmed to respond to this request and transmit the message. If a copy is not stored, the operator at the originating station must be asked to resend the message. The operator may of course ignore the request, in which case the information processor is unable to take further action except to notify supervisory control (which is described in Chapter 14).

All of the discussion to this point has been directed toward non-interactive input. Interactive input is much more difficult to protect against loss or duplication than batch or message input. To some extent such protection is less critical because interactive input errors are usually apparent to the terminal user; this is not generally true of other input. In many cases even input duplication could occur without damage. (Obviously, in other cases it could not be tolerated.)

Protection of interactive input is difficult, because the technique just described requires some type of identifier to be associated with each transmission so that the identifier can be used to check for loss or duplication. When terminals are used interactively, such an identifier would be required on each separate piece of data sent: for example, each input line of a time-sharing conversation. This would be unacceptable to terminal users if the identifier had to be manually provided, because of the extra effort involved.

If loss/duplication control is required at interactive terminals because data loss or duplication would not be noticed and/or would be damaging, it can be provided in other ways. Some types of terminals can automatically provide the identification needed, via hardware logic. Programmable terminals can also do so, via either software or firmware control.

The most common type of input protection required, in practice, for interactive processes, is to retain received input even if the connection between the terminal and the processor is broken. This type of protection can be provided easily by the information processor, and it usually suffices for information integrity. It will protect against the most common cause of data loss, which is terminal or line failure.

Output continuity is provided by the information processor which may attach one or more identifiers to its output. These identifiers can be checked by the person or programmable device receiving the data, and loss or duplication can be detected.

The most common output identifier is a repeat of the input identifier which caused this output to be created. This may be the input sequence number, used for continuity checking, or a separate job or message identifier. In addition to, or in place of, this identifier, output may be sequentially numbered to each destination. If the information processor is associated with a network processor which provides sequence numbering for continuity, it may rely on that feature and not do any sequence numbering itself.

12-2   FUNCTIONAL INTEGRITY

The second Level V entry under Integrity is Functional Integrity, which includes the elements required to ensure the integrity of the information-processing system and of the processes operating within it. This includes procedures to prevent failures when possible and procedures to handle those which do occur. There are a number of interfaces with the information integrity function described earlier, since these are used to prevent information loss when failures occur. There are five Level VI techniques under Functional Integrity.

Test and Diagnostics

The first Level VI entry is Test and Diagnostics (T&D). There are two types of T&D: on-line and off-line. On-line T&D consists of routines executed concurrently with other processes, so that problems can be diagnosed and repaired without interrupting other processing. Off-line T&D is used when the failure is so serious that a major component, sometimes the entire information processor, must be removed from operation until its failure can be diagnosed and corrected.

On-line T&D is generally initiated when an error threshold is reached: that is, when a defined number of errors have occurred. The threshold may simply be an accumulative total of errors, or it may be an error rate. In the latter case, the rate of use over a defined period of time is compared against errors encountered during the same period. Applying the usage factor when performing threshold calculations allows the system to tolerate high error incidence during periods of high usage, which is realistic since error frequency tends to increase with use. Unnecessarily shutting down the processor or some component because of an improperly set error threshold is a very real possibility unless this is handled carefully.

To permit threshold calculation, the system must accumulate usage and error statistics for each component. Threshold calculations are generally made each time an error occurs. When an error threshold is reached, the operating system may automatically initiate T&D, or it may request manual intervention, notifying the operator that T&D is required.

It is also possible to periodically check usage statistics and to call T&D during low-use periods to exercise and test any relatively inactive component. Naturally this mode of operation must take into account the availability of other resources for T&D use; if the system is loaded with application work this type of T&D call must have a relatively low priority. Background T&D is not often used in general-purpose systems, but it is more often found in real-time applications with requirements for high reliability.

T&D can assist maintenance personnel in their error diagnosis by maintaining a record of component failures and the associated repair methods. Each such entry in the record consists of a set or sets of symptoms, and the repair technique used to correct the failure associated with those symptoms.

The field maintenance personnel who repair the equipment must furnish the necessary information describing the repair. The T&D routines can validate this by checking to see if another failure recurs within a predefined time limit. If this happens, the entry is either deleted, or presented to maintenance personnel for conditional deletion. If no failure recurs, the entry is considered valid and retained.

With this base, each time a component error occurs, T&D can compare the apparent symptoms with the entries in the repair record and inform the engineer of any matching entries. Over a period of time this record can provide a significant aid in repairing component failure. Sometimes the record is maintained at a central site belonging to the computer vendor, making it remotely available to all of that vendor's customer installations. This provides a very large historical base on which each customer can draw.

Two types of on-line test and diagnostic packages are described in *Total On-Line Test System (TOLTS) Reference Manual*[1] and *OS On-Line Test Executive Program.*[2]

Checkpoint/Rollback

The second Functional Integrity entry at Level VI is Checkpoint/Rollback. Checkpoints were first used in magnetic tape based applications to reduce rerun time in case of program or system failure.

Taking a checkpoint consists of writing the contents of main memory (or that portion of it devoted to the program being checkpointed) onto the checkpoint medium—usually a magnetic tape or mass-storage device. This memory dump must include enough information to enable files such as magnetic tapes to be repositioned in case of rollback.

Rollback consists of restarting the program execution from a checkpoint dump. In some systems, restart is possible only from the

---

[1] Order No. DA49, Honeywell Information Systems, Waltham, Massachusetts.
[2] Order No. GY28-6551, International Business Machines Corporation, White Plains, New York.

latest checkpoint, while in others any checkpoint can be used. The latter is much preferable. Restart consists of reloading main memory, then positioning all external files (magnetic tapes, principally) as they were when the checkpoint was taken. Control can then be given to the program at the point just following the request for checkpoint, and it can continue execution as though no interruption had occurred.

Checkpoints are extremely useful in large, long-running tape applications: tape sorts, for example. In a sort, a checkpoint is usually taken at the beginning of processing for each output and/or input reel. A restart need not normally go back farther than one reel.

Unfortunately, today's mass-storage-oriented applications, run under complex operating systems, are not nearly so easy to checkpoint as were earlier applications. The need for such protection, however, may be even greater than it used to be. The difficulties in providing this function arise from the concept of update in place, used on mass storage, as contrasted to update by copy, used on magnetic tape. When a checkpoint is taken in a mass-storage update process and execution then continues beyond that point, a restart from the checkpoint requires that all updates subsequent to that point be removed. Note the difference between this and a magnetic tape update; in the latter, repositioning the output tape to the checkpoint wipes out updates past that point.

To allow checkpointing of mass-storage jobs, the techniques described earlier for File Protection/Recovery are used. Either Before images are kept for the updated file(s), or delayed update is used. When Befores are used, a special Before record or marker is written each time a checkpoint is taken. Rollback requires that all Befores following the selected checkpoint be written back to the file, thus restoring it to its checkpoint status.

When delayed update is used, each checkpoint causes updates to be applied to the file. Rollback causes those not applied to be dropped. This of course implies that rollback can only be to the latest checkpoint; it is also possible to separate delayed updates by checkpoint and selectively apply them at rollback. This is extremely complex and builds up considerable overhead, so it is not a recommended method.

These methods are complex and often time consuming; however, the result is the same as tape repositioning.

Another major problem in providing a general-purpose checkpoint/rollback facility has to do with the operating system. Writing out main memory for the job being checkpointed may not be easy. Much information concerning each task may be stored in the operating system's tables, rather than in the task's memory area. The task's input and/or output files may exist on mass storage, under operating-system control. This is shown conceptually in Figure 12-5. If the object is simply to roll back the execution to a previous checkpoint and then restart it at once, these problems can usually be solved.

It is, however, much more complex to completely remove the job from the computer, later return it to the system, and then restart it from the checkpoint. Its input, output, and any working files must be dumped at the checkpoint, along with memory contents. Restart requires that peripherals, memory, etc. be reallocated, and that the job be linked into all operating-system tables as though execution had

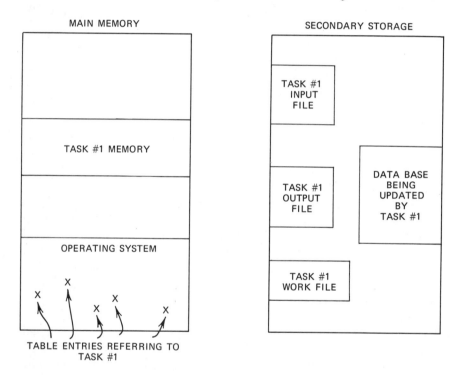

Figure 12-5 Complex checkpoint conditions.

previously been in process. These are such complex problems that no general-purpose operating system today provides a satisfactory checkpoint/rollback system which will handle all types of tasks with equal facility. Magnetic-tape-based applications still receive the primary emphasis in providing checkpoint capabilities.

Still another major problem which has not, to my knowledge, been solved is how to handle checkpoint/rollback when multiple concurrent updating programs are involved. Because any two or more programs updating the same file, and possibly even the same records, may be dependent upon each other, it appears impossible to checkpoint or roll back one such program without doing the same to all related programs. If this is not done, the program which continues to run may produce erroneous output based on a view of the file prior to the other program's rollback. The general subject of concurrent update was covered in Section 6-3. The problems here are too complex to go into in detail; it must suffice to say that this is an unsolved problem area.

Restart/Recovery

The third of the Level VI entries under Functional Integrity is Restart/Recovery. This consists of the procedures necessary to restart after a system failure and to recover so that no information loss results from the failure.

It is useful to think of a system failure as the simultaneous failure of a number of tasks, some of which are problem-program owned and some of which are operating-system owned. Restart consists of restarting each of these separate tasks without damaging any of the files being used. Thus the major problem to be solved is the same as that involved in successful checkpoint/rollback: that is, remembering a point at which task status is known to be correct, returning the task to that state, and then allowing it to continue execution.

The major difficulies arise in obtaining checkpoints, or the equivalent, for all executing tasks, including those of the operating system. There are two basic approaches to this problem: one is to force a system checkpoint periodically throughout normal operation and the other is to force a system checkpoint only if a failure appears imminent. Each of these has both advantages and disadvantages. Periodic checkpoints add to system overhead, but they guarantee that a restart point will be available. A checkpoint taken at the time of failure minimizes overhead, but if it cannot be obtained successfully restart will involve data loss.

Restart consists of reloading the information processor's operating-system code. This is usually done as a precaution in case the operating system was erroneously modified as a result of the system failure. Memory content is usually treated as unreliable, and it is therefore reloaded during restart.

Recovery takes place as part of restart. The restart process uses the latest available system checkpoint to reestablish system status as of a point prior to the failure. Any file changes made between the checkpoint and the time of system failure must then be removed, either by repositioning for files such as magnetic tape or by rollback for mass-storage files. Just as in problem-program rollback, this provides a clean starting point for each execution.

Operating-system processes may not fit neatly into the same framework of checkpoint/rollback, but with care they can be made to do so. Restart/recovery is greatly simplified if the same procedures can be used for operating-system and application tasks.

The continuity controls described earlier, under Information Integrity, also come into play during restart/recovery. System input and output must be recovered without allowing any data to be lost or duplicated. Often this involves interaction between the system and the operators/users at various I/O devices, using their analytical capabilities to assist the system in its recovery. For example, the console operator may be told the identity of the last local input processed before the failure. It is then up to him to determine if any later inputs were partially processed and if so to reenter those.

When the information processor is part of an information network, communication must be reestablished with its associated network processor(s) as part of restart. This generally includes a resynchronization procedure by which two processors agree on the identity of messages which were being exchanged between them at the time of failure and restart those messages. In a multiple information-processor network, it may also be necessary during restart to exchange messages with the other information processor(s) to resynchronize data exchange.

If terminal interactions were in process at the time of failure, restart must also take these into account. Interactive tasks which update files may be handled by the rollback procedures just described, although in some cases files may instead be left in their state as of the failure. In the latter case the interactive user is expected to take any action required to correct file content. Which approach to use is dependent on the type of processing which predominates interactively.

The information processor may also reestablish contact with its interactive users if it can do so. Private-line terminals and those which can be contacted via dial-out will usually be called immediately as part of restart, so that the users are aware that the system is operational again. A user at a dial-up terminal which cannot be contacted by the system must initate a new call to the system.

This is an area in which an independent network processor can be of great help in maintaining system continuity. The network processor can determine that the information processor has failed, and it can then take steps to partially or completely mask this failure from users.

When noninteractive data is being exchanged, the network processor can frequently continue this operation, stacking information processor input on mass storage until the processor is available again. Similarly, output being transmitted from shared mass storage (the delta configuration described in Section 5-2) can continue unaffected.

The network processor may also be able to provide a short-term buffering of interactive traffic, and then if necessary notify the users that there will be a short delay. An information processor with a good automatic restart system can generally be operational again within 1 to 2 minutes after a failure. This does not mean that all file rollback is complete, but that the computer is again under operating-system control and able to converse with interactive users. If the network processor maintains the line connections and keeps users informed during this short period, the interruption is much less traumatic than is an abrupt loss of contact with the information processor.

One of the most annoying problems in an information-processing system is the syndrome known as recursive system failures. This condition is said to exist when the same, or a related, system failure recurs immediately after restart, or perhaps even during restart.

The most common cause of recursive failures is an operating-system error which creates an invalid condition in some system file or table. This invalid condition is later discovered, usually by some other operating-system component, and that component then initiates a system stoppage. Since restart tries to keep all system data intact, it usually succeeds in retaining the invalid data. Predictably, this situation becomes self-sustaining and further operation is impossible.

Although recursive failures usually involve repeated occurrences of the same fault, this is not always the case. In complex failures the same invalid condition may be discovered by more than one system component, each of which may react with a different failure.

The original cause of a recursive failure can usually be traced to operating-system processing of a particular job or message (input or output). The cure therefore is to identify the job/message and eliminate it. (Although failure could theoretically involve a timing problem, this is not normally the case. Timing is seldom at fault in interrupt-driven systems. Even when it is, failures involving timing relationships do not usually recur after restart, since timing almost always varies.)

Recursive failures can, in most cases, be cured by controlling job execution after restart so that only one task is executed at a time. If the failure occurs again, the job in execution at that time is identified as the cause, and it can then be eliminated. Unfortunately, if the failure is not caused by a task execution but by some other process, this procedure will not identify the cause of failure.

For those cases not identifiable by sequential uniprogramming job execution, and for those situations where the failure makes a restart impossible (the system fails while still performing restart), the only possible action is to restart from some earlier system checkpoint. (Normal restart is from the latest system checkpoint.) This is a gamble, but it is based on the assumption that the invalid condition may not recur if restart goes back to a time before the error happened. Since there is usually no way to discover positively when the error occurred, this type of restart may be a trial-and-error process.

There are no really good generalized techniques for handling recursive system failures. Unfortunately they do occur, and they are a potential problem in any system.

Reconfiguration

The fourth Level VI entry is Reconfiguration. It is listed under Integrity since it is most often used as part of this function, but it is also used for load-leveling purposes.

Reconfiguration consists of changing the physical (or sometimes the logical) form of the computing system. Most frequently, peripheral devices are removed for repair or to be used with another computer (perhaps for load leveling). Another reconfiguration may occur later to return the peripherals to their normal connections.

A very simple logical reconfiguration occurs when an unrecoverable error is sensed on a magnetic tape or disc pack. One of the techniques frequently used is to request the operator to move the reel to a different handler, or the pack to a different spindle. Often the error will disappear when this is done. This is a logical reconfiguration since the file is reassigned to a different device, but no physical change is made to the hardware. Sometimes operators use physical reconfiguration for the same purpose, altering tape handler or disc pack spindle assignments on the hardware.

Reconfiguration of peripheral devices is quite common. Less common is the ability to add and/or remove central system components such as processors and main memory. For example, a processor in a multiprocessor system may be taken out of the on-line configuration so that it can be tested off-line. Failing areas of memory may similarly be removed from active use temporarily. When this type of reconfiguration takes place it may involve only software, or both software and hardware. Software reconfiguration simply makes a processor, memory area, or other component logically unavailable. This may be accompanied by manual (or perhaps software-directed) changes to the hardware which cause the component to also be physically unavailable. Reversal of this process, to make the component available again, will similarly require software and possibly hardware changes.

While the ability to reconfigure central system elements is quite rare, it is even rarer to find a system with the ability to add totally new components while it is in operation. Generally, the operating system requires a complete predefinition of all the components it will manage. Presenting it with a previously undefined component is not normally permitted. Improvements in this area are needed, and they can be expected in future systems.

Reconfiguration is very important in the fail-soft and fail-safe systems described next, and additional aspects of this subject are presented in those descriptions.

Fail Soft/Backup

The final Level VI entry is Fail Soft/Backup. Fail soft is the ability to use available duplicate hardware to survive all except catastrophic hardware failures and continue operation, although with degraded performance. Fail soft is distinct from fail safe, which uses completely redundant hardware for backup purposes only. (Fail safe is described later.) Fail soft, on the other hand, allows use of all available resources in normal operation, but it reassigns responsibilities if some resources become unavailable so that other devices which are still operational perform the necessary functions.

There are several possible levels of fail-soft operation. First, the failure of any peripheral not vital to system operation should not cause the entire system to fail. As a general rule, duplication of any peripheral minimizes the probability that its loss will cause system failure. Most peripherals are not vital to system operations, although a failure may cause one or more functions to be temporarily unusable. As an example, failure of the only card reader on a system will make reader input impossible and prevent execution of jobs (card-to-tape, for example) which use the reader. However, continued system operation, using remote input and/or jobs already with the system, should be possible.

Another type of failure involves the loss of main system components such as a processor, memory, I/O controller, multiplexor channel(s), etc. from the configuration. A fail-soft goal is to survive failure of any duplicated component to the degree that this is feasible within the hardware's capabilities.

For example, fail-soft reconfiguration to drop a processor from a multiprocessor configuration is usually possible. Memory failure affecting only problem programs can usually be handled by marking that section of memory unavailable. Execution can continue using the remainder of memory. The failing area may be assigned to T&D for diagnostic use only and later returned to normal use if the failure is located and repaired.

Although mass-storage-device failure might be considered a peripheral failure, loss of any part of the information-processing system's data base has other implications. For example, in a billion character integrated data base, loss of one device (containing perhaps 20 million characters) must not prevent access to the remainder of the data. It is sometimes possible to handle this condition by recreating the lost data on another device. However, even if this is not possible the system can provide other methods to continue operation.

For example, the system can continue to execute jobs and interactive processes which do not require the absent file(s) or absent file segment(s). These files should be reconnectable dynamically when repaired, and the system can then resume their use after performing any recovery actions required to ensure file integrity.

The loss of vital operating-system data due to mass-storage-device loss may of course cause total system failure. This possibility can be minimized by duplicating this data, as described earlier under File Protection/Recovery.

The information-processing system should also be able to survive the loss of its interface with any associated network processor(s). This prevents execution of some or all interactive tasks and other remote processes, but other operations can continue. When the interface is restored, remote processing should begin without interruption of other events in process at the time. The resynchronization necessary after a network processor failure is the same as that described under Restart/Recovery for information-processor failure.

Completely backed up, or fail-safe, systems are comparatively rare, but they are required in some cases. Manned spacecraft missions, for example, use triplex systems running completely in parallel. Some airline reservations systems and message-switching systems use duplex configurations.

There are two ways of handling backup equipment: "hot standby" and "cold standby." In the first mode, the two (or three) systems run in exact parallel performing all of the same processes. The backup system may not actually output any data, but it does everything else the primary system does. The systems continually exchange data, either simply to determine that both are operational or to check each others' results for accuracy. If the primary system fails or if a discrepancy is noted by the backup system, the hot standby processor can take over immediately with little or no interruption of service. Figure 12-6 shows a hardware configuration for such a system. Both dual information processors and dual data bases are shown, with dual peripheral devices switchable to either processor.

The second mode, cold standby, simply makes a second system configuration available as backup. While the primary system is operating correctly, the backup system may be idle or used for other pro-

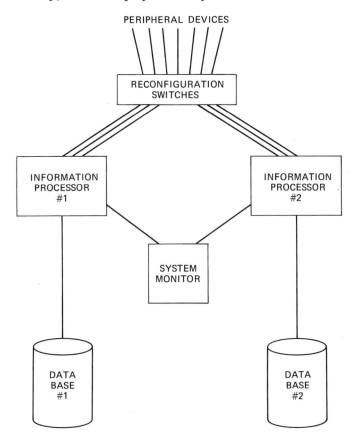

Figure 12-6   Dual backed-up configuration.

cessing. A failure of the primary system causes any processing on the backup system to be dumped, the primary program loaded, and the main load to be picked up by the backup system. This method is very likely to cause noticeable interruption of service when switchover occurs.

Generally, the choice between fail-soft and backed up (fail-safe) information-processing systems is made on the basis of the level of availability required. Trade-offs between availability and cost must of course be considered. Fail safe is considerably more expensive than fail soft, but it may be required if the application needs close to 100% availability. Many applications, particularly those which are not heavily interactive, can tolerate an availability closer to 98 or 99% in return for reduced equipment and software implementation costs.

12-3   SECURITY

The final Level V element under Integrity is Security, which separates into two Level VI entries, User Identification and Access Control. Security has two purposes. It protects the privacy of system users by preventing unauthorized access to their data or to facts concerning their data, task executions, etc. It also improves information integrity by allowing data to be accessed and/or modified only by authorized personnel. This decreases the probability of accidental or willful destruction of information.

User Identification

The first Level VI entry is User Identification, which is the process of establishing the identity of a system user. In a network environment it may be sufficient to conclusively identify the terminal being used and to apply that validation to any user of the terminal. More secure systems may require that both the terminal and the user be validated before access is allowed. Terminal identification and validation are network-processing functions.

User identification is required for two purposes. First, the user's identity must be known in order that his access privileges can be determined (see Access Control, following). Second, his identity must be known so that the user can be billed for the resources he uses.

There are some batch oriented systems which do not require any user identification because they provide no access control. Systems of this type generally use a project identifier for billing resource usage; in this case it serves some of the same purposes as the user identifier.

User-identity checks can be made in either of two ways, based on mechanical or manual methods. In the mechanical method, a badge, identity card, or other similar item is issued to the user. Placing this item in a badge reader or other similar device transmits data which identifies the user as the one to whom that badge was issued. In the manual method, the user is issued only identifying data, such as a user number, passwords, etc. Manual (keyboard, punched card) entry of this data serves to identify the user.

Although user validation is more often important in interactive than in batch systems, some form also appears in most batch processing. For example, the job stack of each batch job may require a user identity card or record, which serves the same purpose as the interactive user validation. More often, only a project identifier is required. This serves as a more general validation: i.e., that the user is working on a known project. Either the project or the user identifier can be used as a pointer to a billing authorization and thus serve the additional purpose of validating the charges incurred by the user.

Access Control

The second Level VI entry is Access Control, which includes techniques provided to protect the system and its users against unauthorized access. There are many levels of access control; the first is control over access to the information-processing system itself. Generally a valid user identifier or project identifier is required to gain access to the system. There are several reasons for this.

One of the reasons of course is billing; the user must be known so that he can be charged for the system resources he uses. Another reason is gross privacy protection; unknown users are not allowed to intrude since they might access private data. The third reason is to protect the system's integrity; an unauthorized user might accidentally or maliciously damage the system or data within the system by using it improperly.

Of these three reasons, the one which deserves further discussion is control over access to data within the system. Data access control is provided to protect the data owner's privacy by preventing others from reading data he wishes to keep secret. Access control is also used to protect data integrity by allowing only authorized users to modify data.

Access control over data stored in user and system files is achieved

by associating a set of permissions with each file. A permission author-
izes a particular person, class of persons, or perhaps all except a specified person(s) to use the file in a particular mode. READ permission,
for example, allows the file to be read but not updated if no other
permissions are granted. The standard set of access modes includes
READ, WRITE, EXECUTE, APPEND, and DELETE. These are
sometimes grouped, for example READ FOR UPDATE (equivalent
to READ plus WRITE), but the principle remains the same.

Permissions can be granted in any of a variety of ways. Generally,
of course, the owner of a file has a full set of permissions granted
implicitly. A file's owner is the person who created it, in the case of a
private file. Shared data bases often have no owner in this sense, but
they may have an owner arbitrarily assigned to whom these permissions will apply. This person is generally one of the technical staff or
a supervisor of the application group responsible for the file. Personnel
of this type often share group user codes under which they can be
assigned various permissions.

Private files are usually created with a standard set of permissions
unless the owner specifies otherwise. One frequently used standard
gives general READ permission, that is, any authorized system user
can read the file (subject to passwords, to be described), but all other
permissions apply only to the file owner. Another standard rule supplies only the owner's permissions, making the file inaccessible to all
others.

Permissions may be granted explicitly by the file owner, either
inclusively or exclusively. He can usually specify general access or
general exclusion, with individual exceptions in either case. Most
often, access is denied to all except a list provided: for example,
"USER-A," "USER-M," "USER-X." Occasionally access is allowed
to all except those specifically excluded, perhaps "USER-Q" and
"USER-Y." This process can be followed for each different type of
access, so that certain persons may have READ access, others WRITE
access, still others EXECUTE access. It is probably most common for
a user to allow general READ permission, but to allow other permissions only on a very restricted basis.

In many cases access is further controlled by the use of passwords.
If a password (or passwords) is associated with a file, this refines
general permissions by requiring that anyone accessing the file know
the necessary password(s).

These permissions and passwords are sometimes applied at multiple levels, providing finer control. For example, a logical file may
be divided into subfiles, and different control over access can be

applied to each. Sometimes permissions are applied to individual record types within a file. For example, if an employee file contains both work history and payroll records, the work history records might be easily accessible while the payroll records with their salary information are tightly controlled. This can even be carried farther, to the field level. In this case, for example, only salary fields in a payroll record might be protected, while other data is readily accessible.

An example of considerable flexibility in providing password/permission access control is found in the Honeywell Series 6000 File Management Supervisor.[1]

The same type of access control can be applied to operating-system files, which are usually tightly protected against modification and often against access of any type. The latter is particularly important when proprietary software is used. To handle this case, the EXECUTE ONLY access permission may be provided. A user can then execute the code, but he can neither modify it nor read it, preventing the creation of unauthorized copies of the software.

SUMMARY

Integrity and its three subdivisions, information integrity, functional integrity, and security are assuming ever greater importance. As information-processing systems become more interactive and are used increasingly to control business activities and industrial processes, integrity of the system and its data bases is absolutely essential. This function is one in which much development effort and many advances in technique can be expected in future systems.

[1] *GCOS File System Reference Manual,* Order No. BR38, Honeywell Information Systems, Waltham, Massachusetts.

CHAPTER **13**

Statistical
Recording

The next Level IV function is Statistical Recording. This includes the recording, reporting, and evaluation of the information necessary to analyze the performance of the information-processing system. This function is subdivided into the Level V and Level VI elements shown in Figure 13-1.

13-1 RECORDING

The first Level V entry is Recording. This covers the accumulation of data required for the other Level V entries: Reporting and Evaluation/Feedback. In practice, an analysis of the statistical recording function should start with these other two items, and from the reporting and evaluation needs which are specified the recording requirements can be determined.

Generally, the data recorded consists of measurements of system performance. Some measurements are used in determining the actual throughput versus theoretical maximum throughput. Often the aim in this case is to look for the causes of poor throughput, if it is less than the level required (or expected). In addition to performance analysis, measure-

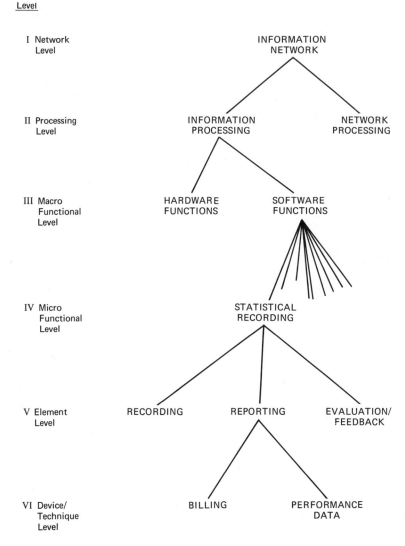

Figure 13-1   **Statistical recording techniques.**

ment data is accumulated for historical purposes (and may later be used for long-range performance analysis) or to aid in billing for the use of system resources.

Although the majority of performance measurement and recording is performed by the operating system, measurement should not be ignored in application system design. It is very important in complex applications to have precise measurements available so that performance can be analyzed in detail. In some cases, all of the required information can be obtained from the operating system, but it is more likely that the application itself will be required to make additional measurements and to record them.

There is a considerable degree of overlap between statistical recording and the supervisory control function described in Chapter 14, at least in the sense that the same information is mentioned in both. However, when this is the case, the data is used for different purposes in the two functions.

Statistical recording accumulates information for relatively long-range purposes, often in fact simply to satisfy legal requirements for record keeping. In general, it provides a long-term record of what happened in the system and how it happened: that is, execution times involved in various functions, and so on.

The logging portion of supervisory control may record some of the same data, but its function is different. The purpose of logging is to display system actions dynamically so that they can be known to the operators and other personnel controlling the system. Generally speaking, each item logged may not require operator action, but only those items of potential interest to control personnel are logged. Data recorded, on the other hand, may be of no interest in system control and have only statistical value.

The following items form a representative list of measurements and other data which should be recorded within the information-processing system.

Task/Job Execution Time is measured and recorded for each execution. In a uniprogramming system, elapsed time and processing time are identical. In multiprogramming systems the two are always different, and they must be measured separately. Often the processing time is used for billing purposes, while elapsed time may be used in system throughput analysis.

Execution time measurements are sometimes recorded in detail: that is, as one or more series of start/stop times; or they may be recorded in summary, as a single total time. Both methods are used; most often a combination is employed. Typically, the execution's first-start and last-stop times are recorded, while processing time is accumulated as a summary total (in seconds or some similar unit). Start and stop times are usually displayed as part of each job output for the user's information.

Task Input/Output Volumes are frequently measured and recorded. The total number of jobs and/or job steps is recorded. The number of records (card images) which comprise job input and job output are also measured. In transaction-processing or message-oriented systems, the measurements are usually in number of input and output messages, and perhaps also in number of characters per message. These measurements are useful in determining average system input and output loading.

Response Time is also measured in interactive systems. Response time can be considered a subset of execution time since it is the time required to execute an interactive command or process a transaction, and to return a response to the input location. However, a response-time calculation within the information processor does not present the complete picture, particularly in a complex communication network. If the I/O data must travel through a remote concentrator(s) and/or network processor(s), this network transit time must also be measured to arrive at the true response time. Measurements within the network environment are generally provided by the network processor(s). (Network processing also includes a statistical recording function.) Their time measurements and those of the information processor(s) can be combined for a complete measurement of system response.

Queue Wait Times may also be recorded and used to analyze system throughput and response. Tasks generally reside in a series of queues as they progress through the processing cycle. While being read into the system the task usually has an entry in an input-in-process queue; when input is complete it may move into a scheduled queue or directly into the queue of jobs in execution. On completion, it may move into an output waiting queue until all of its outputs (reports, etc.) are complete. The system may have many lower-level queues: one in which a task is waiting for in-process I/O to complete, one for tasks swapped out because of higher-priority tasks in process, and others. The time spent in any or all of these queues can be measured and recorded. This type of measurement is particularly important if response time and/or execution time are unsatisfactory; the more detailed data is of great help in analysis.

Queue Size is often a significant measurement. It is important that dynamic records be kept of the size of important queues, so that maximum and average sizes can be determined. Measurements are most often taken of the scheduled job queue(s), but others may also be measured for more detailed analysis.

Resources Used are also measured and recorded. Resources are main memory, processor time (covered in the earlier discussion of execution time measurements), peripherals such as magnetic tapes, card readers, etc., mass-storage space, and so on. These are usually measured in terms of elapsed time in use and also in terms of the quantity used. For example, use of two magnetic tape handlers for 20 minutes would result in entries recording both the use of 2 handlers and 20 minutes usage time on each. Secondary storage quantity is usually recorded in terms of the size of the space. Resource usage records are the most common source of billing data.

There are two particularly important items which should be part of the resources measured. These are I/O-channel-time use and I/O-device-time use. These items are important because I/O time is frequently one of the scarcest resources in an information processor. Detailed measurements can be used to calculate actual use versus theoretical maximum capacity, determining what potential the system has for expansion and/or pointing out poor use of these resources.

Error/Fault Statistics are accumulated as part of statistical recording. These are very useful in plotting long-term trends of hardware errors, and sometimes of software errors. This data can be used in conjunction with external data such as frequency of preventative maintenance, software changes made, etc. to determine the effect of these actions on system performance.

Overhead Time/Percentages may be measured and recorded, although this is seldom done except when an information-processing system is still being tested and debugged or is performing inadequately. Overhead is at best a difficult term to define, but it is loosely used to refer to software execution time not directly tied to the execution of problem-program coding.

For example, any I/O execution in a multiprogramming system requires a call from the problem program to the supervisor. It may then involve transformation from symbolic to actual execution commands and queueing if the device is busy. Data movements between the problem-program area and an operating-system I/O buffer may also be required. All of these items of processing may in some cases be regarded as overhead. They are, of course, also necessary to allow multiprogrammed execution, and the resulting overhead should be trivial if weighed against the time required to run all programs serially rather than concurrently. However, it is certainly true that careless implementation of functions of this type can seriously impair system performance.

System Trace may be part of the data recorded. This may include significant events such as start of job, end of job, start of terminal interaction, etc. generally recorded in time sequence. It may also include a record of internal operating-system actions, such as reading input, queueing input, scheduling a job, and starting or terminating task execution also in time sequence. This trace is a form of Execution Trace described in Section 8-4, and it may be used for purposes of analysis if a system failure occurs.

The items just decribed above are not by any means a complete list of statistical data required, but they are fairly typical of the needs found in most information-processing systems. Generally, the larger and more complex the system, the greater the need for extensive and accurate statistical recording. It is very important that adequate measurement facilities are included in the original system design as it is very difficult to add them later.

13-2   REPORTING

Using the data accumulated, a variety of reports can be prepared. This Level V entry, Reporting, covers the specification of reporting requirements. Reports can be very simple or quite complex in format and content, depending on the purpose for which they are prepared. There are two Level VI entries under Reporting: Billing and Performance Data.

Billing

The first Level VI entry, Billing, covers reports prepared to show how users are being charged for system resources. Perhaps the most common report of this type is the accounting data usually reported at the completion of each job or interactive execution. The report is sent to the user for whom the execution was performed. It shows the resources used, execution time, perhaps counts of records processed as input and output, and other similar data. Frequently the billing charges for the execution are computed, based on this recorded data, and included in the report. Alternatively, the user may be given only the accumulated detail data at this time and billed at a later date.

Billing data is generally accumulated and used to produce periodical reports, most often on a weekly or monthly basis. Billing reports may be sent directly to the users with copies to control personnel or used as input to a manual billing process. Manual billing should be avoided if possible, particularly in large systems.

Performance Data

The other Level VI entry is Performance Data. It includes reports consisting of the system performance measurements discussed earlier under Recording. Reports fall into two classes: those prepared dynamically in response to a request and those prepared cyclically at some predefined interval.

Reports of accumulated performance data, in detail and/or summary form, are most often prepared at predefined intervals. The most common interval is daily; detailed reports of performance statistics are difficult to comprehend if they cover too long a period. Sometimes, however, it is useful to maintain cumulative data and prepare summary reports weekly and/or monthly. A longer reporting period tends to smooth out unimportant variations, which often erroneously appear more significant in detailed daily reports.

A useful feature is the ability to combine reporting with evaluation (described next). If the data being reported is analyzed for normality or abnormality, unusual items can be flagged in the reports. This is of considerable help if the bulk of the evaluation and feedback process is manual.

It is often very useful to have performance report data available on a request basis. For example, a report of queue wait times and response times, current to time of request, can be very helpful in analyzing a system overload problem. The ability to obtain such reports on demand of course costs some software effort, as well as some processing time, but it is well worth it if the reports can be put to good use. This feature is an aid to supervisory control and is also discussed in Chapter 14.

13-3   EVALUATION/FEEDBACK

Evaluation/Feedback is the final Level V entry under the Statistical Recording function. It covers the use of the data recorded, and later reported, to evaluate operation of the information-processing system. This evaluation may lead to feedback in the form of adjustments to the system, modifying its mode of operation and thus potentially its performance. Evaluation in simpler systems is often manual, while in more complex software it may be performed by the information-processing-system software itself.

Evaluation consists of analyzing the available statistical data in accordance with some set of rules. Generally the analysis includes processes such as comparing data with specified acceptable limits, and noting cases which do not fit within these limits. Setting acceptable limits is generally an iterative process, and it cannot realistically be done until significant statistics are accumulated reflecting actual performance. As experience in operating a system grows, its acceptable and expected performance levels can be defined more accurately and in more detail.

Many of the items listed in Section 13-1 will be found to have acceptable limits within which performance is satisfactory. Response times of course must be kept within reasonable limits, or interactive users will be dissatisfied. This particular performance factor has sometimes been shown, in practice, to be self-adjusting. If response is unsatisfactory, some users simply will not use the system. This causes a decrease in the load, which causes response to improve for the remaining users. This is a unique case; most unsatisfactory performance does not resolve itself. Of course the example given may not really be an acceptable way to improve response.

Queue wait times and queue sizes can be shown, by experience, to have optimum limits beyond which performance deteriorates. Reasonable numbers of errors and faults can be computed readily; this topic is discussed under Error Detection/Correction in Section 12-1. Other items may similarly have acceptable limits determined, either empirically or using statistical techniques.

Rules can also be set for considering out-of-limits cases significant. For example, items 1–5% out-of-limits might be considered unimportant unless this condition occurs above a specified frequency. On the other hand, any item 30% or more out-of-limits might trigger special action, perhaps consisting of output for manual analysis and possible action.

Having evaluated the data, we may want to use the results of this analysis as feedback to the system. Generally, out-of-normal recordings, such as abnormally long response times or long queue wait times, will result in a modification of system algorithms in an attempt to correct the problem. Some of the feedback possibilities include changing the system's scheduling algorithms, modifying the peripheral and/or memory allocation priorities, changing the processor allocation algorithm, etc. Changes of this type will usually have some effect, although perhaps not exactly the desired effect.

Experience has shown that it is difficult to anticipate the effect of changes of this type in complex multiprogramming and multiprocessing systems. Simulation and modeling techniques can be used to great advantage to predict the consequences of various changes.

These techniques, however, are not generally feasible while the system is in production operation. Feedback is therefore often a trial-and-error procedure rather than a logical process. Manual monitoring is necessary to insure that undesirable results do not follow system modification.

The detailed functions performed when feedback is manually controlled are covered under Control in Section 14-3.

SUMMARY

The need for a satisfactory set of statistical recording, reporting, and analysis techniques cannot be too strongly emphasized. Particularly in large systems, effective performance evaluation is impossible without a base of good measurement data. This should be kept in mind throughout system design, since effective measurement tools must be an integral part of the system. Attempting to tack these capabilities on later will not result in satisfactory system evaluation. This is particularly true in the operating system, but it is equally true in large-scale or complex application software.

CHAPTER 14

Supervisory Control

The final Level IV entry under Software Functions is Supervisory Control. This covers all man/machine interfaces provided for control purposes. Supervisory control in its local form consists of control of the information processor only, but in the larger sense it extends outward into the information network. Supervisory control also appears as a software function under network processing; the two functions have much in common. Together they provide control over the entire information network.

When we discuss the control function, the concept of interaction between people and the system is important. This is a different type of interaction than that involved, for example, between the system and a time-sharing user. Interaction in the latter case is between the system software and a person using services and features provided by that software.

The interaction involved in supervisory control is quite different. It is an interaction between system software, generally the operating system, and people who are responsible for operation of the information-processing system. The interaction involves output from the software, notifying of events occurring within the system. These notices may or may not require responsive action by control personnel. The interaction may also originate externally and take the form either of inquiries to be responded to by the software or of control commands causing some software action. All of these interactions have to do with the full range of events transpiring in the system rather than being limited to a single process, as is the case with the time-sharing interaction used as an example earlier.

In general, when we consider the subject of supervisory control, the tendency is to think of the computer console operator. Certainly one of the most direct forms of supervisory control is that which is exercised by the console operator(s). However, this is only part of the control function, particularly in large and/or complex information-processing systems. Too often, the other aspects of control are ignored or slighted.

The console operator has several clearly defined functions. He feeds local job/task input into the system and removes local report output from it. He mounts and demounts file storage such as magnetic tape reels and disc packs when notified by the system to do so. He attempts to recover from peripheral errors when manual assistance is required for error correction. These are quite standard functions, needed in all systems. To simplify the discussion, the person performing these duties is referred to as a console operator, although in practice this is often not the case. In a large installation, for example, the input function may be handled by input preparation specialists, who see and use no component of the computer hardware except card readers and possibly an associated typewriter or other console device. Other specializations, such as tape/disc librarian, often exist to handle other functions. It is simpler, however, to refer to all of these people as console operators, since they perform a subset of the operator's function.

The additional functions associated with supervisory control are not nearly as well-defined, but they are equally important. They are the functions of monitoring the system and reacting to current or potential problems which develop or appear likely to develop. This type of monitoring is performed by the console operator for small information processors. It may be partly performed by the operator in larger systems, but in general the function is assigned elsewhere.

It is necessary to introduce here the concept of a technical staff or techniques group. These are the individuals (or possibly only one person) who are responsible for the more technical aspects of system operation. They may also be the software technical experts to whom designers and programmers come for expert advice and assistance.

The two duties are often combined, because similar technical expertise is required in each case.

The technical staff may assist in controlling system operation by monitoring events, by determining whether or not performance is satisfactory in the present circumstances, and by taking steps to modify operation when this is necessary. They may also cope with system errors, hardware and (particularly) software, which call for more complex treatment than the operators can normally handle. For example, the technical staff often decides what action to take if a software error in the operating system causes the entire information processor to fail.

Given the fact that there are at least two types of people involved in controlling the system, one can formulate the concept of hierarchical supervisory control. This concept consists of categorizing all control functions and placing each in a specific hierarchical level of control. One can then assign responsibility for each level to a particular person or type of person.

For example, the lowest level of hierarchical control includes the simple functions normally performed by the operator: handling input, output, mounting files, and peripheral error correction. The next higher, or more privileged, level might include functions such as setting relative priorities for user task executions, assigning file storage space or space limits for system users, and other similar functions. The next higher, and still more privileged, level might consist of changing system scheduling algorithms, dynamically modifying the rules for load leveling between two information processors, etc. The highest control level might allow dynamic modification of the coding of the operating system itself. Obviously the functions included at each level would vary in different installations, and possibly at different times within a single installation, due to varying circumstances.

This approach to supervisory control gives great flexibility while protecting the system against improper handling. Generally speaking, it is inappropriate to allow a console operator to perform the higher-level functions, because the operator has neither sufficient training nor enough knowledge of the total information-processing system. For example, changing job priorities requires a good idea of what the result of this change will be and how it may affect the business. In transaction-processing systems, changing the priority of one type of transaction may alter response times for all other transaction types. Actions of this type obviously should not be taken without a thorough understanding of the consequences.

Privileged supervisory control functions may be protected against misuse by allowing them to be performed only from a specific terminal or console device. Further protection may be given in the form of password keys which must be entered to perform privileged functions. It may even be desirable to provide another level of protection in the form of a physical key required to unlock and use the privileged terminal or console.

It is sometimes the case that the higher-level supervisory control functions are physically (not logically) consolidated with the similar functions for the network of which the information processor is a part. By assigning similar functions to a single terminal, it is possible to view overall network performance from one location.

It is very important that the information-processing system provide for the full range of control interfaces. Many software systems provide only the lowest-level interfaces, those usually associated with the console operator. This makes it very difficult to accurately monitor the system and even more difficult to modify its actions when necessary. The ability to dynamically modify important system parameters is really a necessity in a large-scale system. This point is stressed because so many software systems are inadequate in this respect. The whole subject of supervisory control, in fact, is an iceberg, only the tip of which is recognized in many software systems.

Supervisory Control breaks into Level V and Level VI entries as shown in Figure 14-1. Each of these entries is discussed in the following pages.

14-1 LOGGING

One of the Level V entries is Logging. This is the software function of outputting data which is of interest, or potential interest, to people controlling the system. There are several levels of control possible, and data logged may be associated with each of these. Data logged may therefore be separated into groups as part of the definition of hierarchical control. Certain groups may be associated with each level, and possibly each type will be logged at a different location.

Logging falls into the two basic types which form its subsidiary Level VI entries: Historical Logging and Action Requests.

Historical Logging

The first Level VI item, Historical Logging, includes output which, generally speaking, requires no responsive manual action. For exam-

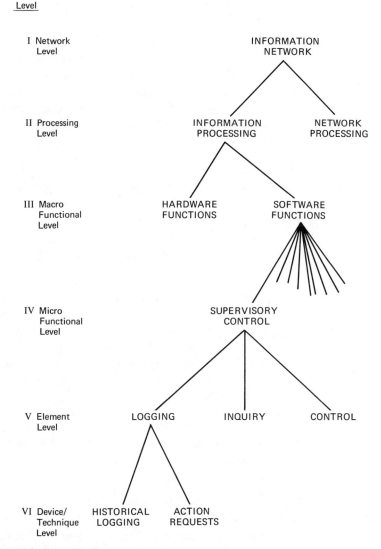

Level

I Network
Level

II Processing
Level

III Macro
Functional
Level

IV Micro
Functional
Level

V Element
Level

VI Device/
Technique
Level

INFORMATION
NETWORK

INFORMATION
PROCESSING

NETWORK
PROCESSING

HARDWARE
FUNCTIONS

SOFTWARE
FUNCTIONS

SUPERVISORY
CONTROL

LOGGING   INQUIRY   CONTROL

HISTORICAL   ACTION
LOGGING   REQUESTS

Figure 14-1 **Supervisory control techniques.**

ple, normal event occurrences are often logged simply to provide a running record of what is happening in the system. This type of notice may cause action indirectly. For example, the operator's action of distributing printed reports is an indirect reaction to notification that the job which prepared the reports is complete.

In determining which items should be logged, it is well to make a clear distinction between those needed dynamically and those which should be part of the statistical recording function described in Chapter 13. Events which should be noted for monitoring purposes are part of logging, while those which are of truly historical interest are part of statistical recording. Often, the need for detailed logging can be dramatically reduced if the inquiry function described in Section 14-2 is well developed. It is generally better to be able to obtain rapid answers to specific questions about system status than to receive comparable data in a stack of logged output.

Although there is certainly a distinction between logged and recorded data, this does not mean that there should be no duplication. Whenever data is required in logging because of dynamic system control, there is a strong probability that it should also be recorded for statistical or historical purposes. As long as the reason for doing so is clear, information duplication is perfectly legitimate.

The following is an incomplete but representative list of items which are generally required in the historical logging category.

System Trace consists of a continuous record of significant, user-oriented events occurring in the system. Start of job, start of job step, start of terminal interaction, and end of any of these are typical of the items included. This type of logging may be unnecessary if the control personnel use the inquiry function (Section 14-2) instead to determine system status. Sometimes the trace takes the form of a continually updated CRT picture of system status—jobs active, resources in use, etc. The only disadvantage to the exclusive use of the more dynamic displays is that it is difficult to trace back on prior system actions when this is needed. A hard-copy log is often useful in looking back at earlier system status and in obtaining a running picture of system activity.

Periodical Status Reports were mentioned earlier in the example of system status displays via CRT. Logging may periodically report queue sizes and wait times, users/tasks active, and other similar data. The reports in this category do not indicate out of normal conditions, but they simply record status as of a given point in time.

Peripheral Errors Corrected are also logged for information to control personnel and possibly to field maintenance personnel. These are errors or failures handled automatically; in some cases hardware reconfiguration may have taken place to correct the problem. The latter would of course indicate the need for repair action on the device which failed and was configured out of the system.

Automatic Switchover is a major form of reconfiguration, in which an entire information processor is taken off-line because of errors or failure and automatically replaced by another duplicate system. This is described in Section 12-2 under Fail Soft/Backup.

Deadly Embrace Resolved is another recording entry for information only. In systems which allow multiple concurrent update users of a single file, conflicts which cause a total deadlock between two or more users must be resolved. If the data management software does so automatically, that fact is generally logged.

Action Requests

The second Level VI entry, Action Requests, includes system outputs which require a fairly immediate human response. The most common event of this type is a peripheral error which requires human intervention for correction (device-not-ready, card jam, etc.). The event is logged by the system software, and the operator is requested to take appropriate action. Generally a choice of actions is explicitly or implicitly available, with the decision of exact procedure left to the operator. The following are items which fall into this category of action request logging.

Uncorrected Peripheral Errors are the most common of the items logged for operator response. Logging may occur because the error cannot be corrected without manual intervention: for example, a device is powered off. Logging may also occur because automatic error correction was attempted but was unsuccessful. Any further action to be taken must therefore be determined by the operator.

Switchover Required is an event logged in a dual backed-up system where switchover to the second information processor does not occur automatically. This notice is generated when an error occurs, and is detected by software, and is analyzed as a reason to switch.

Deadly Embrace Exists notices occur in systems which allow multiple concurrent update but do not automatically resolve deadlock situations. If the occurrence is infrequent, manual action may be satisfactory.

Abnormal System Performance notices may also be generated. For example, the system may have a set of built-in parameters defining acceptable performance levels. If so, it will continually or periodically compare its actual performance with these specified norms. If they are not met and if the divergence is significant, an action request may result. This is the type of notice which would be addressed to one of the higher hierarchical levels of control. The action taken in response might be to alter the software processor allocation methods, its scheduling methods, its priority structure, or other similar parameters.

It would certainly be possible for the software to take these actions automatically, and sometimes this is done (see Evaluation/Feedback, Section 13-3). It is very difficult, however, to do this. Successfully modifying the processing in a large, sophisticated system is not a simple process, and the effects of any modification are hard to predict. The normal approach, therefore, is to do the majority of such modifications manually, monitor the results, and make further modifications if necessary.

14-2   INQUIRY

The second Level V entry under Supervisory Control is Inquiry. This function allows personnel such as operators, technical staff, and sometimes individual users to request status information from the system. Inquiry is usually arranged hierarchically by levels of privilege. Thus, some queries may be permitted to anyone, others only to console operators, still others only to more privileged personnel. This structure may be related to Security (see Section 12-3) since one of its aspects is privacy.

In this context, users are generally not allowed to make any inquiry which would result in the disclosure of private information belonging to another user. Similarly, even control personnel may be prevented from learning certain facts if user privacy is involved. Obviously, there must be reasonable trade-offs; control personnel must have enough information to be able to operate the system successfully. This may cause some degree of privacy invasion, but this is necessary.

Although this function is not subdivided into Level VI entries, it includes a variety of different types of inquiries. Some representative examples are listed in the following paragraphs.

Job/Task Status Requests are a major form of inquiry. A wide variety of status requests are usually required. A basic request is used to obtain the current status of a particular job, task, or process. The response will be that it is in one of a variety of statuses: being input, queued waiting to execute, executing, completed execution but output not complete, and all processing complete. An alternate response, of course, is that it is not in the system at all.

This is an area in which many software systems are deficient, and it should therefore be carefully investigated. Many systems furnish too little detail; for example, they may say simply that a job is waiting in queue. This is not sufficient if the particular job being investigated has been waiting for some time. The reply should indicate what the job's position is in the queue and give the reason if it cannot execute. For example, it may be waiting for a tape to be retrieved from the library, it may need too much memory to execute while another long-running job already in memory is still executing, etc. These facts are extremely important when attempting to analyze a problem, and inquiries are most often made when a problem exists (or is thought to exist).

Another irritating deficiency in many systems is their inability to remember completed work. For example, an inquiry response that the job is not in the information processor may mean that it was never received or that it was completely processed. This is not satisfactory, particularly when remote tasks are involved. The system should retain a record of what it has processed for a reasonable period of time—at least several hours but preferably a full day.

Inquiries about the status of a specific job can usually be made by any of the control personnel and also by the person who sent the job in. An individual user will normally receive no response to a query about any job(s) he did not originate.

Output Status Requests are also required. These are used to determine the status of task output (SYSOUT) waiting for local printing/punching, etc. and/or remote output awaiting transmission over the communication network.

One form of output inquiry requests the status of output produced by a specified job or process. This feature is often used by the owner of the output to determine which of his available output reports he wishes to receive first.

Another version of output status inquiry, used by control personnel, gives a complete list of all waiting output. This can also be used to load level; some reports may be directed to tape or to a remote printer, leaving the most urgent items to be printed locally. Alternatively, output addressed to a remote station which is out of operation can be redirected to an on-line printer or punch and delivered in some other way (mail, messenger) to the remote location.

Peripheral Status Inquiries are needed by the console operators. For example, they should be able to inquire about a tape handler and be told its status; it is off-line, on-line, assigned (and to what job) or unassigned; its accumulated error statistics; and any other significant data. This capability is very useful both for the operators and for maintenance personnel.

File Status Inquiries allow operators or other control personnel to determine the status of files cataloged by the system (as described in Chapter 9). These inquiries may request the status of a particular file or of all files known to the system. The response should generally give the file identity, perhaps its size, its physical location(s), its attributes such as format, etc., if known, and its current status. The status may be: idle (not in use); being accessed and in what mode(s); locked because of an error detected in its content; or being recovered after a problem-program or system failure.

If privacy is important, the detail displayed in response to file status inquiries should be analyzed carefully. Sometimes, for example, exact file identity and/or file ownership should be displayed only to the file's owner and perhaps to the control personnel at the highest privilege level.

System Status Requests allow display of significant data concerning the entire system rather than some individual task or job. For example, it should be possible to obtain a display of all system queues showing either totals or details of tasks/jobs in each status. It should also be possible to display current use of resources such as peripherals, memory, storage, etc.

In all information-processing systems, the type of data which can be obtained on demand is very important. The inquiry function should therefore be given considerable emphasis to ensure that appropriate functions are available.

14-3   CONTROL

Control is the third and final Level V entry under Supervisory Control. It encompasses all facilities for external control over major system operation. Often the features provided by this function are used as an indirect response to output from the logging function described earlier. They may also be used without any trigger from the system software.

Control is an interactive function. The interaction consists of a command input to the system, some action taken (if possible) by system software, and finally a confirming (or denying) message from the system to the originator of the command. There are a number of commands which can be included within the control function. As in inquiry, these are generally grouped into hierarchical levels with different persons allowed to execute commands associated with each level.

Some commands cause changes in status, either of a single job or process or of a homogeneous group. For example, a particular job can be forcibly removed from the system, adjusted in priority, or perhaps put into a holding state (or queue) while other action is taken. These changes may be performed by the job's owner or only allowed to control personnel.

Generally speaking, the control functions permitted to individual users should be carefully considered. It is normally harmless to allow a user to eliminate his job or place it in hold. However, allowing him to change its priority (particularly to increase the urgency) may disrupt the priority scheme of the entire system. Each such function should be analyzed for possible misuse, and that should be weighed against the convenience to the user of having the function available. Decisions of this type are often application dependent, and general rules are difficult to establish.

Control is not separated into any Level VI items. The following paragraphs describe some of the commands provided as part of this function.

Job/Task Status Changes were referred to earlier. They cause a particular job's status to be changed in any of a variety of ways. Similar status change commands may affect all of a class of jobs. For example, all jobs or tasks of a particular type may be given a higher or lower priority, may be put into hold status and later returned to normal, etc. These commands are used to make relatively gross changes in system processing.

Output Status Change Requests include commands which cause waiting output to be processed and sent either to its original destination (peripheral or remote terminal) or to an alternate.

Reconfiguration falls into the control function when manually requested. This may take many forms, including removing a peripheral or main-system component from use, exchanging the functions of two similar components, or switching to the backup system in a dual failsafe information-processor configuration. It is particularly important that the supervisory console device or devices be reconfigurable, either manually or automatically, so that failure of a console does not cause the entire system to fail.

Initiate Test and Diagnostics is another control feature. T&D is discussed in Section 12-2. Even in systems which automatically call T&D when errors are sensed, manual calls should be available for use in preventative maintenance.

System Status or Parameter Changes are another type of control function which is used to adjust the system's operating parameters. For example, in a partitioned memory system, memory allocation can be changed. In a system which dedicates a certain percentage of resources to interactive processing and the remainder to batch, the percentages can be altered. In cases where individual users are given resource allowances to be used, these can be allocated and modified via control functions. A very wide range of system parameters is theoretically available for modification, although in practice most systems are rather deficient in allowing dynamic change.

Send Message is a very useful control function if the system supports interactive processing. Control personnel can use this feature to send a single message to all users or to all users of a defined class (such as time-sharing users). The message might notify of an impending system shutdown, inform users that a new software feature is available, or provide other similar information. This function may be unnecessary if the information processor is part of a network which includes message-switching capability, since in that case any network terminal can be used to send these messages.

Investigate/Correct Problems is a function sometimes allowed interactively but generally only to very priviledged control personnel. Using these features one can view and modify memory contents and possibly secondary storage contents. This is obviously a very sensitive function, but if it is used properly it can be very helpful in software error diagnosis in systems which run 100% of the time (providing little opportunity for off-line analysis).

Utility Functions may be used by supervisory control personnel. They may be able to initiate tasks such as file dumps or other media conversions using control commands rather than by setting up normal job input. This may not be really necessary, but it is often very convenient.

System Startup/Shutdown must be controlled by operators and/or technical staff personnel. Generally these functions require interaction between software and people. At startup, for example, the software must be given the current date and time. It may also require input of the scheduling algorithm, allocation scheme, or other similar parameters to be used. Shutdown is manually initiated via the control console, and the actions to be included (file dumps, for example) may also be specified by control personnel.

Control functions should cause a record of the action taken to be logged. If the control command originates at a lower privilege level location (a tape console, for example), it may be desirable to log it also at a high privilege system monitor station. This will insure that significant changes are noted by the people most responsible for successful system operation.

SUMMARY

Supervisory control is a function often taken for granted by information-processing-system owners and designers. In fact, many present software systems are noticeably deficient in this area. In large-scale systems, in particular, the requirements for successful system monitoring and control should be considered in as much detail as are languages, utilities, etc. Good control features can make the difference between a system which is awkward and difficult to operate and control and one which is relatively simple.

CHAPTER 15

Trends in Information Processing

After digesting the effects of the original computer revolution, information processing today is going through another revolution which consists of an explosive growth in the use of communications-based systems. This, far more than new "generations" of computer hardware, will cause fundamental changes in the way information is processed.

Complex network-based systems are, in fact, the main reason that the functional approach is so important. Information processing as a whole is moving more and more rapidly toward ever greater degrees of complexity. This is borne out by the findings of a number of recent market research studies of trends in computer use.

The average computer installation is moving, and will continue to move, toward remotely oriented network-based systems. The "small batch system" of today will continue to be used, but it will frequently be a node in a large information network. Large and very large-scale computers will increasingly be used in such networks, providing focused computing power at central and/or regional locations. However, centralization is not a universal trend as networks can equally well serve the customer with medium scale computing sites at several locations, tied together via data communications to exchange information as needed.

Information networking is the generic term used to describe these remotely oriented systems, but this includes many different types of processing. Probably the most rapidly growing type of application today is the transaction-processing system, which appears to be the wave of the future. Systems of this type are becoming essential to many industries and government agencies because they provide the rapid information flow and dynamic control so necessary to these enterprises. Examples of transaction-processing systems include on-line banking with immediate account update, point-of-sale credit checks in large department stores, on-line entry in wholesale and/or retail outlets, and other similar applications.

As information-processing systems of this type continue to be developed, their owners become more and more dependent on them. The data bases around which such systems are centered tend to become the only repository of vital information describing the business. Inability to access the data base, or to make use of the computer, becomes intolerable.

Systems of this type therefore require levels of reliability and integrity which are orders of magnitude greater than the requirements of batch processing systems. These needs are frequently complicated by the use of large shared access data bases. Although these levels of integrity are difficult to provide, they are vital. Once a business or government agency is committed to information networking as a way of life, its very existence depends on the network, the information processors, and the data bases.

Although the need for integrity and reliability continually increases, the probability of fulfilling such requirements generally decreases with the complexity of the system. Both hardware and software reliability decrease with the addition of components which are interdependent with the other surrounding components. In the case of hardware, there are mathematical equations which can be used to compute the reliability of a system from the reliability of its individual components. There are no similar equations for determining software reliability, but experience has shown that as complexity increases and the number of software components grows, the reliability decreases significantly.

Another important aspect of the new on-line systems is that they must often support a wide range of users. Managers, clerks, engineers, programmers, and others may share the use of a single system. Because these different types of users have such varied backgrounds and such differing needs, many varieties of user facilities must be provided. In particular, the "noncomputer professional" user of an information-processing system requires much greater software support than a "computer professional" user does, because he has less knowledge and background in the computer field to draw on. It is a characteristic of transaction-processing systems that most users are not computer oriented; more often they are drawn from clerical personnel and other similar sources.

It can therefore be concluded that there are at least three outstanding traits which distinguish today's and tomorrow's information-processing systems from those of the past:

- They are heavily network oriented.
- They have high requirements for integrity, availability, and reliability.
- They must support a wide range of users, including many without programming or other computing background.

Some systems of this type have already been installed and can be said to be sucessful in the sense that they generally perform the functions required. Few, if any, can be said to have reached this level at a reasonable cost in design and implementation. As large numbers of complex, on-line systems become necessary in the future, such costs will be increasingly unacceptable. To bring costs into line requires many improved techniques, first and foremost of which is the use of formalized and standardized design principles and methods. The functional approach provides a starting point for the development of the required principles and methods.

To date, the design of complex systems of the type just described has been a real problem to system designers. Designers have, in general, been forced to rely on intuition, native talent, and personal experience. Although all of these are necessary in a good designer, they are not a substitute for well-defined and proven methods and techniques for system analysis and design. Given this lack it is amazing that any large-scale system is adequately designed, and certainly the high cost can be easily explained.

One of the goals of the functional approach is to provide a useful and formal method of attacking design problems. With such a method, designers will be able to produce good results much more consistently and with fewer variations because of the designer's experience and background. There is no intent to downgrade individual talent; the simple fact is that there are not, and will not soon be, enough designers who can overcome the existing obstacles and successfully design complex systems.

This problem is both real and serious, and it will continue to be so in the future. The 1970s and beyond will see increasing needs for complex information networks to assist managers who control complex businesses. Unless design tools such as the functional approach can be made available, many of these complex information networks will be poorly designed and will be much more costly than necessary, because of the trial-and-error approach to analysis. Some, in fact, will no doubt be both expensive and totally unsatisfactory for their stated purposes.

Perhaps equally important, in a long-range sense, is making the design of complex systems modular, flexible, and easy to customize and maintain. Because on-line systems are so intimately related to the organizations they serve, they must be able to adapt readily to changing business conditions. Such change is impossible or impractically expensive without formalized methods of achieving modularity. Here again, the use of the functional approach, which is itself formalized and modular, should aid in achieving this goal.

To restate the basic premise of this book, every system is built from common functions and elements. The bulk of this volume, Chapters 5 through 14, consists of lists of the functions and elements which form the common ingredients of all information-processing systems. Further investigation and use may uncover other Level VI items which must be added to make these lists comprehensive, but it is felt that they are substantially complete.

These lists, used as the base for system design, have been applied successfully to the analysis and design of one system. Such experience is of course necessary to prove the validity and usefulness of the functional approach.

The basic procedure for using the function lists is to compare each item (hardware and software) on the functional tree structure against the requirements of the system being analyzed. If there is a match, the function is required. It is then necessary to analyze that function in detail within the context of the system and decide how it should be provided, what its exact characteristics must be, and so on. This may lead to an iterative process of reconsidering other functions previously thought unnecessary. This matching and analysis process still requires further study. It should be possible to reduce this to a set of relatively formal procedures which will further simplify the design process.

This continuing study of the functional approach must also determine if there are computerized tools (simulations, for example) which can be used to advantage in the design process. Very little assistance of this type is normally available to the software designer, but there is real promise in the use of such techniques, particularly when dealing with complex systems.

Although, as indicated, there is much additional work to be done in formalizing the system analysis and design process, the functional approach is the necessary first step. The use of the functional approach can materially aid the designer of complex information systems. It can, in fact, much simplify his effort while providing him with guidelines to insure that no significant functions are omitted. This should prove to be of great assistance in the design of the complex information-processing systems of tomorrow.

Bibliography

2 Evolution of Information Processing Systems

Baldwin, F. R., Gibson, W. B., and Poland, C. B., "A multiprocessing approach to a large computer system," *IBM Systems Journal*, 1, Sept., 1962, pp. 64–76.

Becker, H. B., "Time-sharing: the next step," *Computers and Automation*, Oct., 1966, pp. 18–20, 28.

Critchlow, A. J., "Generalized multiprocessing and multiprogramming systems," *AFIPS Conference Proceedings*, 24, 1963 Fall Joint Computer Conference, Spartan Books, New York, pp. 107–126.

Plugge, W. R., and Perry, M. N., "American airlines' "SABRE" electronic reservations system," *Proceedings of the Western Joint Computer Conference*, 1961, pp. 593–606.

Steel, T. B. Jr., "Operating systems," *Datamation*, 10, May, 1964, pp. 26–28.

Wimbrow, J. H., "A large-scale interactive administrative system," *IBM Systems Journal*, 10, 1971, pp. 260–282.

"An Introduction to CP-67/CMS," Document Number 320-2032, Printed May, 1969 for Spring Joint Computer Conference, Scientific Center Report, IBM Corporation, Cambridge Scientific Center, Cambridge, Massachusetts.

3 Definition of the Functional Approach

Corbato, F. J., and Vyssotsky, V. A., "Introduction and overview of the MULTICS system," *AFIPS Conference Proceedings*, 27, 1965 Fall Joint Computer Conference, Spartan Books, New York, pp. 185–196.

5   Hardware Functions

Auf der Heide, R., "More bits/inch," *Datamation,* **16,** July 15, 1970, pp. 66–71.

Bauldreay, J., "Mark reading," *Datamation,* **16,** Oct. 1, 1970, pp. 34–38.

Brening, R. L., "External control," *Datamation,* **16,** Sept. 1, 1970, pp. 48–55.

Chu, Y., *Introduction to Computer Organization,* Prentice-Hall, Englewood Cliffs, New Jersey, 1970.

Durao, M. J. Jr., "Finding happiness in . . . extended core" *Datamation,* **17,** Aug. 15, 1971, pp. 32–34.

Eadie, D., *Modern Data Processors and Systems,* Prentice-Hall, Englewood Cliffs, New Jersey, 1971.

Hillegass, J. R., "Memory upgrades provide 360's with more processing punch," *Computer Decisions,* **3,** Dec., 1971, pp. 28–32.

Murray, J. T., *An Introduction to Computing: IBM System/3,* McGraw Hill, New York, 1971.

Tucker, S. G., "Microprogram control for SYSTEM/360," *IBM Systems Journal,* **6,** 1967, pp. 222–241.

Optical Character Recognition and the Years Ahead, International Business Forms Industries, The Business Press, Elmhurst, Illinois, 1971.

6   Languages

Byrnes, C. J., and Steig, D. B., "File management systems: a current summary," *Datamation,* **15,** Nov., 1969, pp. 138–142.

Centefelli, A. R., "Data management concept for DOS/360 and TOS/360," *IBM Systems Journal,* **6,** 1967, pp. 22–37.

Clark, W. A., "The functional structure of OS/360 data management," *IBM Systems Journal,* **5,** 1966, pp. 30–51.

Flores, I., *Data Structures and Management,* Prentice-Hall, Englewood Cliffs, New Jersey, 1970.

Gass, S. I., *Linear Programming Third Edition,* McGraw Hill, New York, 1969.

Kiviat, P. J., Villanueva, R., and Markowitz, H. M., *The Simscript II Programming Language,* Prentice-Hall, Englewood Cliffs, New Jersey, 1968.

Lefkovitz, D., *File Structures for On-Line Systems,* Spartan Books, New York, 1969.

McCracken, D. D., and Dorn, W. S., *Numerical Methods and FORTRAN Programming, With Applications in Engineering and Science,* John Wiley and Sons, New York, 1964.

Patterson, A. C., "Requirements for a generalized data base management system," *AFIPS Conference Proceedings,* 39, 1971 Fall Joint Computer Conference, AFIPS Press, Montvale, New Jersey, pp. 515–522.

Rishel, W. J., "Incremental compilers," *Datamation,* 16, Jan., 1970, pp. 129–136.

Sammet, J. E., *Programming Languages: History and Fundamentals,* Prentice-Hall, Englewood Cliffs, New Jersey, 1969.

Sharpe, W. F., and Jacobs, N. L., *BASIC An Introduction to Computer Programming Using the BASIC Language,* The Free Press, New York, 1971.

Stabley, D. H., *Logical Programming with System/360,* John Wiley and Sons, New York, 1970.

Feature Analysis of Generalized Data Base Management Systems, CODASYL Systems Committee Technical Report, The Association for Computing Machinery, New York, 1971.

A Survey of Generalized Data Base Management Systems, CODASYL Systems Committee Technical Report, The Association for Computing Machinery, New York, 1969.

7   Applications

Bromberg, H., "Software buying," *Datamation,* 16, Sept. 15, 1970, pp. 35–40.

Gabrieli, E. R., "Medical network," *Datamation,* 16, Oct. 15, 1970, pp. 42–45.

Hodges, J. D. Jr., "Law enforcement communication and inquiry systems," *AFIPS Conference Proceedings,* 39, 1971 Fall Joint Computer Conference, AFIPS Press, Montvale, New Jersey, pp. 281–293.

Markuson, B. E., "An overview of library systems and automation," *Datamation,* 16, Feb., 1970, pp. 60–68.

Minini, D. J., "Implementing the very large applications-software package," *Datamation,* 15, Dec., 1969, pp. 141–144.

Reenshaug, T., "Some notes on portable application software," *Datamation,* 16, April, 1970, pp. 104–106.

8   Utility

Barron, D. W., "Assemblers and Loaders," *Macdonald/Elsevier Computer Monograph,* American Elsevier Publishing Company, New York, 1969.

Bernstein, W. A., and Owens, J. T., "Debugging in a time-sharing environment," *AFIPS Conference Proceedings,* 33, 1968 Fall Joint Computer Conference, The Thompson Book Company, Washington, D.C., pp. 7–14.

Grishman, R., "The debugging system AIDS," *AFIPS Conference Proceedings,* 36, 1970 Spring Joint Computer Conference, AFIPS Press, Montvale, New Jersey, pp. 59–64.

Hanford, K. V., "Automatic generation of test cases," *IBM Systems Journal,* 9, 1970, pp. 242–257.

Siegel, S., "WATFOR . . . speedy Fortran debugger," *Datamation,* 17, Nov. 15, 1971, pp. 22–26.

9   File Management

Madnich, S. E., and Alsop, J. W. II, "A modular approach to file system design," *AFIPS Conference Proceedings,* 34, 1969 Spring Joint Computer Conference, AFIPS Press, Montvale, New Jersey, pp. 1–13.

10   Task Management

Bouvard, J., "Operating system for the 800/1800," *Datamation,* 10, May, 1964, pp. 29–34.

Ramamoorthy, C. W., and Gonzalez, M. J., "A survey of techniques for recognizing parallel processable streams in computer programs," *AFIPS Conference Proceedings,* 35, 1969 Fall Joint Computer Conference, AFIPS Press, Montvale, New Jersey, pp. 1–15.

Ryder, K. D., "A heuristic approach to task dispatching," *IBM Systems Journal,* 9, 1970, pp. 189–198.

Witt, B. I., "The functional structure of OS/360 job and task management," *IBM Systems Journal,* 5, 1966, pp. 12–29.

11   Resource Management

Baskett, F., Browne, J. C., and Raike, W. M., "The management of a multi-level non-paged memory system," *AFIPS Conference Proceedings,* 36, 1970 Spring Joint Computer Conference, AFIPS Press, Montvale, New Jersey, 459–465.

Cohen, L. J., *Operating System Analysis and Design,* Spartan Books, New York, 1970.

Marshall, B. S., "Dynamic calculation of dispatching priorities under OS/360 MVT," *Datamation,* 15, Aug., 1969, pp. 93–97.

Meinstein, L. S., "RCA's time-sharing operating system," *Comparative Operating Systems—A Symposium,* Brandon/Systems Press, Princeton, New Jersey, pp. 1–10.

Rosenberg, A. M., "Resource allocation and system management in the timesharing era," *Data Processing Magazine,* May, 1969, pp. 38–44.

Strauss, J. C., "A simple thruput and response model of EXEC 8 under swapping saturation," *AFIPS Conference Proceedings,* 39, 1971 Fall Joint Computer Conference, AFIPS Press, Montvale, New Jersey, pp. 39–49.

12   Integrity

Bates, W. S., "Security of computer-based information systems," *Datamation,* 16, May, 1970, pp. 60–65.

Carroll, J. M., Martin, R., McHardy, L., and Moravec, H., "Multidimensional security program for a generalized information retrieval program," *AFIPS Conference Proceedings,* 39, 1971 Fall Joint Computer Conference, AFIPS Press, Montvale, New Jersey, pp. 571–577.

Friedman, T. D., "The authorization problem in shared files," *IBM Systems Journal,* 9, 1970, pp. 258–280.

Gustlin, D. P., and Prentice, D. D., "Dynamic recovery techniques guarantee system reliability," *AFIPS Conference Proceedings,* 33, 1968 Fall Joint Computer Conference, The Thompson Book Company, Washington, D.C., pp. 1389–1397.

Hansen, M. R., "Insuring confidentiality of individual records in data storage and retrieval for statistical purposes," *AFIPS Conference Proceedings,* 39, 1971 Fall Joint Computer Conference, AFIPS Press, Montvale, New Jersey, pp. 579–585.

Lancto, D. C., and Rockefeller, R. L., "An application-oriented multiprocessing system—the operational error analysis program," *IBM Systems Journal,* 6, 1967, pp. 103–115.

Molko, L. M., "Hardware aspects of secure computing," *AFIPS Conference Proceedings,* 36, 1970 Spring Joint Computer Conference, AFIPS Press, Montvale, New Jersey, pp. 135–141.

Nagler, H., "Recovery for computer switchover in a real-time system," *IBM Systems Journal,* 2, March, 1963, pp. 76–83.

Nelson, G. W., "OPTS-600—on-line peripheral test system," *AFIPS Conference Proceedings,* 33, 1968 Fall Joint Computer Conference, The Thompson Book Company, Washington, D.C., pp. 45–50.

Suda, R., "An application-oriented multiprocessing system—the diagnostic monitor," *IBM Systems Journal,* 6, 1967, pp. 116–123.

Van Tassel, D., "Cryptographic techniques for computers," *AFIPS Conference Proceedings,* 34, 1969 Spring Joint Computer Conference, AFIPS Press, Montvale, New Jersey, pp. 367–372.

Wessler, J., Myers, E., and Gardner, W. D., "Physical security . . . facts and fancies," *Datamation,* 17, July 1, 1971, pp. 34–37.

13   Statistical Recording

Campbell, D. J., and Heffner, W. J., "Measurement and analysis of large operating systems during system development," *AFIPS Conference Proceedings,* 33, 1968 Fall Joint Computer Conference, The Thompson Book Company, Washington, D.C., pp. 903–914.

Cantrell, H. N., and Ellison, A. L., "Multiprogramming system performance measurement and analysis," *AFIPS Conference Proceedings,* 32, 1968 Spring Joint Computer Conference, Thompson Book Company, Washington, D.C., pp. 213–221.

Kolence, K. W., "A software view of measurement tools," *Datamation,* 17, Jan. 1, 1971, pp. 32–38.

Selwyn, L. L., "Computer resource accounting in a time sharing environment," *AFIPS Conference Proceedings,* 36, 1970 Spring Joint Computer Conference, AFIPS Press, Montvale, New Jersey, pp. 119–130.

Yourdon, E., "An approach to measuring a time-sharing system," *Datamation,* 15, April, 1969, pp. 124–126.

14   Supervisory Control

Andrews, D. W., and Radice, R. A., "Multiple consoles: a basis for communication growth in large systems," *AFIPS Conference Proceedings,* 36, 1970 Spring Joint Computer Conference, AFIPS Press, Montvale, New Jersey, pp. 131–134.

Index